Using Literature to Help
Troubled Teenagers
Cope with Societal Issues

Using Literature to Help Troubled Teenagers Cope with Societal Issues

Edited by Pamela S. Carroll

The Greenwood Press "Using Literature
to Help Troubled Teenagers" Series
Joan F. Kaywell, Series Adviser

Greenwood Press
Westport, Connecticut • London

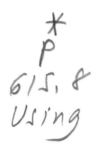

P
615, 8
Using

Library of Congress Cataloging-in-Publication Data

Using literature to help troubled teenagers cope with societal issues
/ edited by Pamela S. Carroll.
    p. cm.—(The Greenwood Press "Using literature to help
troubled teenagers" series)
  Includes bibliographical references and index.
  ISBN 0–313–30526–9 (alk. paper)
  1. Bibliotherapy for teenagers. 2. Young adult literature—Study
and teaching (Secondary) 3. Teenagers—Social conditions.
I. Carroll, Pamela S. II. Series.
RJ505.B5U85 1999
615.8'515'0835—dc21   98–55348

British Library Cataloguing in Publication Data is available.

Library of Congress Catalog Card Number: 98–55348
ISBN: 0–313–30526–9

First published in 1999

Greenwood Press, 88 Post Road West, Westport, CT 06881
An imprint of Greenwood Publishing Group, Inc.
www.greenwood.com

Printed in the United States of America

The paper used in this book complies with the
Permanent Paper Standard issued by the National
Information Standards Organization (Z39.48–1984).

10 9 8 7 6 5 4 3 2 1

Copyright Acknowledgments

The author and the publisher gratefully acknowledge permission for the use of the following
material:

Joy G. Dryfoos, *Adolescents at Risk: Prevalence and Prevention* (New York: Oxford University
Press). Copyright © 1991 by Joy G. Dryfoos.

Excerpts from personal writings by Brian Strehle.

B&T 39.95 net
4/09/01

Contents

Series Foreword

The idea for this six-volume series—addressing family issues, identity issues, societal issues, abuse issues, health issues, and death and dying issues—came while I, myself, was going to a therapist to help me deal with the loss of a loved one. My therapy revealed that I was a "severe trauma survivor" and I had to process the emotions of a bad period of time during my childhood. I was amazed that a trauma of my youth could be triggered by an emotional upset in my adult life. After an amazing breakthrough that occurred after extensive reading, writing, and talking, I looked at my therapist and said, "My God! I'm like the gifted child with the best teacher. What about all of those children who survive situations worse than mine and do not choose education as their escape of choice?" I began to wonder about the huge number of troubled teenagers who were not getting the professional treatment they needed. I pondered about those adolescents who were fortunate enough to get psychological treatment but were illiterate. Finally, I began to question if there were ways to help them while also improving their literacy development.

My thinking generated two theories on which this series is based: (1) Being literate increases a person's chances of emotional health, and (2) Twenty-five percent of today's students are "unteachable." The first theory was generated by my pondering these two statistics: 80% of our prisoners are illiterate (Hodgkinson, 1991), and 80% of our prisoners have been sexually abused (Child Abuse Council, 1993). If a correlation actually exists between these two statistics, then it suggests a strong need for literacy skills in order for a person to be able to address emotional turmoil in healthy or constructive ways. The second theory came out of work I did for my book, *Adolescents at Risk: A Guide to Fiction and Nonfiction for Young Adults, Parents and Professionals* (Greenwood Press, 1993), and my involvement in working with teachers and students in middle and secondary schools. Some of the emotional baggage our youth bring to school is way too heavy for them to handle without help. These students simply cannot handle additional academic responsibilities when they are "not right" emotionally.

THEORY ONE: BEING LITERATE INCREASES A PERSON'S CHANCES OF EMOTIONAL HEALTH

Well-educated adults who experience intense emotional pain, whether it is from the loss of a loved one or from a traumatic event, have several options available for dealing with their feelings. Most will find comfort in talking with friends or family members, and some will resort to reading books to find the help they need. For example, reading Dr. Elizabeth Kübler-Ross's five stages for coping with death—denial, anger, bargaining, depression, and acceptance or growth—might help a person understand the various stages he or she is going through after the death of a friend or relative. Sometimes, however, additional help is needed when an individual is experiencing extreme emotions and is unable to handle them.

Consider a mother whose improper left-hand turn causes the death of her seven-year-old daughter and the injury of her four-year-old daughter. It is quite probable that the mother will need to seek additional help from a therapist who will help her deal with such a trauma. A psychologist or psychiatrist will, more than likely, get her to talk openly about her feelings, read some books written by others who have survived such a tragedy, and do regular journal writing. A psychiatrist may also prescribe some medication during this emotionally challenging time. This parent's literacy skills of talking, reading, and writing are essential to her getting through this difficult period of her life.

Now, consider her four-year-old daughter who is also experiencing extreme grief over the loss of her beloved older sister. If this child is taken to counseling, the therapist will probably get her to talk, role-play, and draw out her feelings. These are the literacy skills appropriate to the developmental level of a four-year-old child. Such a child, if not taken to a counselor when needed, will manifest her emotions in one of two ways—either by acting out or by withdrawing.

Lev Vygotsky, a well-respected learning theorist, suggests that without words there could be no thoughts and the more words a person has at his or her disposal, the bigger that person's world. If what Vygotsky suggests is true, then a person with a limited or no vocabulary is only capable of operating at an emotional level. *The Story of My Life* by Helen Keller adds credibility to that view. In the introduction to the biography, written by Robert Russell, he describes Helen Keller's frustration at not being able to communicate:

> Perhaps the main cause for her early tantrums was plain frustration at not being able to communicate. . . . Not being able to hear, Helen had nothing to imitate, so she had no language. This meant more than simply not being able to talk. It meant having nothing clear to talk about because for her things had no names. Without names, things have no distinctness or individuality. Without language, we could not describe the difference between an elephant and an egg. Without the words we would have no clear conception of either elephant or egg. The name of a thing confers identity upon it and makes it possible for us to think about it. Without names for love or sorrow, we do not know we are experiencing them. Without words, we could not say, "I love you," and human beings need to say this and much more. Helen had the need, too, but she had not the means. As she grew older and the need increased, no wonder her fits of anger and misery grew. (pp. 7–8)

Helen, herself, writes,

> [T]he desire to express myself grew. The few signs I used became less and less adequate, and my failures to make myself understood were invariably followed by outbursts of passion. I felt as if invisible hands were holding me, and I made frantic efforts to free myself. I struggled—not that struggling helped matters, but the spirit of resistance was strong within me; I generally broke down in tears and physical exhaustion. If my mother happened to be near I crept into her arms, too miserable even to remember the cause of the tempest. After awhile the need of some means of communication became so urgent that these outbursts occurred daily, sometimes hourly. (p. 28)

If Vygotsky's theory reflected by the illuminating words of a deaf, blind, and mute child is true, then it is no wonder that 80% of our prisoners are illiterate victims of abuse.

THEORY TWO: 25% OF TODAY'S TEENAGERS ARE "UNTEACHABLE" BY TODAY'S STANDARDS

Teachers are finding it increasingly difficult to teach their students, and I believe that 25% of teenagers are "unteachable" by today's standards. A small percentage of these troubled youth do choose academics as their escape of choice, and they are the overachievers to the "nth" degree. That is not to say that all overachievers are emotionally disturbed teenagers, but some of them are learning, not because of their teachers, but because their very survival depends upon it. I know. I was one of them. The other adolescents going through inordinately difficult times (beyond the difficulty inherent in adolescence itself) might not find the curriculum very relevant to their lives. Their escapes of choice include rampant sex, drug use, gang membership, and other self-destructive behaviors. Perhaps the violence permeating our schools is a direct result of the utter frustration of some of our youth.

Consider these data describing the modern teenage family. At any given time, 25% of American children live with one parent, usually a divorced or never-married mother (Edwards & Young, 1992). Fifty percent of America's youth will spend some school years being raised by a single parent, and almost four million school-age children are being reared by neither parent (Hodgkinson, 1991). In 1990, 20% of American children grew up in poverty, and it is probable that 25% will be raised in poverty by the year 2000 (Howe, 1991). Children in homeless families often experience developmental delays, severe depression, anxiety, and learning disorders (Bassuk & Rubin, 1987).

Between one-fourth and one-third of school-aged children are living in a family with one or more alcoholics (Gress, 1988). Fourteen percent of children between the ages of 3 and 17 experience some form of family violence (Craig, 1992). Approximately 27% of girls and 16% of boys are sexually abused before the age of 18 (Krueger, 1993), and experts believe that it is reasonable to say that 25% of children will be sexually abused before adulthood (Child Abuse Council, 1993). Remember to note that eight out of ten criminals in prison were abused when they were children (Child Abuse Council, 1993).

Consider these data describing the modern teenager. Approximately two out of ten school-aged youth are affected by anorexia nervosa and bulimia (Phelps & Bajorek, 1991) and between 14% to 23% have vomited to lose weight (National Centers for Disease Control, 1991). By the time students become high school seniors, 90% have experimented with alcohol use and nearly two-thirds have used drugs (National Institute on Drug Abuse, 1992). In 1987, 40% of seniors admitted they had used dangerous drugs and 60% had used marijuana (National Adolescent Student Health Survey). In 1974, the average age American high school students tried marijuana was 16; in 1984, the average age was twelve (Nowinski, 1990).

By the age of 15, a fourth of the girls and a third of the boys are sexually active (Gibbs, 1993), and three out of four teenagers have had sexual intercourse by their senior year (Males, 1993). Seventy-five percent of the mothers who gave birth between the ages of 15 and 17 are on welfare (Simkins, 1984). In 1989, AIDS was the sixth leading cause of death for 15- to 24-year-olds (Tonks, 1992–1993), and many AIDS experts see adolescents as the third wave of individuals affected by HIV (Kaywell, 1993). Thirty-nine percent of sexually active teenagers said they preferred not to use any method of contraception (Harris Planned Parenthood Poll, 1986).

Ten percent of our students are gay (Williams, 1993), and the suicide rate for gay and lesbian teenagers is two to six times higher than that of heterosexual teens (Krueger, 1993). Suicide is the second leading cause of teenage deaths; "accidents" rated first (National Centers for Disease Control, 1987). An adolescent commits suicide every one hour and 47 minutes (National Center for Health Statistics, 1987), and nine children die from gunshot wounds every day in America (Edelman, 1989). For those children growing up in poor, high crime neighborhoods, one in three has seen a homicide by the time they reach adolescence (Beck, 1992).

Consider these data describing the dropout problem. In 1988, the dropout rate among high school students was 28.9% (Monroe, Borzi, & Burrell, 1992). More than 80% of America's one million prisoners are high school dropouts (Hodgkinson, 1991). We spend more than $20,000 per year per prisoner (Hodgkinson, 1991) but spend less than $4,000 per year per student. Forty-five percent of special education students drop out of high school (Wagner, 1989).

Numbers and statistics such as these are often incomprehensible, but consider the data in light of a 12th grade classroom of 30 students. Eight to 15 are being raised by a single parent, six are in poverty, eight to ten are being raised in families with alcoholics, four have experienced some form of family violence, and eight of the female and five of the male students have been sexually violated. Six are anorectic or bulimic, 27 have used alcohol, 18 have used marijuana, and 12 have used dangerous drugs. Twenty-two have had sexual intercourse and 12 of them used no protection. Three students are gay. Eight will drop out of school, and six of those eight will become criminals. Everyday in our country, two adolescents commit suicide by lunchtime.

These are the students that our teachers must teach every day, and these are the students who need help beyond what schools are currently able to provide. Think about the young adults who are both illiterate and in pain! Is there anything that can be done to help these young people with their problems while increasing their literacy skills? Since most of our nation's prisoners are illiterate—the acting out side—and most homeless people are not exactly Rhodes scholars—the withdrawal side— it seems logical to try to help these adolescents while they are still within the educational system.

Perhaps this series, which actually pairs literacy experts with therapists, can help the caretakers of our nation's distraught youth—teachers, counselors, parents, clergy, and librarians—acquire understanding and knowledge on how to better help these troubled teenagers. The series provides a unique approach to guide these caretakers working with troubled teenagers. Experts discuss young adult literature, while therapists provide analysis and advice for protagonists in these novels. Annotated bibliographies provide the reader with similar sources that can be used to help teenagers discuss these issues while increasing their literacy skills.

Joan F. Kaywell

REFERENCES

Bassuk, E. L. & Rubin, L. (1987). Homeless children: A neglected population. *American Journal of Orthopsychiatry, 57* (2), p. 279 ff.

Beck, J. (1992, May 19). Inner-city kids beat the odds to survive. *The Tampa Tribune*.

Craig, S. E. (1992, September). The educational needs of children living with violence. *Phi Delta Kappan, 74* (1), p. 67 ff.

Edelman, M. W. (1989, May). Defending America's children. *Educational Leadership, 46* (8), p. 77 ff.

Edwards, P. A. & Young, L. S. J. (1992, September). Beyond parents: Family, community, and school involvement. *Phi Delta Kappan, 74* (1), p. 72 ff.

Gibbs, N. (1993, May 24). How should we teach our children about sex? *Time, 140* (21), p. 60 ff.

Gress, J. R. (1988, March). Alcoholism's hidden curriculum. *Educational Leadership, 45* (6), p. 18 ff.

Hodgkinson, H. (1991, September). Reform versus reality. *Phi Delta Kappan, 73* (1), p. 9 ff.

Howe II, H. (1991, November). America 2000: A bumpy ride on four trains. *Phi Delta Kappan, 73* (3), p. 192 ff.

Kaywell, J. F. (1993). *Adolescents at risk: A guide to fiction and nonfiction for young adults, parents and professionals.* Westport, CT: Greenwood Press.

Keller, H. (1967). *The story of my life.* New York: Scholastic.

Krueger, M. M. (1993, March). Everyone is an exception: Assumptions to avoid in the sex education classroom. *Phi Delta Kappan, 74* (7), p. 569 ff.

Males, M. (1993, March). Schools, society, and "teen" pregnancy. *Phi Delta Kappan, 74* (7), p. 566 ff.

Monroe, C., Borzi, M. G., & Burrell, R. D. (1992, January). Communication apprehension among high school dropouts. *The School Counselor, 39* (4), p. 273 ff.

Nowinski, J. (1990). *Substance abuse in adolescents and young adults.* New York: Norton.

Phelps, L. & Bajorek, E. (1991). Eating disorders of the adolescent: Current issues in etiology, assessment, and treatment. *School Psychology Review, 20* (1), p. 9 ff.

Simkins, L. (1984, spring). Consequences of teenage pregnancy and motherhood. *Adolescence, 19* (73), p. 39 ff.

Tonks, D. (1992–1993, December–January). Can you save your students' lives? Educating to prevent AIDS. *Educational Leadership, 50* (4), p. 48 ff.

Wagner, M. (1989). *Youth with disabilities during transition: An overview of descriptive findings from the national longitudinal transition study.* Stanford, CA: SRI International.

Williams, R. F. (1993, spring). Gay and lesbian teenagers: A reading ladder for students, media specialists, and parents. *The ALAN Review, 20* (3), p. 12 ff.

Introduction: The New Realities of Growing Up Today

Pamela S. Carroll

I have comforting memories of growing up with a sister and two brothers within the caring sphere of loving parents, of living in a comfortable home outside of town, right next door to my grandparents, of having good friends, making good grades, achieving in athletics. I have comforting memories of enjoying the passage from childhood to adulthood. Yet these memories are inadequate as a vehicle for helping me make sense of what it means to be an adolescent in today's world. In order to work effectively with today's youth, I must step beyond my memories and remind myself that adolescence is, for many, characterized by frightening uncertainties and unrealistic expectations.

Life had not prepared me to deal with some of the secondary school students whom I found myself teaching in the 1980s. I did not know how to reach students like the tough 16-year-old who came to class with a huge bite mark on his neck and, in tears, explained that his father had gotten drunk and attacked him the night before. My adolescence was far removed from that of the 12-year-old student who told me she had to miss class in order to go to court, where she would be forced to testify against members of a gang who raped her. My teen years were nothing like those of the 14-year-old student who was constantly ridiculed because of his effeminate speech and mannerisms. I had to struggle to try to comprehend how the mother of a young gymnast could push her daughter into one competition after another, with little regard for the consequences related to the girl's social and educational opportunities.

I had to learn about those worlds from the students themselves. They taught me that I cannot draw solely on my own life to try to make sense of the world inhabited by today's youth; no adult can. In the following pages, I will address two significant questions in an effort to help teachers and other adults who, like me, find the need to update their understanding of contemporary adolescents and adolescence. Two core questions are: (1) What do we really know about predictable physical, psychosocial, and intellectual transitions that characterize puberty and adolescence, and about the impact these characteristics have on adolescents' social realities? (2) What do we need to recognize and understand about the ways that adolescence today is different than it has ever been before?

In this introduction, I will provide a few answers to the first core question. This introductory section is intended to help readers establish an updated frame of reference about adolescents—a frame of reference from which the ideas presented in the remainder of the book might be considered. The second core question is outlined in this chapter and addressed in the eight chapters that follow. Only a few of the most serious issues that are currently associated with growing up in the United States can be discussed in a single book. Nevertheless, the contributing writers have devoted effort to bring further attention to specific contemporary social realities that shape, in part, our adolescent students' worlds. Their goal is to suggest ways in which teachers, media specialists, and other adults can work alongside students toward an understanding of those issues, within the low-risk environments of secondary English classrooms and through class assignments that require experiences within the broader community.

Each writing team is led by a specialist in secondary school literature; the literature specialist has collaborated with a medical, social, psychological, or ethical specialist in order to bring our attention to ways in which teachers, media specialists, and other adults can use literary resources as a means of beginning meaningful conversations with today's youth about some of the social realities that influence them as they come of age.

As adults who work with teens, we must draw on updated knowledge instead of relying solely on our own memories of what it was like to be a teenager. Those who have collaborated to write the chapters in this book have chosen to focus on several touchstones for beginning to understand the world inhabited by adolescents at the beginning of the twenty-first century. The topics include complications of the following in adolescents' lives: contemporary music; sexuality, sexual activity, and gender confusion; violence, gang participation, and high-risk behaviors; rape as one kind of abuse; body image and self-esteem; the confusing transition from high school to college; ethical questions surrounding coach and athlete relationships; and explicit and implicit demands of sports participation.

This list of topics, though far from complete, offers a beginning for teachers, media specialists, and other adults who, like me, have too long relied on their own memories of adolescence and have found that their experiences do not help them make sense of adolescence as it exists here and now.

In order to effectively bring an understanding of social realities to bear on our understanding of adolescence, we need first to consider some of the characteristics that define adolescents today. It is these characteristics that begin to answer the first core question.

CORE QUESTION ONE: WHAT DO WE REALLY KNOW ABOUT PREDICTABLE PHYSICAL, PSYCHOSOCIAL, AND INTELLECTUAL TRANSITIONS THAT CHARACTERIZE PUBERTY AND ADOLESCENCE, AND ABOUT THE IMPACT THESE CHARACTERISTICS HAVE ON ADOLESCENTS' SOCIAL REALITIES?

Changes in the Onset and Duration of Adolescence

Recently, I told a group of adults that I am a former teacher of middle and high school students, and that I am now involved in teacher education. Their responses were predictable: "Adolescents? Are you crazy?" "Teens today don't want to learn—they just want to enjoy themselves." "No one could possibly pay me enough to teach middle or high school students!" Most teachers of secondary school students have probably had similar experiences. I believe that responses like these are perhaps in part the products of adults' personal contacts with teens. However, the generally negative impressions of today's youth that are reflected in these adults' comments are also fueled by indirect contacts with youth. When we pay attention to print and nonprint advertisements, we see renderings of apathetic, egocentric, and aimless teens. When we read and watch national news, we are horrified, with legitimate reason, by stories of a disturbed and increasingly violent teen population. When we watch television and movies, we see young people portrayed, on one hand, as cavalier about sexual activity, vocations, and values; on the other hand, we see teens portrayed as hostile toward the adults who have control of the social power and economic resources to which teens, especially poor and minority ones, are denied access. What do we really know about the physical, psychosocial, and intellectual changes that are typical of adolescence?

Physical Characteristics of Adolescents and Social Consequences

Hans Sebald (1992) explains that, while "adolescence refers to the period of social maturation, pubescence refers to the physiological development during which the reproductive system matures" (103). Because we are adults, it is sometimes difficult for teachers to recall the rapid and often confusing physical changes of pubescence that occur during middle and high school. For girls, a major growth spurt that marks puberty normally occurs between the ages of 10 and 14; adult size is usually reached between ages 15 and 18 (Wolman, 1998, p. 9). Besides an increase in height, this growth spurt is usually outwardly apparent in the softening and rounding of hips and the development of breasts; girls also see the growth of body hair under the arms and in the pubic area, and at an average age of just over 12, they begin to menstruate. These changes are brought about by hormonal changes, which can easily affect a young female's emotional condition as potently as her physical one. The changes are manifested in classroom interactions in which young females appear to be gloomy and irritable at times, and cheerful and enthusiastic the next day—or the next minute. Girls develop earlier than they did a century ago, when menstruation typically began not at age 12, but at age 17. Further, females in the second half of the twentieth century are four inches taller and twenty-two pounds heavier than they were in the late 1880s (Sebald, 1992, p. 106).

Boys usually have their major growth spurt between the ages of 12 and 17; adult size is reached between 17 to 20 years of age (Wolman, 1998, p. 9). For young adolescent males, the growth spurt is outwardly apparent in increased height and weight, and in muscular definition. Underarm and pubic hair growth is followed by the emergence of upper-lip hair. Adolescent males are often embarrassed during classes when they call out answers, because their voice cracks as it begins to deepen. Males are interested in the growth of their testes and their penis. Between the ages of 13 and 14, the testes grow rapidly; between 14 and 17, the penis typically doubles in size. Another indicator of puberty for males is the beginning of nocturnal emissions that accompany the development of their sex organs. Boys whose physical development is slower than that of those with whom they must shower during physical education classes or other sports participation often experience anxiety about their development. On average, boys today are five inches taller and twenty-four pounds heavier than they were one hundred years ago (Sebald, 1992, 106). All of these physical changes weigh heavily on the minds of many of the students who are in our middle and high school classrooms; therefore, they have an almost tangible impact on the academic environment.

In most respects, early physical maturation is negative for females and positive for males. Females who develop before their classmates are often ostracized and ridiculed by members of both sexes. Girls may make ugly comments to and about them out of jealousy, while males are more likely to make comments out of desire and curiosity. Females who develop early may feel removed emotionally and socially from the friends they had relied on before they began to show signs of physical development; the abandonment can easily damage, at least temporarily, females' self-esteem and undermine their self-confidence. As teachers, we need to be aware of the potential impact on behavior that early (or late) physical development may provoke. Because females feel uncomfortable with their new bodies, a problem that is exacerbated by early maturation, they often have trouble in social situations, including classrooms.

In a study conducted in mixed and same-sex schools in New Zealand, A. Caspi (1995) found that girls who mature early have more problems in school, particularly in mixed-sex schools. Caspi notes that earlier research in the United States identified the following as problems experienced by early maturing females: body image disturbance, lower academic success, and conduct problems in school. Similar problems were found in the New Zealand students. Caspi suggests that "the early onset of menarche was associated with the most disruptive psychosocial reactions in adolescence" and hypothesizes that these effects are more pronounced when a girl enters a coed school than when a girl enters a same-sex school, because coed schools expose girls to "a greater variety of social and sexual pressures from peers" and possibly to "predatory attention of males" (63). Caspi further notes that coed schools are more " 'pleasure oriented' than single-sex schools; they appear to place more emphasis on social affiliation and less emphasis on the control and discipline of students" (63). In terms of their time management, students in single-sex schools "have less free time, spend less time on extracurricular activities, and spend more time on homework . . . institutional pressures that would curb their inclination to misbehave" (64). The researchers conclude that "the cultural and social organization of coed schools may complicate girls' responses to the onset of puberty, especially if it is early" (67). They provide teachers an indirect warning that takes into account students' psychosocial development: "Males in the classroom are more disruptive for young women than for little girls (never mind that the 'young women' and the 'little girls' were born in the same year)" (72).

On the other hand, males who become physically mature early are more popular among male and female peers; they are perceived to be leaders even by teachers, regardless of their emotional, social, or intellectual maturity, when they have the physical appearance of an adult. Nevertheless, as Wolman (1998) notes, an advantage for late maturing males and females may be that they are "better able to reconcile physical and social/emotional/intellectual maturation, so they may actually have advantages that are not at first apparent to their peers and to themselves" (12).

Nutritional advances and universal health care account for earlier maturation among American youth in the late twentieth century. Sebald (1992) notes another interesting contributor: "Rate and quality of growth correlate positively with socioeconomic status. The differences are small but consistent from one study to another. Children of professionals are on the average taller and heavier than those from middle class homes, who, in turn, exceed in all aspects of growth the children from the lowest socioeconomic class" (107). Teachers must wonder what kind of influence a small physical stature paired with poverty must have, particularly on adolescent males, who are more likely than females to gauge their maturity on physical development.

Adolescents of the current generation often appear adultlike earlier than teens did in previous generations. This tendency would probably not pose a problem if social conditions were similar to those that existed in the 1800s. However, the biological changes of adolescence have been outpaced by rapid societal changes. The "disjunction between biological and social development" that David Hamburg (1990) identifies means that young people who are physically mature may be granted admission into adult activities for which they are not emotionally, socially, intellectually, or spiritually ready. Middle school–aged girls who engage in sexual intercourse with older males provide a pointed example. These girls, who are physically more mature than their own male age-mates, easily convince themselves that the older males are "in love" with them. Using immature reasoning and emotions, the girls allow themselves to be taken advantage of by males who are interested in physical, not emotional, connection.

Historian Joan Jacobs Brumberg, in her fascinating book *The Body Project: An Intimate History of American Girls* (1997), discusses many examples of the "mismatch between biology and culture" that results in treatment of adolescent females as if they were fully grown and intellectually mature women. The consequences of this equation, according to Brumberg, include the following:

1. teen pregnancy;

2. females' dissatisfaction with their bodies, which leaves them more vulnerable to the males and females who tell them, "I'll love you if you will sleep with me," or "You are so beautiful when you . . .";

3. easy manipulation by media and companies that create perceived needs by playing on teens' vulnerabilities, such as the current "need" for tight bodies and large breasts. (197)

Brumberg explains that adolescent females have a history of falling victim to the "body projects" that they help their culture create. An example of the biological and cultural mismatch exists in the story of acne. In the nineteenth century, pimples were linked with the "nervous excitement" of masturbation and thus improper sexual activity or, at least of "impure or lascivious thoughts" (64). Physicians were taught that if pimples did not clear up, the moral character of the patient must be investigated (64). Acne was also regarded as an indication of "serious disturbances within the body such as smallpox, tuberculosis, or, worst of all, syphilis. . . . Thus, skin was a critical marker of both moral and physical health" (63). In the late 1800s, medical doctors noted that acne was worse among females than males. In our time, as Brumberg notes, "Because of cultural mandates that link femininity to flawless skin, the burden of maintaining a clear complexion has devolved disproportionately upon women and girls" (61). This mandate has led to a growing cosmetics industry that caters to females' fears that their skin is flawed. Further, because acne has grown to be associated with emotional anguish, dermatology has become "a lucrative staple of the trade," and drug companies, as well as medical doctors, have benefited as a result (62).

Clearly, physical development is inextricably linked to development in other aspects of adolescents' lives.

Psychosocial Characteristics and Social Consequences

Why are adolescents often insecure about their changing bodies? Part of the answer lies in the fact that they are also growing psychologically, socially, and intellectually during puberty. Teens begin to move outside of the influence of their families and childhood friendships for emotional and social interaction and validation during adolescence. They may also begin to shy away from coaches, teachers, and others in the roles of adult authority once they enter adolescence. It is helpful for teachers, parents, and other adults to remember that adolescents must move away from the predictable grounding of childhood as a normal and necessary step toward adulthood. Adults who grieve over the fact that a child no longer asks their permission before choosing a new pair of sneakers and those who are shocked when young teens adopt new tastes in music or hairstyles, may not be aware that such changes are normally healthy signs. The signs indicate that the children are growing up, that they are beginning to make decisions as individuals or as members of peer groups outside of the family, and are no longer acting solely as reflections of their parents' and other adults' influences. Nevertheless, we must not confuse teens' apparent self-sufficiency with completed maturation. We need to be able to recognize when they need help, and provide it, even if they do not recognize the need.

According to David Hamburg (1994), adolescents address specific psychosocial developmental tasks; these tasks involve beginning to move away from dependence on their families and lifelong friends while maintaining connections with them; beginning to be more responsible for personal decisions and personal behaviors; beginning to make new friends; beginning to develop personal intimacy and sexuality; and beginning to deal with complex intellectual challenges (184).

Teachers may well be more familiar with the problems associated with psychosocial changes than other adults are because we see the impact in classrooms when students seem to spend more time socializing than working and more time planning ways to make desired connections with others than concentrating on their lessons. However, we need to consider the bigger picture, too, the one we may not regularly notice among our own students.

What do the psychosocial realities of today's students look like? Hamburg (1994) suggests that there is evidence that today's teens must negotiate myriad problems, including increases in these areas:

1. teenage sexual activity, and in pregnancies for teens 15-years-old and younger;

2. drug and alcohol abuse, with adolescent use of marijuana beginning by tenth grade, and binge drinking and intoxication growing most rapidly among young adolescent females;

3. obesity, eating disorders, and poor physical fitness, and resulting low self-esteem;

4. delinquency and violence, not only among poor dropout teens, but now affecting teens from the mainstream communities, and with the incidence of rape, robbery, or assault about twice as high as the rate for people age 20 and older;

5. serious injuries, including injuries that cause 57 percent of all deaths of adolescents who are 10- to 14-years-old

6. suicides among adolescents, with greatest increases among white males, and with those who are intoxicated seven times more likely than other victims to use a gun;

7. single-parent families and stepfamilies, with poverty more closely associated with single-parent than with two-parent families.

Hamburg also notes that adolescent problems frequently are clustered; clustering is seen, for example, in a positive correlation of alcohol use with both serious injuries and suicide by gun shot; in a positive correlation of serious injuries with poverty, low status, high-risk and adult-like behavior, use of alcohol and drugs, easy availability of weapons and other dangerous objects, and lack of information about risks and consequences of behaviors; and in the correlation of poverty and single-parent families (Hamburg, 1994, 188–196).

As adults who work with today's adolescents, we must be willing to acknowledge that the world our students inhabit is territory that is, in many ways, frightening and unfamiliar to us. With this awareness, we study that world and attempt to see it—from their eyes. In order to understand their psychosocial realities, we must also consider the ways of thinking that characteristically emerge during adolescence.

Intellectual Characteristics and Social Consequences

Many teachers are acquainted with the basic premises of the theory of intellectual development that has been espoused by Jean Piaget (1990).

Of particular importance here are his distinctions between the kind of thinking that children do between the ages of approximately 7 and 11, which he calls "concrete operational thought," and the kind of thinking that older children, adolescents, and adults are capable of, which he labels "formal operational thought." It is important for teachers to realize that, while cognitive development is predictable and regular, the speed of development can vary from one individual to another, and from one social environment to another; therefore, we might find an intellectually advanced 12-year-old and an intellectually immature one in the same seventh-grade class. And the less intellectually mature one may look physically more mature than the other student. This confusing possibility reminds us of the importance of taking time to get to know our students as individuals and of paying regular attention to them as individuals.

In contrast to preadolescent thinking, which involves the ability to think in terms of concrete objects instead of hypotheses and which is characterized by trial-and-error problem solving instead of the testing of various possible solutions, adolescent thinking involves a more complete logic. Adolescent thinking occurs at a level that includes formal reasoning; this kind of thinking, which is frequently referred to as "abstract," allows for "the subordination of the real to the realm of the possible, and consequently the linking of all possibilities to one another by necessary implications that encompass the real, but at the same time go beyond it" (Piaget, 1990, p. 62).

Of special significance to teachers of English/language arts is the fact that this new kind of thinking in hypotheses, with attention to possibilities, allows students to play with language more fully. They can begin to interpret the second symbol system of metaphors and similies; they enjoy puns; they write involved narratives about fantastic people and places.

This new kind of thinking also has social impact. Teens think about themselves and their problems in ways that children do not. David Elkind (1998) notes that this new thinking includes what he calls the "imaginary audience" and "personal fable." The "imaginary audience" is manifested in the "assumption that everyone around them is preoccupied with the same subject that engrosses them: namely, themselves," and it is this notion that everyone is watching every move they make that accounts for teens' heightened self-consciousness (40). The "personal fable" rests upon adolescents' assumption that they are "special, different from other people" (43) and that laws of nature and other forces that apply to other people do not apply to them. For example, Elkind says that when teens smoke "under the belief that they are invulnerable to any harm from this habit" (44) and when a young girl feels that no one has ever suffered in love like she has (45), they are demonstrating the idea of the personal fable.

Children do not have metacognitive abilities that allow them to think about their own thinking in the ways that teens do. The nature of their participation in classroom discussions grows in depth and creativity because adolescents can look at issues from a variety of stances. They can suspend judgment until they have heard ideas other than their own. They can agree to disagree and can even accept ambiguity when no definite answer is possible. Wolman (1998) reminds teachers that intelligence and good grades are not necessarily paired during adolescence. Students who earned high grades in elementary school, in part because they were interested in pleasing the teacher, may lose interest in some aspects of school during adolescence; instead of focusing attention on pleasing the teacher, teens may turn to "discussing religion, politics, morals, social order and above all, their own personalities and future" (17). In classrooms, we can either ignore adolescents' interests and push on despite students' lack of attention and effort, or we can incorporate their interests into our curricular plans so that the classroom becomes an extension of, not an intrusion into, students' lives.

Lawrence Kohlberg is well known for his contributions to understanding of moral development as a component of cognitve development. His ideas are significant for us because social behaviors often lie at the intersection of moral and cognitive development. Briefly, Kohlberg posits that people work through the following hierarchical stages, always moving forward, not backward (except in the case of extreme trauma), in the context of the environment and social structures in which they live:

A. *Preconventional Level*: the child knows rules and interprets them in terms of physical or hedonistic consequences of action (punishment, reward, and so on). There are two stages:

1. punishment and obedience orientation—"right" is that which gets reward, regardless of human value;
2. instrumental-relativist orientation—"right" is that which satisfies one's own needs; reciprocity, such as "You scratch my back, I'll scratch yours," is a useful guide.

B. *Conventional Level*: the person sees that maintaining the values of his or her family or group is valuable in its own right, regardless of consequences; this level is marked by conformity and loyalty to personal expectations and social order, and it has two stages:

3. interpersonal concordance, or "good boy, nice girl" orientation, in which "good" is that which pleases others; behavior is judged by intention, so that "He means well" becomes an important concept;
4. law-and-order orientation, in which "right" is that which is in line with fixed rules and laws and the maintenance of social order for its own sake.

C. *Postconventional, Autonomous, or Principled Level*: the person makes an effort to define values that are valid, regardless of the authority of a group or an individual's identification with a group; it has two stages:

5. a social contract, legalistic orientation, which has utilitarian overtones and in which "right" is what is good for individuals as agreed upon by the society in general; consensus is important as a balance for relativistic values (Kohlberg claims that "This is the 'official' morality of the American government and constitution" [92]);
6. universal-ethical-principle orientation, in which "right" is a decision based on conscience, in accord with self-chosen ethical principles through appealing to logical comprehensiveness, universality, and consistency; according to Kohlberg, "These principles are abstract and ethical (the Golden Rule, the categorical imperative); they are not concrete moral rules like the Ten Commandments. At heart, these are universal principles of justice, of the reciprocity and equality of human rights, and of respect for the dignity of human beings as individual persons" (95).

(Kohlberg's chart, reprinted from the *Journal of Philosophy*, October 25, 1973, is found in Muuss, pp. 92–95.)

It is important for teachers to realize that a student's understanding of the difference between a "right" and a "wrong" behavior is no guarantee that the student will act on that knowledge. For example, a student may realize that it is wrong to cheat on a test, not only because cheating is against the class rules, but also because it, in effect, robs the student who has studied of an ability to distinguish himself from the one who cheats. However, when this student finds herself in a pressing situation, she may cheat in order to maintain her grade average. Ability to use moral reasoning does not ensure the use of it. How might we encourage students to enact moral decision making and thus to grow in terms of moral development?

Kohlberg (1990) does not believe that "character education," "value education," or "affective education," with an emphasis on prescribed values, is the way to help children grow toward moral maturity while they mature cognitively. Instead, he believes that children should learn values through discussion of various possible answers to problems. In classrooms, this might mean the following:

1. give attention to change, in terms of reasoning, not in terms of particular beliefs;

2. do not seek consensus, since students in the class are at different stages of moral development;

3. do not stress your opinions as the teacher, but treat yours as only one of many views;

4. promote the notion that some judgments are more adequate than others, instead of setting up "right" and "wrong" possibilities; at the same time, present students with problems that urge them to the next level of moral reasoning. (98)

Kohlberg's former collaborator, Carol Gilligan (1990), who is well known for her work on gender differences in moral judgment, poses a major challenge to Kohlberg's theory by introducing a feminist perspective to moral development. She contends that neither males nor females are genetically more moral, but that they approach moral dilemmas in different ways. The tests of moral development that Kohlberg designed recognize only male ways of thinking as legitimate. Gilligan compares the moral reasoning of an 11-year-old boy and an 11-year-old girl, and shows how the female is disadvantaged by the way the test questions are asked and interpreted. Jake's and Amy's responses differ greatly when each is asked to respond to the prompt: Mr. Heinz's wife will die without medicine, and he can't afford the extravagant price asked by the pharmacist. Should he steal the medicine? (This question is modeled after the one Kohlberg asked in the study that led him to the design of the model for stages of moral development.)

Jake sees the problem as " 'sort of like a math problem with humans' " (104), one he solves by saying that Heinz should steal the drug because human life is worth more than money. Jake adds that the druggist will not die without the money for the drug, but the wife will die without the drug itself—and that the druggist can get more money from rich patients, whereas Heinz cannot replace his wife. Jake's moral development, according to Kohlberg's scheme, then, is at the conventional level, a mix of stages 3 and 4; he differentiates morality and law, sees that laws can have mistakes, and ultimately, in saying it is the right thing for Heinz to steal the drug, "points toward the principled conception of justice that Kohlberg equates with moral maturity" (104).

Amy seems more perplexed by the problem posed by the interviewer. Her response is circular, and it is scored lower on the scale of moral development than is Jake's, indicating that she has less moral development than he does. But there is a problem in that the questions asked don't fit her construction of the problem itself, so her answers don't "fit" the scale. Amy says that Heinz should talk to his wife and/or the druggist and find another way to get the drug, maybe by borrowing the money, because if he steals it, he might go to jail and thus be unable to help his wife in the future.

What Gilligan notes is that the interviewer does not really hear Amy's answers. Amy does not interpret the problem as a math problem that involves humans. Instead, for Amy, the problem lies in the fact that the druggist fails to respond to the wife. Amy's approach to the problem is different from Jake's approach; the interviewer seems to accept Jake's logic and to reject Amy's. Gilligan explains that the different kinds of logic are complementary, not contradictory: "Both children thus recognize the need for agreement but see it as mediated in different ways: he impersonally through systems of logic and law, she personally through communication in relationship. As he relies on the conventions of logic to deduce the solution to this dilemma, assuming these conventions to be shared, so she relies on a process of communication, assuming connection and believing that her voice will be heard" (105).

Gilligan offers today's teachers an intriguing area to investigate when we engage in self-evaluation of the ways we treat and evaluate students' ideas. Her work raises new questions about our understanding of the intermingling of biological, psychosocial, and intellectual development; it provides a natural segue into the second core question on which this book is based.

CORE QUESTION TWO: WHAT DO WE NEED TO RECOGNIZE AND UNDERSTAND ABOUT THE WAYS THAT ADOLESCENCE TODAY IS DIFFERENT THAN IT HAS EVER BEEN BEFORE?

Changes in the onset and duration of adolescence have had an important impact on the way that teens grow up today, and on the way adults and youth perceive the dynamic period called adolescence. However, there are other characteristics that are unique to today's adolescents because they are unique to contemporary society. Each team of writers who have contributed chapters to this volume present classroom-oriented considerations of a particular aspect of one of the realities of society with which adolescents are faced.

Kathryn H. Kelly, with Elaine Beaudoin, addresses the issue of the crime and violence that are facts of life for members of gangs in chapter 1, "Society's 'At Risk' Teenagers: What It Means."

M. Linda Broughton and Mae Z. Cleveland address one aspect of the concept of teen identity when they focus on the impact of body image on adolescents' social interaction and development in chapter 2, "Body Image and Society's Impact."

Elizabeth L. Watts and LaShawnda Eggelletion address teenage sexuality and suggest ways of discussing it through attention to literature in high school classrooms, in chapter 3, "Society's Impact on Adolescents and their Sexuality."

Gail P. Gregg and Maureen Kenny, along with an anonymous contributor, present one example of a violent crime to which teens fall victim in chapter 4, "Adolescent Rape." This chapter includes the anonymous contributor's painful personal recollection of her own rape and the life-long impact the event had on her development. The riveting recollections emerged when the contributor read the book that is featured in Chapter Five, as a vehicle for addressing the issue of rape with mature high school students.

Pamela S. Carroll and Steven B. Chandler use young adult literature, and suggest ways to teach it, as they use sports participation as a metaphor for the struggles of adolescents, with special attention to teens who are left to make their own decisions in a confusing world, in chapter 5, "Sports in the Life of Today's Adolescents."

Lawrence Baines, Elizabeth Strehle, and Steven Bell, with Josh Murfree, provide us with a view of a broader spectrum of adolescents' music and suggestions for including their music in classroom assignments, in chapter 6, "Music and Musicians' Effects on Adolescents."

Chris Crowe and Mel Olson discuss problems in modern athletics, with particular attention to male coach/male athlete relationships, and how these problems might be addressed through literature study in high school English classes, in chapter 7, "Ethics in Athletics for Adolescents."

Connie S. Zitlow, with Janet M. Rogers, discusses the role of adults during teens' transition from the world of home and high school to the unknown territory of being away from home in college in chapter 8, "Leaving Home: Transitions and Independence."

The contributing writers address the issues from a particular perspective. Because there are many ways to approach the topics, readers may find that they want to explore a particular topic in greater depth. The following are texts that I have found useful in my quest to better understand the issues introduced within this volume.

RECOMMENDED READINGS

General Overview

Snyder, Thomas D., and Linda L. Shafer. (1996). *Youth Indicators 1996: Trends in the Well-Being of American Youth*. Washington, DC: US DOE, Office of Educational Research and Improvement. 167 pp. (ISBN: 0–7881–4010–8).

The Influence of Music and Media

Arnett, Jeffrey Jensen. (1996). *Metalheads: Heavy Metal Music and Adolescent Alienation*. Boulder, CO: Westview Press. 196 pp. (ISBN: 0–8133–2812–8).

Arnett takes readers into the world of heavy metal music and culture. This is a place that features "harsh, dark sound" and lyrics that focus on "alienation and anger" (41), and that does not readily admit adults. Arnett's book is a sometimes frightening guide to the fierce, abrasive, chaotic world in which many teens find a sense of belonging.

Giroux, Henry. (1997). *Channel Surfing: Race Talk and the Destruction of Today's Youth.* New York: St. Martin's Press. 248 pp. (ISBN: 03–12–1626–50).

Giroux points, without flinching, to the current crop of television situation comedies, movies that depict American teen life, and visual advertisements to deliver an indictment of the adult-controlled, "electronically mediated culture" (5) that characterizes youth as "demonized or trivialized" (2) and as a social "menace" (5).

Strasburger, Victor C. (1995). *Adolescents and the Media: Medical and Psychological Impact.* Thousand Oaks, CA: Sage Publications. 137 pp. (ISBN: 0–8039–5499–9).

Strasburger presents statistics about the ubiquitous presence of television in American homes, the television viewing habits of teens, the correlation between watching violent television and committing violent acts, and other timely topics. His book offers teachers and others solid evidence for suggesting that families turn off their televisions more often.

Sexuality, Sexual Activity, and Gender Confusion among Adolescents

Coles, Robert E. (1997). *The Youngest Parents: Teenage Pregnancy as It Shapes Lives.* Durham, NC: Center for Documentary Studies, in assoc. with New York: W. W. Norton. 223 pp. (ISBN: 0–393–04082–8).

This book uses excerpts from interviews conducted by Coles, a child psychiatrist and Pulitzer Prize–winning writer, and his sons, with teen parents in cities and towns across America. Complete with poignant photographs, this book succeeds where statistics fail, in bringing to life the overlapping layers of problems associated with teen parenthood.

Due, Linnea. (1995). *Joining the Tribe: Growing Up Gay and Lesbian in the 90's.* New York: Anchor. 272 pp. (ISBN: 0–385–47500–4).

In this book, Due, a gay-rights activist and journalist, shares her conversations with gay and lesbian teens with whom she talks in cities across the United States. Due's book, though it will be controversial for some teachers and in some communities, has the potential of helping teachers learn how to talk with gay and lesbian teens, and how to help them face their own questions.

Portner, Jessica. (1998). "U.S. Teenage Birthrate Tops Industrial Nations." *Education Week* (May 20), 5.

This article is an example of many that are included in this weekly newspaper, one that deals with events and trends that affect American education. Portner's comparisons of the rates of sexual activity among American teens and teens worldwide may help teachers grasp the scope of the problem and begin to regard teenage sexual activity in concrete terms.

Violence (Including Rape), Crime, Gangs, and Other High-Risk Activities

Barr, Stephen. (1998). "Thrilled to Death." *Reader's Digest* (June), 74–81.

This article could be considered melodramatic if the stories it includes were not true. Barr recounts the risks taken by several teens who died as the result of activities including car surfing (riding on the hood of a car while it is in motion), dinking (driving at a high speed while jerking the steering wheel from side to side), and crowding too many people into one car, then driving at excessive speeds. In none of the stories does alcohol provide an almost easy explanation; instead, the teens depicted were involved in their own, or a friend's, conscious and deadly choices.

Hamburg, David A. (1994). *Today's Children: Creating a Future for a Generation in Crisis.* New York: Time Books. 376 pp. (ISBN: 0–8129–2208–5).

Hamburg, a medical doctor and currently the president of the Carnegie Corporation, gives attention to the predictable aspects of adolescence that are discussed in Core Question One, but also addresses the prevalence of violence, crime, and high-risk activities among today's teens. He does a particularly effective job of linking criminal and violent behavior with other problems among youth, such as drug and alcohol abuse, poverty, and lack of education.

Huizinga, David. (1995). "Developmental Sequences in Delinquency: Dynamic Typologies." In Lisa J. Crockett and Ann C. Crouter (Eds.), *Pathways through Adolescence: Individual Development in Relation to Social Contexts*. Mahwah, NJ: Lawrence Erlbaum Associates, 15–34. (ISBN: 0–8058–1500–7).

This article, like others in the volume cited, presents research-based findings to clarify terms and behaviors associated with youthful criminals. Huizinga's article gives teachers specific risk factors to look for so that we might be able to intervene on behalf of students who, because of their life situations and choice of friends, develop the potential to become involved in crime.

Ambiguity and Absence of Direction from Adults

Brown, Bradford B., Mary Jane Lohr, and Carla Trujillo. (1990). "Multiple Crowds and Multiple Life Styles: Adolescents' Perceptions of Peer-Group Stereotypes." In Rolf E. Muuss (Ed.), *Adolescent Behavior and Society: A Book of Readings*, 4th ed. New York: McGraw-Hill, 30–36. (ISBN: 0–07–044164–2).

In this article, the writers summarize their study of teens' perceptions of stereotypes. Their work helps us understand how teens identify groups and how they decide to associate themselves with particular ones, at a time in their lives when age-mates take on a greater significance and the influence of adults diminishes. Teachers should not ignore or underestimate the power of peer influence; although we commonly think of this influence in negative terms, this article helps us recognize that peer influence can be a positive contributor to adolescents' classroom behavior, too.

Elkind, David. (1998). *All Grown Up and No Place to Go: Teenagers in Crisis,* revised ed. Reading, MA: Addison Wesley. 290 pp. (ISBN: 0–201–48385–8).

Child and adolescent development specialist David Elkind contends that today's adolescents are struggling as the result of a shift in society to a "postmodern" period. In this period, "the needs of children and youth are often weighted less heavily than are the needs of parents and the rest of adult society" (xiii). Elkind believes that, as a result, "we as a society have abrogated our responsibility to young people" (xiv). Elkind explains how, in this postmodern period, adults mistakenly treat adolescents as though they were already competent and sophisticated, and therefore do not guide them from childhood into adulthood, as youth were guided in previous generations. His words sound a clear warning to teachers and other adults who tend to confuse adolescents' physical maturity with emotional, psychological, social, intellectual, and spiritual maturity. A useful feature is his discussion of how the "growth markers" that were formerly available to guide children into adolescence and teens into adulthood are now absent. Examples include girls of all ages now being encouraged to wear makeup and sophisticated clothes, and boys of all ages being encouraged to participate in high-stakes competitive sports teams.

Kozol, Jonathan. (1995). *Amazing Grace: The Lives of Children and the Conscience of a Nation.* New York: Crown. 284 pp. (ISBN: 0–06–097697–7).

This book is a gem, one that I wish all teachers had the opportunity to read, though it is not intended for educators per se. Through Kozol's careful and respectful depiction of the people he spent time with in one of New York City's poorest neighborhoods, we become more aware of the almost unthinkable realities that some of our students bring with them to our classrooms. The book raises questions about adults' political, ethical, and social responses to extreme poverty and homelessness among children, teens, and adults.

The issues addressed herein are important problems, and therefore offer teachers and other adults with a place to begin revising our knowledge of what it means to be a young person in today's world. Throughout the remainder of this book, you will find suggestions for addressing some of the contemporary problems of adolescents. Each team of chapter writers has included carefully constructed classroom activities and attention to specific literary texts that might be used as whole-class or independent readings, depending on your own goals, students, school, and community. Most chapters conclude with a list of issue-related questions that the literature specialist asks an expert on behalf of readers. You will have other questions, we are sure, but we hope that the ones here address some of your concerns. Each of the remaining chapters also includes an annotated bibliography, a resource list that will allow you to bring into your classrooms and media centers contemporary texts that will speak to adolescents and the adults who work with them.

Despite the different backgrounds of the many contributing writers, each has one perspective in common: each of us has worked directly with adolescents. Each of us recognizes that although literature alone cannot change the world for today's youth or alter the social conditions that delight and plague them, books can help us make connections with students. Through proposing the pairing of well-chosen texts and lessons that invite students into consideration of those texts, we hope that we will offer young people lenses through which they can see their worlds more clearly and more fully. We hope, too, that the books will offer adult readers a means of vicariously stepping into the world that our youth inhabit, so that we can understand that world with more clarity.

REFERENCES

Arnett, Jeffrey Jensen. (1995). *Metalheads: Heavy Metal Music and Adolescent Alienation.* Boulder, CO: Westview.

Barr, Stephen. (1998). "Thrilled to Death." *Reader's Digest* (June), 74–81.

Brown, Bradford B., Mary Jane Lohr, and Carla Trujillo. (1990). "Multiple Crowds and Multiple Life Styles: Adolescents' Perceptions of Peer-Group Stereotypes." In Rolf E. Muuss (Ed.), *Adolescent Behavior and Society: A Book of Readings*, 4th ed. New York: McGraw-Hill, 30–36.

Brumberg, Joan Jacobs. (1997). *The Body Project: An Intimate History of American Girls.* New York: Random House.

Caspi, Avshalom. (1995). "Puberty and the Gender Organization of Schools: How Biology and Social Context Shape the Adolescent Experience." In Lisa J. Crockett and Ann C. Crouter (Eds.), *Pathways through Adolescence: Individual Development in Relation to Social Contexts.* Mahwah, NJ: Lawrence Erlbaum Associates, 57–74.

Coles, Robert E. (1997). *The Youngest Parents: Teenage Pregnancy as It Shapes Lives.* Durham, NC: Center for Documentary Studies, in association with New York: W. W. Norton.

Due, Linnea. (1995). *Joining the Tribe: Growing Up Gay and Lesbian in the 90's.* New York: Anchor.

Elkind, David. (1998). *All Grown Up and No Place to Go: Teenagers in Crisis.* Rev. ed. Reading, MA: Addison-Wesley.

Gilligan, Carol. (1990). "New Maps of Development: New Visions of Maturity." In Rolf E. Muuss (Ed.), *Adolescent Behavior and Society: A Book of Readings*, 4th ed. New York: McGraw-Hill, 101–110 (reprinted from *American Journal of Orthopsychiatry*, 1982, vol. 52, pp. 199–212).

Giroux, Henry. (1997). *Chanel Surfing: Race Talk and the Destruction of To-day's Youth*. New York: St. Martin's Press.

Hamburg, David. (1990). "Preparing for Life: The Critical Transition of Adolescence." In Rolf E. Muuss (Ed.), *Adolescent Behavior and Society: A Book of Readings*, 4th ed. New York: McGraw-Hill, 5–10.

Hamburg, David. (1994). *Today's Children: Creating a Future for a Generation in Crisis*. New York: Times Books.

Huizinga, David. (1995). "Developmental Sequences in Delinquency: Dynamic Typologies." In Lisa J. Crockett and Ann C. Crouter (Eds.), *Pathways through Adolescence: Individual Development in Relation to Social Contexts*. Mahwah, NJ: Lawrence Erlbaum Associates, 15–34.

Kohlberg, Lawrence. (1990). "The Cognitive-Developmental Approach to Moral Education." In Rolf E. Muuss (Ed.), *Adolescent Behavior and Society: A Book of Readings*, 4th ed. New York: McGraw-Hill, 91–101 (reprinted from *Phi Delta Kappan*, June 1975, vol. 56, pp. 670–677).

Kozol, Jonathan. (1995). *Amazing Grace: The Lives of Children and the Conscience of a Nation*. New York: Crown.

Piaget, Jean. (1990). "Intellectual Evolution from Adolescence to Adulthood." In Rolf E. Muuss (Ed.), *Adolescent Behavior and Society: A Book of Readings*, 4th ed. New York: McGraw-Hill, 61–66 (reprinted from *Human Development*, 1972, vol. 15, pp. 1–12).

Portner, Jessica. (1998). "U.S. Teenage Birthrate Tops Industrial Nations." *Education Week* (May 20), 5.

Sebald, Hans. (1992). *Adolescence: A Social Psychological Analysis*. 4th ed. New York: Prentice-Hall.

Strasburger, Victor C. (1995). *Adolescents and the Media: Medical and Psychological Impact*. Thousand Oaks, CA: Sage Publications (volume 33 in *Developmental Clinical Psychology and Psychiatry*, series ed. Alan E. Kazdin).

Synder, Thomas D. and Linda L. Shafer. (1996). *Youth Indicators 1996: Trends in the Well-Being of American Youth*. Washington, DC: US DOE, Office of Educational Research and Improvement.

Wolman, Benjamin. (1998). *Adolescence: Biological and Psychosocial Perspectives*. Westport, CT: Greenwood.

CHAPTER ONE

Society's "At Risk" Teenagers: What It Means

Kathryn H. Kelly
with Elaine Beaudoin

As teachers, educators, media specialists, parents, and concerned citizens, we have often heard the term "at risk" applied to some of the students in our schools. Although we are familiar with the term, and in some instances have worked with students identified as "at risk," many of us do not know what the label actually means or how to work with this type of student.

Many books classified as young adult literature show teenagers facing problems as they grow up. For the majority of teenagers, the passage from adolescence to adulthood is a difficult journey. But, for some teens—those identified "at risk"—this growth is complicated by lives that are often embroiled in seemingly insurmountable problems. When reading books that have troubled teens as protagonists, I wonder if the pictures painted in the books are true to life. Further, I wonder if "at risk" teens will be able to identify with the characters and situations in the books. If so, will troubled teens be able to find solutions for some of their problems within the pages of these books? In other words, will reading about teenagers like themselves help them handle real-life situations?

To begin answering these questions, we first need to have a clear definition of the term "at risk." One of the foremost researchers in the field of adolescent behavior, Joy G. Dryfoos, defines the term in her book, *Adolescents at Risk: Prevalence and Prevention* (1990). According to her, problem behaviors exhibited by at risk teens fall into four areas: (1) delinquency, (2) substance abuse, (3) teen pregnancy, (4) and school failure. Dryfoos says these problem areas often overlap, with at risk teens exhibiting inappropriate behaviors in two or more of the areas. In addition, she identifies six common characteristics of high-risk youth that can be associated with each of the problem areas. The characteristics are the following:

1. *Age.* Teens who begin to exhibit antisocial behavior at a young age will usually become heavily involved in the behavior and will experience negative consequences.
2. *Educational Expectations.* Students who expect to do poorly in school do have lower grades.
3. *General Behavior.* Teens who fall into any one or all of these problem areas act out bad behaviors such as truancy, antisocial behavior, and other conduct disorders.
4. *Peer Influence.* These teenagers have a low resistance to peer influences and have friends who participate in the same behaviors.
5. *Parental Role.* Most at risk teenagers have parents with whom they have not bonded sufficiently, or parents who do not monitor, supervise, offer guidance, or communicate with them. Their parents tend to be either too permissive or too authoritarian.
6. *Neighborhood Quality.* Usually these teens live in a poverty area or in a densely populated, urban community. (94–95)

In addition to the identification of the four problem areas and the six common characteristics of at risk teenagers, Dryfoos states, based on her research, that one in four adolescents can be labeled at risk and, therefore, has limited potential to become a productive adult. Thus, we must find ways to help our at risk teenagers. Can young adult literature that is written about and for troubled youth help solve the problem?

Since we now have a definition of the term "at risk," we can take a close look at two books written for young adults that center around the lives of troubled teens, in order to see how close to reality they are. The first, *Crews: Gang Members Talk to Maria Hinojosa* (1995) by Maria Hinojosa (with photographs by German Perez), consists of a series of interviews with actual teenage gang members from Queens in New York City. The second, *Don't You Dare Read This, Mrs. Dunfrey* (1996) by Margaret Peterson Haddix, relates the story of 15-year-old Tish Bonner as her life veers out of control. While both of these books focus on teenagers classified as at risk, each delves into different sets of problems faced by troubled teens. Let's take a closer look at them to see if they are accurate depictions of the lives of at risk teens.

The following discussions of each of the selected works include a summary of the book and an analysis of one person or character in the work. The basis of the character analysis, in both cases, is Dryfoos's four problem areas and six common characteristics of at risk youths. Following the discussion of the two selections is a question-and-answer section in which Elaine Beaudoin, a social worker at a large urban high school, talks about her experience working with at risk students. Beaudoin gives us some insight into what school systems are doing to help at risk students, as well as suggestions for what we can do to help these students realize their potential and become productive adults.

CREWS: GANG MEMBERS TALK TO MARIA HINOJOSA

Summary

Crews is a "no-holds-barred" book about the reality of life on the streets of Queens, in New York City. Through interviews with Hispanic gang members, both male and female, we get a very disturbing picture of the lives these teenagers lead.

Hinojosa was prompted to write this book by the senseless murder of an 18-year-old visitor to New York City. Brian Watkins was killed trying to defend his mother from an assault by Gary Morales, a gang member of Flushing's Top Society (FTS). Through the legal proceedings that followed this murder, the public learned that Brian was killed because Gary, called "Rocstar" by his friends, wanted money "to go dancing." To mainstream Americans, this desire seemed to be a frivolous reason to kill someone, but to fellow gang members of FTS, it was understandable. In fact, one member, Coki, says about the incident and Rocstar's sentence: "it's not right that the kid got killed first of all, but it's not right that the man [Rocstar] is gonna spend twenty-five years to life in jail for something he didn't mean to do" (11). Through the pages of this book we begin to see the frightening rationalization behind the gang members' understanding.

Each chapter focuses on individual crew members, either from FTS or another crew, known as 20 Park. Her interviewees consist of five male crew members and six Puerto Rican female crew members who live in the projects of Queens in New York. Hinojosa devotes one entire chapter solely to the girls. Through her questions, Hinojosa finds out what life is like for teenagers growing up as gang members in Queens. The picture is one that shows what it is like to live in an area surrounded by poverty and high crime—an area in which violence is a way of life. Also, Hinojosa asks the members about their plans for the future, their dreams and aspirations, and how they intend to make their dreams become realities. Through the words of these crew members, we are introduced to a subculture of our society that has its own set of values and code of conduct—both of which are alien to mainstream American society.

Every one of these teenagers is surrounded by violence. All of them know someone their age who has been killed. In fact, the interview session with the girls was delayed a couple of days because one of their friends had been killed over a pair of sunglasses earlier in the week. While the girls were upset over the death, they accepted the event as a part of everyday life. Perhaps this acceptance comes from seeing daily acts of violence in their lives—few of which make the headlines. These girls have built a tough outer shell around them to protect themselves from the abuse they suffer at the hands of their parents, boyfriends, peers, and fellow crew members.

This acceptance of violence is also prevalent among their male counterparts. These teenagers have to resort to violence as a way to survive on the streets. Without being abusive, or tough, to other people, they would never gain the "respect" of their crew members. They project the image of "Don't mess with me—I'm bad!" This image is a protective device that they employ to keep from becoming victims of the streets.

Along with the general acceptance of violence, these young adults are surrounded by the ready availability of drugs and alcohol. To them, selling drugs is an acceptable way to make money on the streets. In fact, since the only jobs these teens and their parents can get are low-wage ones that keep them at poverty level, many see drug dealing as a quick and easy way to make a better life for themselves. However, their view of drug users/abusers varies. For the most part, users of hard drugs like cocaine or crack are looked down on, even though the majority of these teens readily accept the use of marijuana and alcohol as a part of their lives.

In order to survive in a world full of violence and substance abuse, these teenagers band together in crews. Crew members watch out for each other and serve as a kind of support system. In fact, "i trust the crew more than i trust any guy" is the title of the chapter about the girl members. But while the crew provides protection, the peer pressure exerted by the members also forces teenagers to stay on the streets. Therefore, the crew actually becomes the main deterrent to their making a better life for themselves—to their reaching their dreams. This book captures the futility these teens face as they try to survive in their world.

Analysis of Teenagers in *Crews*

When I apply the four problem behavior areas identified by Dryfoos to the people in *Crews*, it becomes obvious that much overlap of at risk indicators occurs. While not all crew members exhibit the same extent of behaviors in all the problem areas, they all have some degree of problem in every area. For instance, all members exhibit behaviors associated with the first problem area, delinquency; however, the degree to which each individual takes part in criminal activities or antisocial behaviors varies. These teens talk about actions as inconsequential as jumping a subway turnstile to get a free ride and writing their "tags" (graffiti writer's street name) on public property to events as grave as the armed robbery of a drugstore and the murder of an 18-year-old tourist in a robbery attempt.

Involvement in the second problem area, substance abuse, also varies by degree. Still, all of the crew members, male and female, admit that they have either used or abused drugs or alcohol at some time in their young lives. The level of their experience with consuming these substances varies from occasional use of marijuana and alcohol to actual addiction to cocaine or crack. While a few stop using drugs, some sell drugs on the streets. They rationalize this by believing that selling drugs is not as bad as using them; for gang members, dealing is a quick, easy, legitimate way to make money. Some of these teens come from homes where parents abuse drugs and alcohol. Some also come from homes that shun drugs and alcohol. Further, as Dryfoos points out, there is an overlap between delinquency and substance abuse in their lives. Crew members admit that many of the violent acts and serious crimes they commit are done while they are under the influence of drugs or alcohol.

Teen pregnancy, the third area, is also a huge problem. Of the eleven crew members Hinojosa interviewed, five are either fathers, mothers, or soon to be mothers. For both males and females, having a baby is a very adult thing to do. These teenage parents know that responsibility goes along with parenthood; most of them want to be better parents than theirs have been. The problem is, they do not know how to be parents. They know they should change their violent lifestyle and get off the streets for the sake of their child, but they don't know what to change into. Therefore, most only stay off the streets temporarily. One interesting fact is that having a baby gives these teens an acceptable way to leave crew life without losing "respect." Some actually do leave the crew for a while, but usually they are back shortly after the birth of the child. After all, now they need to find a way to support their family. These teen pregnancies are also a contributing factor to the fourth problem area, school failure.

These young adults see school and a high school diploma as their ticket to a brighter future. But the life that surrounds them often contributes to their failure to stay in school. For example, two of the girls interviewed who were pregnant dropped out of school to have their babies. Both plan to return to school later, but the additional pressure of raising a child may prove to be a barrier to doing so. Another reason these teens do not stay in school is that school is a source of frustration for them. Not only is school "boring," but it is also a place where they are *controlled*—not *in* control. Therefore, some drop out of school in order to get control over their lives, only to find their lives further out of control on the street.

Coki, a leader in FTS, tells Hinojosa that he dropped out of school for a while in order to "hang" on the streets. As a leader in FTS, he gets the sense of being in control through being on the streets. However, he now calls himself an "intelligent hood" because he is back in school to get his diploma. He now realizes that he will need the diploma at some time in the future. These two examples illustrate why school failure for these teenagers is partly due to the lives they lead outside of school. Once again, the degree of failure in school varies among these teens, but the majority of them experience some form of frustration and failure in school.

Thus, all of the teenagers in this book are at risk according to the first part of Dryfoos's definition. All of them exhibit behaviors in all four problem areas. Now, in order to analyze the book in terms of the six common characteristics of at risk students, let's look at perhaps the most troubled of the teens interviewed by Hinojosa, a male named Shank.

Shank is a senior in high school; he exhibits problem behaviors in three of the four areas named by Dryfoos: delinquency, substance abuse and school failure. For all of these problems, Shank displays the six common characteristics.

The first characteristic concerns the age when the person begins to engage in problem behaviors. At age thirteen, Shank enters the crew life. He joins a Chinese gang and begins running with the 20 Park crew in the space of one year. As a member of these gangs, Shank begins to take part in delinquent behaviors. In fact, the first night he hangs out with 20 Park, he drinks Southern Comfort, smokes marijuana, and beats up a victim. For Shank, this is the first time he helps beat someone up for no particular reason. After that night, Shank says, "I was a new person. I wasn't the Shank that came from Columbia that was a nice kid. All of that was put in a closet, or maybe outrun by the new me" (25). Later he hooks up with FTS and continues his delinquent behavior with that crew. Eventually, Shank's criminal activity leads to the armed robbery of a drugstore and two stints in Rikers jail. While incarcerated there, he learns a lot about crime that he uses when he returns to the streets. So, Shank takes part in the delinquent activities at an early age, suffers negative consequences for those actions, but does not change his ways.

The second characteristic involves educational expectations. Before Shank comes to this country, and before he joins with the crews, he is a good student who tries hard in school. He wants to be a Marine. However, he barely manages to pass tenth grade because he spends most of his time hanging out with FTS. Following is his description of school: "Like with school I was messing up and I wanted to do better and then the teachers start messing with you, saying, oh no, you can't be good enough for this and smart enough for that. And you know how smart you are. I knew how smart I was. In eleventh grade around this time, I tried to do good in school and they look at your grades and say bullshit. And instead of believing in yourself and how smart you are, you give up. You give them the power to decide about your life" (33–34). The last words of this statement are pivotal. When Shank stops believing in himself, he gives the power to control his destiny to others. He gives up part of his "power."

The loss of this power leads Shank into "acting out" other inappropriate behaviors in general, which is the third common characteristic of at risk adolescents that Dryfoos identifies. Shank is an angry young man before he begins to hang out with the crews, but he still maintains control over his actions. However, the first time he beats up a person for no apparent reason, he discovers a way to release some of his anger. Yet at the same time, he loses some of his power to the crew because he lets them determine his actions. This makes him mad. As Hinojosa points out, anger is Shank's constant companion and is the prime motivator in his life. As a result, it is not uncommon for Shank to beat up victims, or "vics." Every time Shank sees someone on the street who he thinks is more privileged than he is, Shanks gets mad. He keeps thinking about how he has no money and no job, which adds to his hatred of the victim. As his anger grows, he looks for a way to vent it. Usually, he ends up hanging out with the crew, looking out for potential "vics." When Shank finds one, he and the rest of the crew beat the victim up and steal his money—if he has any on him. If not, at least Shank is able to feel better about himself because he has vented some of his anger. Obviously, Shank is caught up in a vicious cycle of anger and violence—one which he constantly acts out.

The fourth common characteristic is peer influence. Shank is very susceptible to the influence of his peers, as is evident in the preceding scenarios. In the company of his crew, he has many first-time experiences. The first time he gets drunk, smokes marijuana, and beats up an innocent person, he is hanging out with the crew. He goes along with everything his crew decides to do, including the armed robbery of a pharmacy. Although he really does not want to take part in that crime, he does in order to avoid looking bad to his friends. In fact, Shank still sees the fear in the eyes of the young girls he held at gunpoint during that robbery, but, he assures Hinojosa, he will never share that with his crew members. Thus, Shank goes along with many things simply because of the influence of his peers. However, Shank learns something else from his peers; he learns from his initiation into the crew that he can never trust any of its members.

Shank's initiation consists of having to fight his way out of a circle of all the members—as they all hit him as hard as they can. He has to do this to gain their "respect." If he can fight them and win, he gets their respect. As Shank puts it, "Respect is another thing, but trust—nobody trusts nobody. Nobody" (26). At times, Shank wants to break away from the crew and try to make something of himself. He is attempting to stay in school, even though his peers keep trying to get him to cut class and hang out with them. So far, he has been able to hang with the crew on weekends and stay in school during the week. But Shank readily admits, "I can't stop the way I am and become whatever it is I want to be unless everyone goes along with that change, too" (27).

The fifth characteristic deals with the role the parents play in the life of their child. For Shank, this is another problem area. He lives with his mother, who he says does not care about him. He says she does not set rules for him to follow, and she never asks him where he gets the money he gives to her—even though he has gotten it illegally. He describes their relationship with the stark comment: "I know she is my mom and I care for her, but there is no connection" (39). The story is no different with his father. His father is an alcoholic whose erratic treatment of Shank was a source of confusion for him when he was young. Shank could not understand how his father could be playing with him one minute, and the next be verbally and physically abusing him. One of Shank's earliest memories of being with his father is of the time he witnessed the murder of one of his father's friends. Shank was only four or five, but he had already seen a man executed. Other memories of his father are of times when he would come home drunk and beat up Shank's mother. Eventually, his parents get divorced. For a while Shank tries to stay in touch with his father by writing to him. His father's reaction to this is to tell Shank not to write so much "because we don't have stuff to talk about if you wrote every week" (39). After that response, Shank never writes to his father again. Thus, when we apply Dryfoos's common characteristic of insufficient bonding with parents and permissiveness of the parents, it is no wonder Shank fits in perfectly.

Dryfoos's sixth and final characteristic concerns the type of neighborhood the teenager lives in. In the preceding discussion of Hinojosa's book, it is evident that Shank does not live in the best of neighborhoods. While on the surface it appears to be a nice area of single-family homes and condominiums, after dark it turns into a battleground for the children who live there. Most of the families are existing at the poverty level, even though the parents go to work every day—some have two or three jobs. While they work, their children rule the streets. The various crews are out every night, protecting the neighborhood from others. When gangs come in from other areas of the city, the crew members see it as an intrusion on their territory, and they fight off the trespassers. This environment is a perfect place for violence to breed. And so Shank, and other teenagers like him, continue in their violent cycle while they protect the "hood."

In summary, when we analyze this book using Joy Dryfoos's definition of "at risk" teenagers, we see that the picture painted within its covers is a real one. These teenagers are definitely at risk and seemingly have a very slim chance of becoming productive adults. Now let's take a look at a fictional story about troubled teens to see if it is close to reality according to Dryfoos's guidelines.

DON'T YOU DARE READ THIS, MRS. DUNFREY

Summary

In this ALA Best Book for Young Adults, written by Margaret Peterson Haddix, the story of 15-year-old Tish Bonner unfolds through a series of journal entries she writes as a part of her English class requirements. This is the type of assignment that Tish and her friends usually scoff at, but as her life spins out of control, Tish finds that writing in her journal is one way to think through her problems. Mrs. Dunfrey, her teacher, promises not to read entries that are marked "Do Not Read." The first entries Tish writes are a test to see if Mrs. Dunfrey really will honor her request not to read the journals. As she realizes that Mrs. Dunfrey is true to her word, Tish begins to write about more and more personal things that are occurring in her life.

Tish and her younger brother, Matt, live with their severely depressed mother in an impoverished area of town. Although Tish's mother has a job, she is not able to support her children. Therefore, Tish works at a local fast food restaurant in order to buy clothes and food for the family. Tish tries to cope with her mother's neglect, her abusive father's unannounced visits, and her little brother's confusion about the family situation.

Eventually, Tish's mother deserts the children in order to follow her husband to California. Then, all the responsibilities and bills fall on Tish. Tish has no one to turn to in her time of trouble. She is afraid that if she tells anyone, including her friends, what is going on at home, she and Matt will be separated and her mother will lose her parental rights. In addition, she does not trust school officials because of stories she has heard about other students whose family problems have been dealt with through the "system."

Finally, Tish's last journal entry states, "Do read this, Mrs. Dunfrey." Tish decides to confide in her teacher and asks Dunfrey to read all of the entries in her journal. As Tish says, "The reason I am doing this is, I realized I have to tell someone about Mom and Dad leaving us. I thought I could take care of everything myself, but I just can't. I'm too tired. I'm too hungry. Maybe I'm too stupid, too. I don't know" (114).

Tish is one of those students that teachers see as unmotivated and a low achiever, but not necessarily "at risk." However, she is perhaps an example of a teenager who slips into the at risk category without the knowledge of school officials. But just how much at risk is she, according to Dryfoos's definition?

Analysis of Tish Bonner

Of the four problem areas Dryfoos identifies, Tish exhibits problem behaviors in two—school failure and, to a lesser degree, delinquency. However, in both of these areas Tish exhibits all six of the common characteristics of an at risk student.

School failure is the area in which Tish exhibits the most problem behaviors. At the beginning of the novel Tish says that she is a C student, although she knows she can do better if she studies. She says that school is not one of her priorities and really only goes to school to see her friends. As the problems in her life outside of school intensify, Tish begins to be absent more often (ten days in four weeks); her grades fall, and she begins to think about dropping out of school in order to get a full-time job.

Delinquency only applies to Tish in a peripheral sense, until she needs to resort to crime to feed her brother. Tish's friend, Sandy, often shoplifts merchandise from stores in the mall, even though she has the money to buy the items. Tish has been with her on several of these occasions; however, Tish never shoplifted until after her parents left. Having seen Sandy get away with this so often, Tish resorts to shoplifting food from the grocery store when she runs out of money to buy food for Matt. After this episode, even though Tish does not get caught, she feels dirty. One other delinquent activity Tish gets involved in is fighting in school. When her friends tell her she stinks, Tish, who has no money to wash her clothes, starts a fistfight. While her reaction is very understandable, fighting is still viewed as an antisocial, somewhat delinquent behavior.

Now let's look individually at each of Dryfoos's six common characteristics of the problem areas to see how applicable they are to Tish. The first indicator, early age initiation into problem behaviors, is evident. Tish is just 15, but she has experienced problems in school all along. Teachers view her as a "tough girl," and she describes herself as a "big hair girl who sits at the back of the class." She enjoys thinking that teachers are afraid of her and her friends. It is obvious that she and her friends have acted this way for quite some time since they have this kind of reputation. In addition, Tish has, on occasion, skipped school for various reasons. However, she only begins to miss school on a regular basis after her mother abandons the family. Her excessive absences during this period of time put her in danger of flunking her sophomore year. Tish and her friends are involved in shoplifting at an early age, too. They have been hanging out at the mall for a while, as is evident by Sandy's well-honed shoplifting skill. In a sense, since Tish goes along with Sandy's crime and does nothing to stop her, she is guilty. This type of experience also makes it easier for Tish to resort to shoplifting when she feels she has to steal food to feed Matt and herself. While Tish never gets caught shoplifting, she does feel guilty when she has to steal. Thus, Tish begins to exhibit these behaviors at an early age, and eventually, suffers negative consequences from them.

As cited by Dryfoos, Tish's educational expectations for herself are very low, even though she knows she is capable of doing better in school. For example, in ninth grade Tish decides to do the best she can on an aptitude test and actually scores higher than any other student in the class. For about a week teachers and guidance counselors are, as Tish says, "swarming all over me. I can still hear Mrs. Anthony saying, 'Now that we all know what you are capable of, Tish, I'm going to expect a lot more out of you.' . . . Mrs. Herzenburger started talking to me about college. Then it's like everybody remembered what they were dealing with and forgot me" (9). Then, in her sophomore year, as Tish is working thirty-five hours a week at Burger Boy and contending with her mother's neglect and her father's abuse, she fails to see how what is being taught in school is relevant to her life. She says to Mrs. Dunfrey in one journal entry: "It's not your fault that none of us really care about Shakespeare or . . . Faulkner? Neither one of them has anything to do with my life. . . . Did either of them have a father that left them and a mother who might as well be a zombie? Did either of them have to work at a dumb job like mine frying up thousands of French fries for all those kids who don't have to work? I don't think so" (19–20). Overwhelmed by responsibilities for herself and her brother, Tish sees school as a low priority—eating comes first. When Mrs. Dunfrey talks to her about a research paper that has to be written in order for Tish to pass English for the year, Tish feels that paying the bills and feeding Matt are more urgent than writing a paper. Thus, Tish decides school is relatively unimportant and opts to work and take care of Matt instead.

The third indicator, acting out bad behaviors, is definitely one that Tish exhibits. In addition to the fistfights and skipping of school already mentioned, Tish has a quick temper, which flares up at both home and work. In both cases, her anger is totally justified, but the way she reacts is unacceptable. For instance, she lashes out verbally at both her mother and father in response to their constant and often violent fighting because she sees how much Matt is frightened by the fighting. She tries to stop it by yelling at them. This results in a physical fight between her father and Tish; as a result of the fight, Matt becomes even more frightened.

At work, Tish often acts like a smart aleck—especially when her boss punishes her for refusing his sexual advances by making her clean the bathrooms and cutting her work hours. However, she tries to hold her temper during these forays because she knows she has to keep her job, no matter how unfairly she is treated. Therefore, Tish often "acts out" because she knows of no other way to react.

In the area of peer influence, Tish is more susceptible in the beginning of the novel. For instance, she dresses like her friends, acts like they do, and hangs out with them at the mall. Also, she often attends unchaperoned parties with them and stays out until two or three in the morning. She does these things not because she wants to, but mainly because she does not want them to ridicule her for not going along with them. In another way, she goes along with Sandy's shoplifting as long as she and Sandy are alone, but when Matt is with them, she refuses to let Sandy shoplift anything. Tish learns something else from her friends that directly affects her actions. She has seen her friends take other girls into their confidence only to turn around and gossip about them. From this behavior, Tish realizes that when she has serious problems, like her mother's abandonment, she cannot confide in her friends. Therefore, Tish is only influenced by her peers to a certain extent; she still has the guts to stand up to them when the situation warrants it.

Another indicator that Tish exhibits is the role played by her parents. Both of her parents dropped out of high school and therefore do not place much emphasis on the importance of education. Both her mother and father are substance abusers—her father is an alcoholic and her mother is constantly under the influence of some kind of drug. Her mother is very permissive; she does not even question Tish when she comes home very late at night. Her father, conversely, when he is around, is very authoritarian and demands that Tish obey his every command or suffer the consequences. In both cases, the bonding between parent and child, which Dryfoos cites as essential for healthy development of adolescents, has not occurred. In fact, Tish serves the role of parent to both her mother and her little brother by constantly trying to take care of both of them and protect them from the father.

The last indicator, living in a poor neighborhood, also applies to Tish's existence. Because her mother can only get a low-paying job at a local grocery store, the family is forced to live in a run-down house in a poor section of town. Even though Tish's mother inherited the house from her parents, she is not able to keep up with the maintenance. In fact, she cannot even pay all the bills on her salary; therefore, Tish is forced to work to help keep food on the table and clothes on their backs. Tish is caught in the vicious cycle caused by poverty—having to work to keep food on the table instead of attending school, where she could learn the skills necessary to become a productive adult.

In summary, Tish can definitely be labeled at risk in terms of Dryfoos's problem areas and common characteristics. In this case, *Don't You Dare Read This, Mrs. Dunfrey* appears to be a realistic account of a teenager growing up at risk.

We still need to address the question of how students like Tish Bonner and the teenagers in *Crews* are helped in the real world of public education. What follows is an interview with Elaine Beaudoin, a person who works with at risk youth on a daily basis.

AT-RISK TEENAGERS IN THE SCHOOL SETTING: PERSPECTIVE FROM A HIGH SCHOOL SOCIAL WORKER

Elaine Beaudoin is a high school social worker who helps at risk teenagers learn how to cope with the world around them. Through a question-and-answer format, Elaine tells us about the types of programs public schools offer to at risk students, and gives suggestions to teachers, media specialists, and other educational professionals regarding what they can do to help these students realize their potential and become productive adults.

Beaudoin works in a large urban high school that is populated by a wide spectrum of students. It is an urban school that has students from affluent, middle-class, and poverty-level homes. Some students are from families who have been in the area for generations, and some are newly arrived immigrants from Poland, Laos, Thailand, Puerto Rico, and other countries. Some of the students live in two-parent homes; others live in single-parent or no-parent homes (where parents are absent because of work, prison sentences, or chronic substance abuse). But no matter where students come from in this spectrum, there is a chance that they are at risk. In addition, the degree to which each student is at risk also varies. Some are highly at risk because of their involvement with gangs, their home environment, or other factors. Others are at risk to a lesser degree because of specific circumstances in their lives at a given time. So, how does the school system address the problems of these at risk students?

QUESTIONS AND ANSWERS

How are at risk students identified in your school setting?

We have Pupil Assistance Support Services (PASS), which is a early intervention program to help kids before they get into major problems. Students are identified on the basis of academic concerns, behavioral concerns, truancy, and/or an infraction against the substance abuse policy. If students get caught on campus in possession of drugs or are under the influence of drugs or alcohol, they are automatically referred to us. Teachers, guidance counselors, parents, peers, and the individual student may identify an at risk youth and request an evaluation of that student. These referrals may be submitted in either written or verbal form, but once made, the student is assigned to a case manager who follows up on the case. The case manager sends out a "Behaviors of Concern Checklist" to every teacher that child has. In this way, we can analyze the information from the forms to find out what is going on with this person.

Students are also identified in other ways. For instance, some students who are chronically truant are identified after a certain number of absences and are referred to our program. Then, we have a Planning and Placement Team (PPT) meeting, in which an administrator, a social worker, school psychologist, and a guidance counselor confer with the parent or parents and the student to outline a course of action to help this student. This plan is then forwarded in a written report to the juvenile court. Or, sometimes, I will see a kid who I think needs some kind of social work, and I will just bring him or her in and won't go through the whole official process of referral.

Another way to identify at risk kids is through our middle school referral program. The eighth-grade guidance counselors from the three middle schools that feed into us identify thirty to thirty-five students who are at risk for dropping out or at risk for major problems in any aspect of their lives. The problem with this is that there are so many children who fit into this category that it is really hard for the counselors to narrow the number down to thirty-five. We have received a grant to work with the local university to set up a mentor program for these kids. These kids are then paired up with a mentor—a teacher, a college student—and with tutors. Nelson Villa, the social worker who is responsible for this program, also involves parents in implementing strategies to help the child and will, on occasion, make home visits if necessary.

What kinds of programs does the school have in place to address the problems of at risk students?

The PASS program is the main one in place in our school to deal with at risk students in the early intervention phase of treatment. We have three teams that work with at risk students. Each team is composed of guidance counselors, teachers, social workers, and psychologists. All of these team members have gone through a training program that focuses on working with at risk students. These team members are involved in different stages of the program, from identification through group and individual treatment sessions. We also have peer counselor and peer mediation groups to work with some of the students in the PASS program.

In my position as a school social worker, I run various support groups on specific topics for these kids if there are enough students to warrant a group. I have done groups for survivors of incest and children of alcoholics. Right now, I am running a bereavement group. These are definitely high-risk kids because they have just recently lost a parent or loved one.

And then, I conduct "life skills" groups. We base all our groups on some type of curriculum. So, the kids who come into the life skills groups are ones whom guidance counselors or teachers have identified as having problems with family, relationship issues, depression, or just problems in general. I break these students up into grade level groups—say ninth and tenth graders and then eleventh and twelfth graders. Then, over a ten- to twelve-week period, the groups address various life skills topics that the students themselves have suggested. Usually, I will bring in a handout or pamphlet that has information about a particular topic they want to discuss, but sometimes, if students have a particular issue or problem they want to discuss, we will address it. I also recommend books for the kids to read, but whether or not they read them is up to the students.

One of the big concerns working with all types of these groups is the issue of confidentiality. Members have to understand how important it is that the information shared in the group is not discussed outside the group. If this happens, I usually tell the student that he or she cannot be in the group anymore.

In your experience have at risk teens ever found help, or even solutions to their problems, through reading a book?

I don't really know. I do know that I sometimes suggest that students read a book about the problem they are facing—especially in the group setting, so we can talk about the problem. However, since most of my work is done outside of the classroom, I don't really assign books to read. Another problem with this approach is that many of our high school students classified at risk are not reading at a high school level; therefore, many of the self-help or fiction books that I would suggest are inaccessible to them.

What can teachers or other educational professionals do if they think a student is going through some situation that puts him or her in the at risk category, temporarily? Are there any types of intervention programs or procedures in place to deal with these situations?

Teachers or educational professionals can get the student some help immediately. They should talk to the guidance counselor or mental health professional in the school.

Many times the teacher is the first to notice problems—especially English teachers, because of their use of journals. Once the teacher is aware of a problem, he or she usually talks to the student and either gets the student's permission to alert one of us to the problem or brings the student down to my office. Then I can do individual counseling or solution focused work, in which I work one-on-one with the student for several sessions on one particular issue or problem. In these sessions we establish a specific goal and then devise ways to reach the goal. Because we are in a school setting, it is hard to find time to meet with such students. But it is not unusual for me to meet with a student during the lunch period, or before or after school. The main thing is that once a teacher or educational professional is aware of an at risk situation, he or she should not ignore the problem. They should try to find help within the school setting for the student.

What suggestions do you have for teachers to help at risk students realize their potential, set goals, and become productive adults? What specific things can a teacher do in the classroom to help these students?

I think teachers need to set up situations in which students can feel success, even if it's a small area of success. It is essential that teachers try to draw all students into classroom activities—even the quietest kids because, often, these are the kids with the most problems. Also teachers need to avoid belittling kids. Many of these students come to school with little self-esteem and need to have positive experiences.

I know that teachers have a hard time dealing with all the kids who come into their classrooms, but they need to be aware that what they say in the classroom affects the students. This is not easy, but that awareness must always be there. School should be a safe, warm, accepting place for students, and teachers should foster that kind of environment in their classrooms.

I am not a teacher, and I do not like to tell teachers what to do, but I think it is important for teachers to make what they do in the classroom relevant to the students' lives. I think they need to bring in materials that students can connect to, and I think that is where young adult literature can help. I know there are a lot of things the curriculum dictates, but I think teachers should look for opportunities to bring in other relevant sources of information. That's one way to make education real to the students.

What is the most frequently asked question by parents of at risk teenagers?

Most of the time parents do not ask questions of me. They usually come in and demand that I "fix" something. They say, "Fix this! Stop this! Fix it! Do something!" I get these kinds of requests more often than I get questions. Sometimes, parents come in and ask questions like, "What can we do? How can we help?" But this happens very seldom on the high school level, except when parents are dealing with a new situation. For example, I had a situation in which a girl was sexually assaulted out of school. Her parents came in and asked what they could do to help her through this. Getting this kind of parental concern and involvement was very helpful and supportive to the student.

As I said before, most often parents demand that the school do something to stop a teenager's behavior, and sometimes they are willing to work with us in the initial stages. I might give them a checklist of things to do or monitor at home, and they may help for a while. But frequently, the parents lose interest because the problem has been going on for so long. Parenting styles have already been formed, and it's very hard to get parents to change their styles at this stage.

Many parents of at risk children are at the poverty level, are working two or three jobs, and simply do not have time to help their children. Some of their parents are so heavily involved with their own addictions to drugs or alcohol that they are not even aware of their own children's problems. In addition, one or both of the parents in some of these families are in jail, so the problem is not single-parent homes, but more specifically, no-parent homes. Therefore, often it is impossible to involve parents in helping the at risk student. It can be very frustrating.

CONCLUSION

As we can see, at risk students populate our schools in both reality and fiction. There are many Shanks and Tish Bonners in our classrooms today. We must figure out ways to help these students cope with their problems and overcome their situations if we expect them to become contributing members of our society. Their fate is in our hands.

RECOMMENDED READINGS

Fiction Works

Young Adult Literature with Troubled Teenagers as Protagonists

Crutcher, C. (1996). *Ironman*. New York: Bantam Doubleday Dell Books for Young Readers. 192 pp. (ISBN: 0–440–21971–X). High School (HS).

Eighteen-year-old Bo Brewster has had one too many run-ins with his English teacher and football coach, Mr. Redman. As a result, he quits the football team and is forced to attend an anger management group. In this group, peopled by other at risk youths, Bo learns how to control his anger and how to cope with his father's malevolent interference in his quest for the Ironman championship.

Gallo, D. R. (Ed.). (1997). *No Easy Answers: Short Stories about Teen-agers Making Tough Choices.* New York: Delacorte. 336 pp. (ISBN: 0–385–32290–9). HS.

Once again Don Gallo has collected a group of short stories that deals with topics of importance to teenagers. In this collection, young protag-onists find themselves in various situations that put them at risk. From pregnancy to gang violence, these teenagers have to make decisions that can alter their lives forever.

Hinton, S. E. (1997). *The Outsiders.* New York: Viking Penguin. 192 pp. (ISBN: 0–14–038572–X). Middle School (MS), HS.

In this young adult literature classic, Pony Boy and his friends, Greas-ers, constantly run into problems with the Socs, a gang of rich kids. This novel gives the reader an inside look at the lives of several at risk teen-agers who have to depend on each other for support and protection. Originally published in 1967.

Mazer, N. F. (1997). *When She Was Good.* New York: Scholastic: 240 pp. (ISBN: 0–590–13506–6). HS.

Em Thurkill's world is full of neglect, abandonment, abuse, and men-tal illness. Still, somehow she learns to survive in a world in which all the odds are against her. This poignant story details the existence of a young girl who is dangerously at risk of becoming just another statistic—just another one of those kids who fall between the cracks.

Myron, L. (1994). *A Shadow Like a Leopard.* New York: HarperTrophy. 192 pp. (ISBN: 0–06–440458–7). MS, HS.

Fourteen-year-old Ramon finds himself all alone on the streets of New York. His mother is in the hospital, and his father is serving a prison sentence. With no one to protect him, he feels he needs to find a gang to join so he will have at least some kind of family. But then in a robbery attempt, he meets Mr. Glaser, a man who changes the direction of Ra-mon's life.

Voight, C. (1987). *Dicey's Song.* New York: Fawcett Book Group. 211 pp. (ISBN: 0–449–70276–6). MS, HS.

Dicey Tillerman is used to the responsibilities of keeping her family together. Although she is just 13-years-old, she has shouldered this responsibility since her father and mother both abandoned the family. In this part of the Tillerman cycle of books, Dicey has to learn how to let her grandmother assume the responsibilities of caring for her brothers and sisters—as well as herself.

White, R. (1992). *Weeping Willow*. New York: Aerial. 256 pp. (ISBN: 0–374–38255–7). MS, HS.

Tiny Lambert's imaginary friend, Willa, helps her cope with an alcoholic stepfather who is sexually abusing her. But when the secret of her abuse becomes the topic of local gossip, Tiny needs help from a real person. She turns to her aunt Evie and her band director, who help her find solutions to her problems.

Nonfiction Works

Hayden, T. L. (1992). *Ghost Girl: The True Story of a Child in Peril and the Teacher Who Saved Her*. New York: Avon Books 320 pp. (ISBN: 0–380–71681–X). MS, HS.

Torey Hayden works with troubled teenagers every day in her job as a psychologist and special education teacher. But when she meets Jadie, she is forced to confront a case of severe abuse that even her colleagues do not know how to handle. Through perseverance and love, Torey uncovers the shocking truth about Jadie's life and helps heal the wounds caused by years of abuse.

Professional Resources

Kaywell, J. (1997). "Young Adult Literature." *English Journal* (September), 91–95.

This article categorizes problems that at risk teenagers confront while growing up, such as sexual abuse, delinquency, pregnancy, divorce, and physical and mental abuse. Kaywell then provides a list of annotated bibliographies that deal with the problem areas. This article is a good source of books that can be used to help teenagers cope with their problems.

McWhirter, J. J., B. T. McWhirter, A. M. McWhirter, E. H. McWhirter. (1997). *At Risk Youth: A Comprehensive Response*, 2nd ed. Pacific Grove, CA: Brooks/Cole Publishing. 384 pp. (ISBN: 0–534–34580–8).

This book, written specifically for teachers, guidance counselors, and human service professionals explores the problems of at risk youths and gives ways for professional educators to help these at risk teens become productive adults. It discusses recent research into each of the categories of at a risk indicators and outlines ways that professionals can best serve the teenagers in each of the problem areas.

Outz, D. T. (1994). "Bibliotherapeutic Literature: A Key Facet of Whole Language Instruction for the At-Risk Student." *Reading Horizons* 35 (2): 162–175.

Outz explains what bibliotherapy is and how it can be used in a whole-language classroom. He also includes a list of titles of young adult novels that can be used to help children cope with various situations in their lives that put them at risk.

REFERENCES

Dryfoos, Joy G. (1990). *Adolescents at Risk: Prevalence and Prevention*. New York: Oxford University Press.
Haddix, Margaret Peterson. (1996). *Don't You Dare Read This, Mrs. Dunfrey*. New York: Aladdin.
Hinojosa, Maria. (1995). *Crews: Gang Members Talk to Maria Hinojosa*. Photographer, German Perez. New York: Harcourt Brace.

CHAPTER TWO

Body Image and Society's Impact

M. Linda Broughton and Mae Z. Cleveland

You can have a lot of good inside you, but if you don't feel good about it, then it is lost.

You can have the best hair, the best eyes, the prettiest complexion, but none of it's gonna get you anywhere if you don't feel something inside.

Jo-Laine, age 14, from Sugar in the Raw (Carroll, 1997, 36)

Body image may be defined as "the perceptions one has about the body." But this perception is not so simple as looking into a mirror and saying, "Oh, I'm average height and weight, with shiny brown hair and eyes, sort of long nose but a nice smile." As Jo-Laine implies, it's what we feel about ourselves that really determines body image and self-concept. We form perceptions of ourselves as a result of several influences, including these: (1) messages we receive about our bodies; (2) an understanding of our bodies as the essence of our being; (3) our feelings about our bodies as influenced by these factors. So, while a body may be a certain height, skin color, and sex, if external messages about these essential features are negative, the person begins to understand that being this height, color, or sex is not as valued as being someone with different features. He or she will begin to perceive his or her body negatively. Repeated comments such as "You need to be tall to play basketball" or "Girls are not good at sports" or "Real men have broad shoulders" can, after a while, influence one's feelings about one's body and self. Thus, the same person in the example above may look into the same mirror and see an entirely different being: "Oh, I'm too short, my chest is too small, my hair is kinky, and my teeth are crooked." This person may add, with a frown, "Aaagh, I just want to hide in my room." And this person is likely to form a slanted self-image, relying on external messages and his or her own interpretations of the messages.

Adolescents are keenly aware of their bodies because of the dramatic physical changes that occur during puberty and the reactions of those around them:

> In the eighth grade, all of a sudden I had a figure: I had hips, and breasts, which was like a complete revelation to me. At a certain point I became glad about it. I thought, "Gee, I'm hot shit!" Boys all of a sudden started taking notice, and it was confusing and sort of bewildering and nice. (Rebekah from *A Totally Alien Life-Form*; Lewis, 1996, 345)

The feelings that accompany these developments vary a great deal, and can range anywhere from awe to fear, from pride to disgust, depending on previous experiences and others' reactions. A young girl may feel good about these changes and respond to puberty as Rebeka above. Conversely, if she is made painfully aware of her developing woman's body by persistent ridicule, catcalls, intimidating stares of men and boys, her feelings about her body and herself will change. As a result, she may become ashamed of her body and want to make it go away. As Leslea Newman points out in *Good Enough to Eat* (1986), girls often become self-conscious victims of boys who taunt them with lines like, "Nice tits ya got there, Honey. Hey, Sweetheart, shine those headlights over here" (Newman, iv). Some decide to hide their bodies in the only way they know how: by getting so thin that they disappear, unnoticed and therefore escaping ridicule and harassment.

Boys learn early what is expected of them as males. They should be tough and "not cry like a girl." At adolescence the image of appearing hard and tough is very important and must not be shattered by a show of feelings or emotions that would imply softness. In "Acting Hard," a poem included in Salisbury and Jackson's *Challenging Macho Values* (1996), David Jackson describes the contradictions within an adolescent male who, "Proud of his blood-grazed knuckles," tries to push his hand through a locked door, but who cries in the school showers, afraid that others will see him naked and "sneer at his hairless dick" (viii).

A GENDER FACTOR: FROM GIRLS TO UNREALISTIC IMAGES

Girls get the message early that their appearance is very important. They go to weight loss clinics with their mothers, diet with the family, hear about what food is "junk food" and should be avoided, and learn to feel guilty about what they eat. Over half of 10-year-old girls have tried some sort of diet to lose weight or "cellulite," and as many girls between ages 14 and 18 think they are too fat. The early lesson is that somehow it's their fault, rather than the fault of society's views, if their body is perceived as not right and does not measure up to the image by which they are judged. Very early, girls internalize the image idealized by society. Various professions, such as fashion modeling, performing arts, and some sports, take pains to use thin women or portray thin women as very attractive. This image is promoted by Barbie, a doll with "perfect" physical features, clothing, and friends.

Popular media messages seem to scream that girls exist to be young, beautiful, sexy, and to make men happy. The ideal woman is one who has a narrowly defined body type, is gorgeously attired, and is having fun. Her image is "to die for." And, in fact, many young girls feel they would nearly rather die than face life in an imperfect body, one that is not model thin or in any way not the attractive image she has come to idealize. This can make life painful to a teenager who sees herself as fat or, in any other way, not fitting the perfect physical image.

During childhood, many girls are enthusiastic about sports. They learn techniques of the sport and get into healthy competition early on. As they develop into adolescence, the enthusiasm wanes because they learn that sports among women is not as acceptable to society as is sports among men. Those who do continue as athletes find the expectations may change a bit. Near puberty, some girls feel pressure to keep their weight and body fat at levels that are unrealistically low for adolescents. This, they are told, will improve their performances; often, they are told that boys are faster or better at sports because they are leaner. What they are not told as often is that girls begin their major growth spurts toward puberty, on average, at age 12, which is two years earlier than when boys' puberty usually begins. The comparison of body types between 12-year-old females and males should be meaningless. Nevertheless, girls learn that looking leaner will help them in sports, where they wear body-revealing outfits and where winning is determined subjectively, by the judges' scores. The winner can be determined by how she looks to the judges. Coaches encourage young female athletes to cut calories, not to "eat like pigs," and to be weighed in front of teammates to determine who has not maintained discipline. A good number of young athletes will engage in some type of pathogenic weight loss method, such as severely restricting calorie intake or abusing laxatives in order to make their bodies *right*.

Poor Body Images and Eating Disorders: One Literary Example

We don't need to wonder why teen girls have such poor body images and cannot accept the natural development of their bodies. Eighty percent of young women worry a lot about their appearance (Canadian Teachers' Federation, 1990). This worry about appearance, body size, and image begins at an early age. Over 50 percent of young girls do not like some part of their bodies (Moore, 1993), and as many as 80 percent of girls have attempted dieting or other means of weight loss to change their body size or shape by the time they reach high school (Mellin, Irwin, and Scully, 1992). Some get more drastic and desperate to change their bodies to match their image of perfection and develop eating disorders: anorexia nervosa, bulimia nervosa, or compulsive overeating. Anorexia is the pursuit of thinness by severely restricting food and calorie intake. Diagnostic symptoms are serious weight loss to more than 15 percent below expected weight delayed onset or loss of menstrual periods, and a distorted body image. In bulimia, binge eating of a huge amount of food in a relatively short period of time is followed by some type of behavior to get rid of the calories and provide relief from the physical effects of eating so much food and from the fear of weight gain. Such "purging" behaviors include self-induced vomiting, overdosing on laxatives, and compulsive exercising. The compulsive overeater binges on food but does not engage in compensatory purging. While less than 10 percent of adolescents develop full-blown eating disorders, about one in five teens engage in disordered eating behaviors to some extent. The behaviors begin as a means to gain some control over their bodies and lives but often lead to explicit eating disorders, depression, obsessive-compulsive disorders, or health problems.

In *Fat Chance* (Newman, 1994), Judi decides she will be happy and her life will be better if she loses weight. A classmate teaches her how to make herself throw up after eating, but Judi only feels her life is getting more and more out of control rather than happier. She has been keeping a journal as an assignment for a class. When she rereads her journal, she realizes that all of her dieting, purging, and restricting behavior have gotten her nowhere—no weight loss, no happiness, no decisions about life. As a result of a crisis at school, the classmate who taught Judi to purge is hospitalized for anorexia nervosa. The principal takes action to have an expert visit classes, talk on the subject, and explain its dangers. This is all Judi needs to talk to her teacher about her problem, to eventually tell her mother, and to get help.

This book should enlighten teachers and parents about the guilt, fear, and self-disgust that are part of the struggle with an eating disorder. *Fat Chance* was written by a woman who herself struggled with her self-image, and draws from some personal experience. Three important events in this novel are worth noting: (1) the school administration takes the subject seriously by inviting a professional to give sound information about eating disorders; (2) the protagonist's use of a journal to record her experiences and her feelings about herself is useful as a vehicle by which she gains insight into her own behavior; and (3) the protagonist confides in her teacher about her eating disorder and shares her journal with her mother. The adults are nonjudgmental and helpful. This story could encourage a student to face her own unhappy experience with dieting, laxative abuse, or bingeing and purging. There is always the risk that a young adult may use it as an explanation of how to try self-induced vomiting, but discussing the book with readers could help teenagers who struggle with self-image realize that engaging in harmful eating behaviors offers no solution to their problems. Together, a teacher and student can follow how Judi, who did not mean to let the problem go so far, almost became powerless to stop her self-destructive thoughts and behaviors.

Poor Body Images and Self-Mutilation: One Literary Example

A growing number of teenage girls engage in self-mutilation, particularly burning the skin or delicate self-cutting with razor blades. Peggy Orenstein, in *School Girls* (1994), tells of one student's attempts to make her emotional pain go away. Lisa is notably overweight. She started at Weston Middle School in seventh grade, and before the school day officially began was greeted by a boy with, "Hi, Miss Piggy!" Her confidence and interest in school plummeted throughout the semester. Previous test scores indicated a "gifted" girl, but now her grades hovered around failing. She began cutting and burning herself:

> "I know I have no self-esteem," she says, beginning to prick her fingers again. "My friends always hit me when I say something bad about myself. I cut myself down all the time, I don't know why. I guess because if I say it first, it's not as bad as if someone else does. But I can take everything—being stupid, being a dumb blonde—just not people saying stuff about my weight. . . . I mean, I know I'm fat. . . ."
>
> Lisa jabs the pin through the left leg of her overalls, hurting herself before someone else can. (108–109)

Physical appearance and gender affect how others react to a person. Beginning in preschool, children indicate a preference for an "attractive" peer and judge this person as more friendly and popular. Both children and teachers perceive more attractive children as smarter, and teachers interact with these children more favorably. By junior high school, girls are treated differently than boys. Teachers call on girls less often than boys and tolerate and encourage more assertive behavior in boys. It is no surprise then that the American Association of University Women's report *Shortchanging Girls, Shortchanging America* (1991) revealed that adolescent girls undervalue themselves. So, it seems, do many others.

MORE GENDER FACTORS: FROM BOYS TO MEN IN NONFICTION AND FICTION

Males are not immune to the cult of the perfect physique. In *Challenging Macho Values* (1996), Salisbury and Jackson discuss the masculine attitudes and behaviors that society approves, and they observe that "Macho values aren't just made and carried around in boys' heads. They are also a part of boys' bodies" (167). Adolescent boys fear appearing weak, which means physically small or short or skinny. In the male world of body culture, males perceive themselves as inadequate and failures as males if they do not measure up to the ideal manly body. When asked what is a "manly" body, boys and men agree that a well-developed upper body is essential. Most frequently mentioned are a large chest, small waist, and narrow hips: a hypermesomorph body type. Height is important, not too short, but not too tall, either. The importance of this body type is really the image it projects. When asked to assign traits to body types, people most often assign positive traits to the mesomorph body type; these people are believed to be better looking, stronger, braver, and happier, and to have many friends. We tend to assign negative traits, such as loneliness, fear, weakness, and sadness, to people with other body types. In movies, character roles with these clusters of traits are usually played by actors who match the body type. Boys want to emulate the popular and successful characters. When Salisbury and Jackson (1996) asked adolescent boys what the ideal would do for them, many felt it would protect them from verbal abuse: "Paul shared his dislike of being called shrimp: 'No one would call me names. I would be bigger and taller.' John also mentions name-calling. He thought that being ideal would stop people from calling him fat. Azzar's concern is his glasses. He is sick of being 'vision express' and 'four-eyes.' He is also taunted with his height and referred to as 'Daddy Long Legs.' Being ideal would protect him too" (198).

Boys are expected to live up to a masculine image on the playing fields. Sport is a primary means for high school males to establish "manhood." They are encouraged and expected to do well, and those young boys who excel get a positive self-image from athletics, as well as a feeling of connection with others. Through sports, men become heroes; young boys worship and want to be like them, with all the glory, strength, and manhood that they embody.

But boys who do not measure up in the sports arena are subject to abusive comments. Coaches, parents, and peers taunt them with comments like "You throw like a girl" or "Don't be a sissy." A salient feature of the male role is the *avoidance* of culturally defined feminine characteristics, or the "antifemininity factor." Such gender-defined characteristics may vary among groups or geographical areas. In "Arturo's Flight," a short story from Judith Ortiz Cofer's *An Island Like You: Stories of the Barrio* (1995), Arturo relates an incident at school where he is called on by his teacher to recite a poem before the class: "I knew my life was over then. See, for the guys of the barrio, reading poetry is like an unnatural act. *Liking* poetry makes you suspicious as to your sexual preference. Unless you're a girl" (31–32). In order to shock his peers into seeing him differently, anything but liking poetry, Arturo dyes his hair purple and spikes it.

Young girls may turn self-dissatisfaction into eating disorders, self-cutting, poor school performance, or other self-destructive behavior in their attempts to gain some control over their bodies, their lives, and their environment. Mary Pipher, in *Reviving Ophelia* (1994), and Peggy

Orenstein, in *School Girls* (1994), share girls' real-life experiences from their interviews with girls and their parents. Young boys are more likely to use verbal abuse, physical threats, and physical aggression aimed at others. Salisbury and Jackson (1996) talk about how boys use language as a weapon and use name calling to regulate girls' lives. But boys also use language to boost their self-image as being strong and in control. "Boys use language as a shield to make sure other boys only see and hear what will be acceptable to ensure status as 'one of the boys' " (167). To counteract the fear of being perceived as not masculine, boys joke, posture, exaggerate, bully, and make fun of those labeled as weak or inferior in some other way, in attempts to guard against being *found out* as other than a real guy.

In the novel *Ironman* (1995), Chris Crutcher delves into the intense struggles teenagers experience in trying to deal with life at home, expectations at school, and peer relationships. Bo struggles with his actions toward others when he thinks he looks bad: "I trash people I care about" (27), and "when my back is against the wall, my mouth is like a machine gun" (8). He also loses himself in his intense training for an Ironman triathlon, a three-sport event of swimming two and a half miles, cycling over one hundred miles, and running a 26.2-mile marathon. His training can get brutal: "I'm able to endure these monster workouts because I welcome physical pain when struggles at school or home heat up. I understand physical pain; I can control it" (6). Other attempts to cover what may be perceived as physical inferiority are threats and physical aggression. The conflict between Bo and Wyrack, a collegiate swimmer, is about Wyrack's reaction at swim practice when Bo finishes the training laps first. Wyrack hits Bo, threatening more to come if Bo continues to swim faster than he does in workouts. While the focus of *Ironman* is dealing with anger, much about how the characters' anger is played out has to do with self-image and a fear of how others might see them—as weak, inferior, or out of control.

With the help of an anger control group at school, Bo gains insight into his actions, finds some stuffed-away emotions, and begins to learn nondestructive ways of expressing feelings. Other members of the group have a way to go in dealing with deep-seated anger, but by talking in the group they learn to trust one another.

HARASSMENT AND BODY IMAGE: NONFICTION
AND REALISTIC FICTION

In *Skin Deep and Other Teenage Reflections*, an adolescent speaker lists different kinds of torture that she would rather subject herself to, such as walking over hot coals in a jungle where snakes are draped across each tree, than suffer the pain of merely walking "through the hall where all the boys hang out" (Medearis, 1995, 7).

While this chapter is not about sexual harassment, the subject must be addressed in a discussion of body image. Verbal abuse and physical assaults have an effect on body image of both the one assaulted and the one harassing. Boys sling verbal abuse at girls because it demonstrates assertiveness and control. Boys also are abused, though girls are the recipients of the majority of abusive behaviors and verbal insults. The extent of harassment in American public schools has been documented in *Hostile Hallways* (American Association of University Women Educational Foundation; 1993), a survey in which 66 percent of girls and 49 percent of boys reported occasional or frequent harassment while at school (7).

A major difference between the sexes is the emotional impact of the harassment. Girls were three times more likely to be upset by the experience, and girls more often stayed home or did not want to go to school. Orenstein gained insight into the impact of harassment on girls when she interviewed over 150 girls from two different middle schools in California. In *School Girls* (1994), she reports her observations and interviews with the students, teachers, and parents, and one school's attempts to deal with harassment. Many girls think they have to tolerate abuse. They are hesitant to speak out when harassed, whether physically or verbally. They don't think they can fight back. In a few years, it will be ingrained in them, and they will accept it as *normal*. By remaining silent, both to school personnel and to peers, girls suffer alone.

Harassment not only hurts the victim's self-image; it hurts those who harass by strengthening their stereotypical view of girls and of their own image as male. Typical of boys' reactions is this comment from a 14-year-old white male: "People do this stuff every day. No one feels insulted by it. That's stupid. We just play around. I think sexual harassment is normal" (American Association of University Women Educational Foundation, 1993, 24). Boys also seem to have the mistaken view that since girls don't say anything, they must not mind, and thus boys remain unaware that girls are intimidated and feel powerless to change male behavior toward girls' bodies. Orenstein (1994) tells of her chat with a boy at Weston charged with grabbing a girl's breasts who said, "All the guys do that stuff, it's no big deal. The girls don't mind. I mean, they don't do anything about it. I'd beat the crap out of someone if they touched me like that. But girls are different, they don't really do anything, so I guess it's okay to do" (128–129).

Physical assault is one focus of Norma Fox Mazer's novel *Out of Control* (1993). Three boys, Brig (the instigator), Candy, and Rollo, assault Valerie Minchon one afternoon while at school. The word gets out that something happened to Valerie in the hall of the third floor. One day Denise, one of the popular girls in school, approaches Valerie in the school cafeteria and asks if they can sit together. Valerie wonders what this is all about. Denise expresses her concern for Valerie and eventually reveals that she, too, was sexually abused last year in the hall at school. Valerie recognizes the emotional pain, humiliation, and anger as Denise tells her story. Soon about half a dozen girls meet every day for lunch and talk about their "third-floor things." Valerie feels she can't keep this hidden and decides to write a letter to the newspaper about her experience at school. She tells her plan to Rollo because she senses that he is "a little different." Rollo obviously has been bothered by his behavior; he had made several attempts to talk to Valerie and hoped to show her that he was sorry, even if he was not willing to admit his guilt and apologize. Although Rollo is frightened when Valerie tells him about her plan to publicize the event, he is also relieved. He also knows this is the end of his friendship with Brig.

A strength of this book is that the protagonist, Valerie, decides to tell about her experience. It is important to let girls, and boys, know they will be supported by administration, teachers, friends, and family, although they may not gain the support of everyone. Administration may see the incident as an embarrassment to the school; adolescents may try to hide the event from their parents in order to spare parents' feelings—which may range from shame to extreme anger and may be aimed at the victim, the perpetrator, the school, or a spouse. A major fear of the one harassed is that she or he will not have the support of peers, and this may sometimes be true. This book could serve as a means of opening discussion about all of these factors.

Another point of discussion is the boys' behavior and attitude. Boys see this abusive or intimidating behavior in adult males and come to think of harassing girls as a rite of passage, both for them and the girls. Boys often don't consider their behavior because they have been protected or excused, as reflected in Brig's statement, "She had it coming to her." Some may feel bothered by what they did, but the sense of belonging to the group and fear of being cast out help them muffle their concerns inside themselves. The three male characters act together, but their individual reactions differ, particularly Brig's and Rollo's. Brig never would admit, even to his friends, that what they did was wrong. He actively tries to convince himself and his friends that they were just playing around. Rollo, on the other hand, was both troubled by his behavior and ambivalent about what to do with how he felt. A discussion about the meaning of personal respect, the effects of harassment on all those involved, and clarification of the law and consequences is essential.

While documentation of the problem of sexual harassment at school and its effects on young girls has grown over the past decades, what to do still remains a problem. Girls' body images and self-concepts are devastated; others come to believe harassment is part of a girl's life and live with it as painlessly as possible. They should understand they don't have to choose either one of these two outcomes.

CULTURE AS A FACTOR: NONFICTION AND FICTION

In the poignant poem "Skin Deep," an anonymous adolescent speaker expresses the wish that he could unzip and step out of his skin whenever he saw fear on the face of someone whose mind is filled with "all those things your momma told you and the newspapers told you . . . about BLACK people" (Medearis, 1995, 9).

Listening to teenagers tell their own stories is the best way to learn how racial and other cultural factors can affect their self-images. Sydney Lewis listened to many teenagers and tells their stories in *A Totally Alien Life-Form: Teenagers* (1996). Some of these teenagers are of Hispanic background, some Asian American, some African American, and others a combination of several racial backgrounds. Akili Merritt, age 14, has a black father and a white mother. "I do feel like I'm in two worlds sometimes—especially when I go home to a white mother. But when I'm out in the world, society names me as a black man, a black teenager" (353). He talks about his alternatives, as far as his own identity, and the effects of each: If he tries to be as white as possible, he will be disowned by the black people; if he tries to be as black as possible, he fears he will be forced to stay away from his white roots. He also describes feeling isolated at times and having fears about how to act around white kids. "If I went and sat with the white kids I would feel uncomfortable; I wouldn't know what to say, I wouldn't know what they wanted me to say. And especially with teenagers, you want to say the right thing" (356).

He makes decisions and does the best he can, although some people may make up their own minds about him. He relates a time when his mom picked him up from school, "and this girl said, 'That's your parole officer?' I said, 'I don't have no *parole officer!*' . . . I have to stuff down a lot of anger—*all* of the time" (357). Akili speaks for many young adults trying to find how they can fit in the world of adolescents and still maintain their own identity.

Blue Tights by Rita Williams-Garcia (1988) is an excellent novel that deals with this aspect of adolescent self-image. An African American girl wants to fit in with the girls in dance class at school, but she has difficulty following her dream because her body doesn't fit the stereotype of that dream. Joyce Collins wants to be a ballet dancer on pointe wearing pink chiffon and satin slippers. Her body has grown beyond what she considers the requirements of a ballet dancer, who, she thinks, should be slender, devoid of hips and breasts. She feels that the dance mistress, Ms. Sobol, doesn't like her because Joyce has a "big butt." A dancer cannot have a big butt and dance. She feels that Ms. Sobol picks on her during dance instruction. Later Joyce realizes that Ms. Sobol "doesn't hate me. She just wants me to be good" (94). Joyce becomes an active member of the African Kuji Je Tea Ujana Dance Ensemble. She finds the dance within herself. She also learns from the director, Haason Carter, that she moves well because of her early ballet training. She needed both.

A young African American girl may find a sense of connection with the protagonist in this novel and feel the frustrations Joyce experiences when not quite fitting in or being able to find a way for her personal form of self-expression. She may at the same time gain a feeling of confidence and even explore her community for opportunities for herself.

Some psychologists think that self-image is tied up with how effective or valued one feels in his or her environment or personal life. A negative self-image develops when self-efficacy is at a minimum. When adolescents have opportunities such as volunteer work, group projects with specific goals, creative endeavors, or learning new skills, they feel valued and effective and, by definition, their self-image improves.

LITERATURE AS A FACTOR

The literature labeled "young adult" or "adolescent literature" usually targets readers between the ages of 10 and 18. The topics introduced for consideration deal with areas including making friends, beginning to develop a personal identity, and experiencing events beyond real time/place constraints. Young readers are searching for answers to questions like: Who am I? Where do I fit in? Where am I going? How will I know when I get there? What do other people think? Young adult literature (YAL) often does not answer questions, but rather posits questions for adolescents to consider. One piece of well-written literature offers various "levels" of concern. Readers (regardless of age) come to any piece of literature from varied places, times, and experiences. Although a book may be associated with a certain primary theme, it is often the subplots and various concerns that affect the reader. Such is the case with the idea of body image (self-perception) in YAL. People are concerned with the way others perceive them. Often this outward perception is developed from within, in the mind's eye of the reader. This inner self-perception grows and develops from early childhood through adulthood. During the adolescent years, young people try on different personas to see if one of them might fit. If, during these developmental years, youngsters are given the opportunity to read about other young people feeling and thinking the same things, perhaps the feelings of isolation, differentness, and "self-loathing" with respect to body image and/or self-perception may be put into some perspective within the readers' experiential backgrounds.

Today's media—all aspects—emphasize the outward, physical attributes of individuals. What is actually viewed by oneself and others differs greatly in many cases. The ways we "see ourselves" and our bodies are embedded within our life experiences and our relationships within our environments.

Few YAL texts deal specifically with body image; however, because of a young person's preoccupation with self-perception ("How do I look?") this topic is subtly layered within almost all literature directed toward the young reader. For example, Chris Crutcher's novel *Ironman*, discussed earlier, is acclaimed as a coming-of-age novel; nevertheless, within the text several characters deal with their self-perception—how they see themselves—and how others see and treat them. A young man named Hudgie, who has been called crazy by his peers, says, "Sticks and stones may break my bones, but names will break my heart" (110). This statement is in reference to how others perceive him and how these misconceptions hurt. Another example is in *The Goats* (1987) by Brock Cole. A young boy, Howie, and a young girl, Laura, are marooned over-night on Goat Island as a summer camp prank. They are stripped naked and left there, as a type of initiation into life. These children are selected because the other camp members "see" them as different. The camp director explains, "I think most kids teased in this way would come back, well, a little proud of themselves, actually. It's the other campers' way of saying, 'Hey, kids, come on! Get with it.' " (65). The young girl's mother, Maddy, thinks how *beastly* this was. Laura and Howie decide to disappear from the island and let the campers suffer the conse-quences—learn a lesson. Parents are contacted and a search begins. Fur-ther in the novel, Maddy "began to wonder if she would ever find her way to Laura. Somehow, in a way she didn't understand, the chance seemed to be slipping away, lost in misunderstandings and *casually in-flicted hurts*" (168) [italics mine].

QUESTIONS AND ANSWERS

Is there an appropriate way teachers, not being professionals in the counseling field, can recommend to young readers a text from which we feel they might benefit? Do we have this kind of authority?

You are an authority in the sense that you know the texts, their content, and your reactions to the stories and characters. So there should be no problem suggesting a book with a particular plot to a student. But be aware of your expectations for a book. Before recommending, ask your-self what you expect from the text for the student. Books are not therapy, so most likely won't solve a problem. Do you expect a particular re-sponse from the reader? People have different responses to subject mat-ter, and a student may not respond as you did. If you expect the reader to see himself or herself and get a particular point, you may be expecting too much. You can suggest a book, but you can't be responsible for how someone else will react to the book.

If we do recommend a text and the student reads it and comes to us to talk about it, what do we say?

A good start is to help the student feel you want to discuss the book. And then listen, a lot. If the student took this step, she or he has some thoughts about it and wants to express or explore them. Think of your role as the audience, responding here and there to show that you are really involved. Most likely the student will gain insights as he or she talks, and the most helpful thing you can do is to allow the opportunity to talk. You can reflect feelings ("I feel you're very upset") or ask open-ended questions ("How does that make you feel?"), but the main thing for you is not to feel the need to analyze or interpret.

Let the student know he or she can come back to talk more about it. You can set up another time, or perhaps suggest another step to take, like how to talk to a parent or introduce them to the school counselor or suggest they start a journal and write about some of the things they think and feel.

Much YAL characterizes adults and authority figures as mean or "out of it" or less than kind. I am an adult; what do I say to the reader?

Most of us see what we're already conditioned to see. For young adults, that's adults as authority figures or "out of it." Make certain they see the examples of caring adults. You may also point out, in a nonauthoritative way, that some "out-of-it" people can be helpful and understanding. People are not either-or, but are complex, just like teenagers. Most books probably have characters of all types. In *Ironman*, Mr. Redman, the football coach and English teacher, is not one you'd want to tell your problems to, but swim coach Lion would probably listen and be nonjudgmental.

If I notice a student puts herself down a lot, or she tries to avoid speaking in class, does this mean the student is developing a negative self-image? If so, can I help change this poor self-conception?

Often negative self-talk reflects a person's inner feelings, and avoiding expressing opinions can mean a lack of self-confidence. Since self-perception is a result of personal experiences and the individual's interpretation of the experiences, it is difficult to teach positive self-concept per se. But it would be of great value to create an environment that fosters self-expression, respect, and trust. Allow adolescents to explore their strengths and not fear their weaknesses. Make honest criticism an enhancing, building experience rather than a negative, destructive experience. Adults often see adolescents as immature and in need of direction. But from the teens' perspective, they are not the immature younger sister or brother or "still my baby." They are emerging from childhood with a maturing body, intellect, and social awareness. They are frustrated and angered when they're seen as immature, selfish, and untrustworthy. If they feel they can make a difference or have an effect, they will gain confidence and feel good about themselves.

It is our hope that, they will begin to develop positive perceptions of themselves and view themselves as capable and worthwhile. Encourage students at every opportunity and allow them to express themselves intellectually and physically through—writing, drawing, acting, dancing, sports and athletics. Have students students write about an experience; for example, ask students to read young adult texts, then ask them to put themselves in a particular position (it might be a teen, a principal, a peer, a teacher, a parent) and write about how it feels or how another individual might think and feel. Another idea is to have students finish a sentence such as. "I have felt like Joyce in *Blue Tights* when . . ." or "Sometimes I'm not sure how I feel, like when . . ." This type of activity can help students clarify (verbally) what they do feel or think.

The next very important step is to give approval, no matter how small you think it may be. An approving comment before, during, or after class, such as "I liked the paragraph (phrase, sentence, word) in your story about . . ." develops self-worth and self-acceptance. Building self-esteem is, in part, a matter of personal interpretation of experiences, but we can help by giving students positive, immediate feedback and room to explore, with encouragement, guidance, and respect.

What are some ways we, teachers and parents, can support young teens?

Whatever would help them feel involved and valued helps. Activities that encourage self-examination and self-expression are valuable. Encourage an interest in sports activities for girls. There are far fewer stories about athletic girls than boys, but teachers can invite local women athletes to participate in special events or career day activities. Parents can take daughters to sports events. Encourage boys to go out for sports other than football, basketball, or baseball. Get track-and-field coaches to demonstrate techniques for different sports or show videos on technique or track meets. As part of a class assignment students could interview different coaches or local athletes or instructors, in fields such as dance, judo, or other sports less familiar to students. Invite students to write a sports story in which they are the protagonists. In surveys that ask adolescents what makes them feel good about themselves, girls and boys both indicate participation in sports as a contribution.

Encourage teens to start a book club. One local club of middle school girls reads a book a month and meets to talk about the book and topics related to the story. These are not self-help groups, and there does not have to be an adult leader with an agenda. Allow the girls or boys to structure the group and do the research for the books they will choose to read, with a parent or teacher as an advisor or facilitator.

Encourage self-expression through writing or acting. Students may write about various experiences and their feelings toward them in a journal for a month, then share whatever parts they want with the group. Or they can write poetry or short stories or choose a novel to adapt for a play that would capture some part of the story. Orenstein tells of assignments Ms. Logan, a teacher at Everett Middle School, gives her students. One assignment was, after the class read "Girl," a short story by Jamaica Kincaid, for students to write their own "girl" or "boy" stories, asking that they look at how stereotypes affect them personally (Orenstein, 1994, 260–261).

The following titles are suggested resources geared toward the young reader (ages 11 through 18) concerned with issues dealing with growing up. Of major concern to young people are the questions: How do I see myself? How do others see me in relationship to my world? All aspects of adolescent development are inextricably linked, and body image (self-perception) is deeply embedded. How one sees oneself is a human concern—one that is omnipresent.

RECOMMENDED READINGS

The annotated texts and novels described below might serve as catalysts for young people and adults as a basis for understanding, recognition, and discussion. Jeffrey Wilhelm (1997) posits that literature is "transcendent: it offers us possibilities; it takes us beyond space, time, and self; it questions the way the world is and offers possibilities for the way it could be" (38). In *"You Gotta BE the Book,"* Joanne, a middle school student, explains to the author, Jeffrey Wilhelm, that the best thing a teacher (or parent) could do is "to recommend a good story to me, and give me a chance to talk about it" (34). Good advice. Enjoy!

Fiction Works

Bauer, J. (1992). *Squashed.* New York: Bantam Doubleday Dell. 192 pp. (ISBN: 0–440–21912–4). Middle School (MS), High School (HS).

This novel is fun. It is about a six-hundred-pound pumpkin named "Max" and his 16-year-old grower, Ellie. Ellie learns that winning is not the only point in competition. She has entered her prize-winning pumpkin in the fall festival events. Her major competition is "Big Daddy," grown by a grouchy, ill-tempered man by the name of Cyril Pool.

Ellie is always talking about her body and its largeness compared to the other, thinner girls. She is always trying to lose five pounds in order to fit into her favorite, appealing outfit—a flowing orange silk shirt, tailored beige slacks, and her deceased mother's shimmering silver earrings. She feels that only by becoming thin can she be attractive to the young man from the agricultural college. Throughout the course of the novel, Ellie realizes that people don't see her as she "sees" herself. Her body image and self-perception have been developed by messages from the media (visual and audio). These messages have been almost subliminal since childhood. Ellie learns to be a gracious winner, a gracious person, and a gracious young woman who is intelligent, humorous, idealistic, loving, and lovable.

This novel will appeal to males and females, from eighth grade through adult. Bauer tells a story that is humorous, touching, serious, and fun. The setting and plot will introduce many readers to an environment that will never be lived for real, but through the words, reactions, and situations that Ellie lives within the pages of this delightful, entertaining story, readers will experience identifiable concerns through a different lens.

Cofer, J. O. (1995). *An Island Like You: Stories of the Barrio.* New York: Orchard Books. 165 pp. (ISBN: 0–531–06897–8). MS, HS.

This is a collection of twelve short stories about young people caught between Puerto Rican heritage and American surroundings. The intriguing concept of this collection is that the characters come and go in each story. The characters live in El Building, a high-rise apartment complex. It, too, is *like an island.* Within the stories and within El Building, the characters interact and react in situations that deal with their own heritage as Puerto Ricans and the clash that sometimes occurs with the American culture. As readers, we meet parents, grandparents, aunts, uncles, siblings, friends, and neighbors and become active participants in their lives. In "Beauty Lessons," Sandra is concerned with her plainness and lack of outward beauty. Her aunt tells her, "You're a late bloomer, Sandra. And flowers that bloom late last longer" (47).

The final story, entitled "White Balloons," deals with a birthday party for Rick Sanchez, who has died from AIDS. The story tells how the barrio doesn't forget and doesn't always forgive. Rick died before he could celebrate his birthday. His friends (most of the characters met in previous stories of El Building) arrange this "building celebration." Everyone in the barrio loves a celebration. The party is held on the roof. White balloons are released during this celebration. The story ends with a line from *Don Quixote*: "I know who I am, and who I may be if I choose" (157). All of these stories deal with self-perception and how each is seen by others. This collection of stories will help readers of all ages understand and accept differences cross-culturally. Readers will empathize with the human need for a positive self-image.

Cole, B. (1987). *The Goats.* New York: Farrar, Straus & Giroux. 184 pp. (ISBN: 0–374–42576–0). MS, HS.

Laura Golden refers to herself as being "socially retarded for her age" (29). She wears glasses, is thin, and is shy. She doesn't fit in. She is picked on. Howie Mitchell is small for his age. His body is immature and lacks hair in the right places. For these reasons, fellow campers decide to make "goats" of them; they are stripped of all their clothing and marooned on Goat Island (hence the name of the prank) for the night. Neither knows the other is on the island until they meet in the only sheltered place on the island. They decide to "get revenge." They decide to disappear and make everyone worry about them. It happens. Howie and Laura find themselves in several tight spots but work their way out of them. Laura remembers that when she "had been little she hadn't been able to hurt anyone. Now she could. She felt glad. She felt real, as if her body had suddenly gained an enormous presence and weight" (179).

As the novel unfolds, Howie and Laura become less worthy of the label "goat." Laura's mother is called. She goes to the camp looking for her daughter. Through Maddy (Laura's mother), the reader begins to see how parents and peers perpetuate images of self-perception that are not healthy. Often, it's not what is done to and for a person, but rather what is *not* done during the formative years of adolescence. Most people (of all ages) have had a joke pulled on them. Reading this novel will cause introspection of what it feels like and what it does to the person(s) on the receiving end of being a "goat."

Crutcher, C. (1993). *Staying Fat for Sarah Byrnes*. New York: Bantam Doubleday Dell. 216 pp. (ISBN: 0–440–21906–X). HS.

Chris Crutcher offers a wonderfully complex novel for the older, mature reader. This novel cannot be labeled as to a specific thematic concern. It addresses prejudice, bigotry, hate, religion, love, sex, personal identity, education, teacher/parent/child relationships, friendship, women's rights, and too many more to list. This novel cannot be read and then forgotten. It is a "major thinker." It is a novel that can be— should be—read several times. Parents, teachers, and students will find almost limitless discussion topics in this novel.

Eric Calhoune is 18 and a swimmer. His nickname is Moby, as in Moby Dick—the whale. Eric says, "I spent years being embarrassed because I was fat and clumsy and afraid. So I developed this pretty credible comedy act—I'm the I-Don't-Care-Kid which is what I assume most other kids do" (56). His best friend since elementary school has been Sarah Byrnes (she would only respond to people who called her both names). Sarah Byrnes at least in her own opinion, is probably the ugliest person he has ever met—or will meet. As a child, she was badly burned on her face and hands, and has never received any reconstructive surgery. Sarah Byrnes "was my friend. She was with me when nobody else was. In the days of my life when my body embarrassed and humiliated me every time anyone laid eyes on me" (74). Eric's body was changing and slimming because of his competitive swimming. He used to stuff himself trying to stay fat for Sarah Byrnes but couldn't. He "stays fat" for her now by remaining her friend and trying to save her from her father's cruel, abusive tendencies. He would not stop being her friend, even when she tried to push him away. He loved her and wanted to do what he could because she was (under her horribly scarred exterior) a warm, loving, kind person. No one had ever gone beyond her external visage to discover her inner beauty and humanity.

Ferris, J. (1994). *Invincible Summer*. New York: HarperCollins; Farrar, Straus & Giroux. 167 pp. (ISBN: 0–374–43608–8). HS.

The title of this novel is part of a quote by Camus—"In the depths of winter, I finally learned that within me there lay an invincible summer" (128). Robin Gregory learns that she has lymphocytic leukemia. She must go through radiation and chemotherapy. While she is in the hospital, she meets a wise young man named Rick Winn, who is also battling this disease. They become friends first and then become emotionally involved. Robin's appearance changes drastically because of the effects of her treatment. She shuns her support group of family and friends, and will not let others see her changed, ugly body. "I'm not angry at everybody who's going to live longer than I am. I'm angry that I have to go through this and be scared and sick and ugly. I'm angry at my body. We've always been friends—I thought I could trust it, and look what it's done to me" (68). Over time her illness goes into remission, and she begins to look like her former self. This is not the case for Richard. He learns that the cancer has spread throughout his body, and there is no hope for a cure.

This is a love story, a romance. It is, however, more; it is a story about human dignity and the human spirit. It is an emotionally powerful novel and would appeal to an older reader. It is intense, humorous, poetic, and well crafted. The reader comes to recognize that illness, accident, and fate are beyond a person's control but do, indeed, affect positively and negatively body image—perception of self.

Feuer, E. (1990). *Paper Doll*. New York: Farrar, Straus & Giroux. 186 pp. (ISBN: 0–374–45724–7). HS.

Leslie Marx is a senior in high school, 17 years old, an excellent student, and a gifted violinist. She neglects typical "adolescent stuff" for school and her music. She loves her violin. She was in a serious car accident when she was 7 and lost both of her legs. She wears artificial legs and limps badly. Because she is not "normal," she has avoided classmates and other girls (and "girl stuff"). She feels that she has no chance to date, love, go out. She meets Jeff. He adores her. He has a mild case of cerebral palsy that affects his legs. He accepts his disability with maturity and a wonderful sense of humor. She realizes, through Jeff's perseverance and sense of humor, that she can love and be loved. Throughout the course of the novel, she discovers that her father pushed her toward music and Juilliard because he felt that she could not have a normal life because of her disability. He wanted to protect her by controlling and directing her life.

She begins to question her music—she wants to punish her dad by giving up her music. She comes to realize that this is foolish. She needed her music. Jeff knew this. Leslie had to realize this and learn that she can do all that she wants to do because of who she is—not what she looks like. She absented herself from her peers because she imagined what they were thinking. She made judgments about people before she really knew what they were thinking and feeling. She felt responsible for others' actions, maybe as a form of self-preservation, because of her perceived body image, which resulted from years of silent direction and guidance by her parents.

This novel will appeal to the older adolescent—male or female. The reader begins to understand why parents sometimes do what they do. Parents cannot control their children's lives and make life-changing decisions for them. This is a concept with which an older adolescent can identify.

Janover, C. (1988). *Josh: A Boy with Dyslexia*. Burlington, VT: Waterfront Books. 99 pp. (ISBN: 0–9149525–10–7). MS, HS.

Concerns of the dyslexic child are voiced through Josh's actions throughout this short novel. Josh doesn't like "regular" school, because the kids call him names and tease him about his specialness. His brother, two years older, calls Josh "retard," "stupid," and "a mental." Because of this, Josh is apprehensive when meeting other kids even though most of the children he meets accept him as a likable person. The neighborhood bully makes life miserable for Josh. Instead of supporting Josh, his brother sides with the bully. Josh begins to question his "ability" as a person of worth. Josh saves the day during a fishing accident and brings help to his brother and Buck (the bully). He tells them how he overcame his dyslexia in order to get help. The protagonist is young; however, readers of all ages should read stories about physical and mental limitations and how individuals learn to cope. By understanding others' limitations, persons of all ages will understand and accept people for what they can offer rather than demeaning them because they are "different."

Kerr, M. E. (1972). *Dinky Hocker Shoots Smack!* New York: Dell. 190 pp. (ISBN: 0–440–92030–2). MS.

"People who don't shoot smack have problems, too" (187). This is the message that Susan "Dinky" Hocker, age 14, is trying to get across to her mother and father. Her mother, Helen, is so concerned with her outside community activities that she doesn't see or feel Dinky's cry for love and support. Dinky is five feet four inches tall and weighs one hundred and sixty-five pounds. Dinky falls in love with P. John Knight, who himself is six feet tall, an overweight boy, and somewhat outspoken and opinionated. Because of Helen Hocker's dislike for P. John, Susan's feelings are pushed aside and ignored by both her mother and father (who is rarely home). Tucker Woolf befriends Dinky because she adopts his cat, Nader (who coincidentally becomes obese under Dinky's care). As the story progresses, Tucker becomes Dinky's friend and confidant. Throughout the novel, Dinky sinks further into her own destructive pattern of overeating and self-indulgence as if no one really cared. Before a prestigious celebration of a community event where Mrs. Hocker is to receive the Good Samaritan Award for helping so many troubled individuals, Dinky plasters the streets with signs of every shape and color stating "Dinky Hocker Shoots Smack." This catches the attention of Mr. and Mrs. Hocker and everyone else at the community activity. Mr. Hocker questions Tucker concerning his involvement. About Dinky's attraction to P. John, Mr. Hocker says to Tucker:

"Well, Helen never really took the thing that seriously. I think it was more than 'a thing' where Susan was concerned. It never amounted to much, after all," Mr. Hocker said.

"If it wasn't much," Tucker said, "it was still all Susan ever had."

"What's this all *about*, Tucker?" Mr. Hocker asked.

Tucker's words came slowly. "I think it's about things amounting to a lot more than people think they amount to—I think it's about having your feelings shoved aside." (186–187)

The story ends on a positive note with hope for the future. Dinky's parents realize what they have been doing to her. She is overweight, unattractive, and crying out for their attention. She saw herself, through their eyes, as less than acceptable because of her physical attributes—not her inner self.

This classic young adult novel is a good read for male or female middle school students, and a quick read for high school students. Readers will begin to understand the need for acceptance of all students regardless of how they look. Beneath the facade of a body, there is something more important.

Lee, L. (1994). *Stella: On the Edge of Popularity*. Chicago: Polychrome. 178 pp. (ISBN: 1–879965–08–09). MS.

Stella Sung Ok Kim is a Korean American is the seventh grade. She wants to be like Americans, but her home life centers around her family heritage. Her father thinks that she is becoming too American and insists that the Korean ways be followed in her home environment. Her grandmother is especially hard on Stella. Stella misinterprets her grandmother's intentions: "she makes me act Korean all the time, so that everybody thinks I'm weird. I hate her" (49). Stella's best friend, Rachel Weinstraube, tries to help her realize that being like everybody else is not always the best policy: "It's good to surprise people, especially if they stereotype you" (55). Rachel plans on helping Stella win the school spelling bee. Stella feels that this feat would help her become more popular with the other girls, whom she so wants to be like.

Stella wants to win for all the wrong reasons. She learns through a series of events that "maybe I'll fight for myself from now on, and maybe I'll just compete. . . . There might be more to friendship than to popularity" (101). Stella also comes to understand what hardships her family had to endure to come to America and have the opportunity to live freely. She learns that there is room for both cultures in her life from her grandmother, who cares for her and her brother while her parents work long hours operating a cleaning business. Her grandmother says, "Honor your history. That is enough. I have nothing to give you; all I can give you is where you are from. That is who you are. It is who I am as well" (138). Her grandmother wants Stella to reach for success on her merits of being a good student. Stella realizes that "maybe she [will] find a place after all" (178).

Paulsen, G. (1993). *The Boy Who Owned the School*. New York: Dell. 85 pp. (ISBN: 0–440–21626–5). MS, HS.

This short, often funny-sad novel is an interior monologue dealing with the methods and strategies 15-year-old Jacob Freisten executes to remain invisible during every school day. Paulsen's farcical humor punctuates many of the inner feelings that a boy (small for his age) has while trying to be "who and what he is." The novel is reminiscent of James Thurber. Events, thoughts, and feelings are magnified through Jacob's imaginings. He spends his entire day trying not to be noticed. This activity is his major concern. His motto: If you get noticed, bad things happen. Solution: Don't get noticed. Until the end of this short novel, he never realizes the people around him see him quite differently than he sees himself. This novel would cause a chuckle and tug at the heart-strings whether read by a 15-year-old or by an older student as a retro-spective piece.

Pitts, P. (1986). *For a Good Time, Don't Call Claudia*. New York: Avon Books. 115 pp. (ISBN: 0–380–75117–8). MS, HS.

Claudia is receiving strange telephone calls. The male callers want "to have some fun." She was no idea why these boys are calling her. She immediately feels that the girls at school are saying awful things about her. Her father and brother have been killed in a car accident, and her mom has become depressed and is drinking. Claudia pretty much has to care for herself. Money is tight, and Claudia cannot afford the "necessary things" to be popular. She describes several girls who are in her eyes, gorgeous. She wants to be their friend. She's sure that "girls who are gorgeous . . . see someone who's just a little different, and before they even try to get acquainted, they start making fun. I make sure I never turn my back on that bunch" (24). She takes a job at a pet store and begins to be friends with herself. The prank calls continue. During the school year, she becomes involved in class activities and begins to slim down naturally. "Then I turned back to my mirror to see if that girl in the reflection was really me, Claudia Baker, formerly Mrs. Jack Sprat" (99). She meets and is enamored with Bill Dangerfield. He seems to be a nice young man. Come to find out, he and his friends put the names and telephone numbers of several girls (who seemed out of the loop) on the boys' restroom wall. It was supposed to be a practical joke. He didn't think anyone ever called those numbers. She was drawn to Bill because of his outer looks, not for who he really was. Claudia realizes that "it's sad when someone judges other people on something insignificant, like clothes, instead of what's really important about them" (107). Readers of all ages need to recognize what harm and hurt practical jokes can cause.

Voight, C. (1986). *Izzy, Willy-Nilly*. New York: Fawcett Juniper. 280 pp. (ISBN: 0–689–31202–4). MS, HS.

Isobel "Izzy" Lingard is a freshman and is invited to a party by Marco Griggers, a popular senior. There are drinking and drugs. On the drive home her date loses control of the car and crashes into a tree. This accident causes Izzy to have her right leg amputated just below the knee.

At first her friends visit her, but soon they stop coming. Izzy has always been popular and well liked, but her physical change affects how everyone sees her. She experiences self-loathing and severe depression. She keeps telling everyone that she is fine, when in reality she is anything but. The young man who caused the accident never contacts her. She feels terribly alone and abandoned. "It was so solitary there inside myself. I just wanted someone to reach in there and connect, just for a minute, just so I would know it could be done" (69). Enter Rosamunde Webber. Rosamunde never "fit in." She wanted to be better friends with the other girls, but she just didn't *look* right. Izzy tells her brother that Rosamunde "is not good looking: she has fuzzy hair, a big nose and a bad figure, I think. She doesn't dress to show off much of her figure. She's intelligent, too" (117).

Later in the novel, Izzy and Rosamunde are talking about being self-conscious because Izzy's mother has suggested that Rosamunde might be self-conscious because of Izzy's situation.

Rosamunde sat down in the chair, her legs looking thick in the overalls and her ankles thick in heavy socks.

"Or maybe," she continued, "it was just my looks." She'd stopped smiling. "You know—there are things about the way you look. . . . That would be the thing about being black—people see it right away, black skin. It means that you have to face up to people's perceptions right away. Don't you see? If you're black, well, the first thing people see is your skin color. You can't hide it. If you see what I mean."

"I see what you mean," I said. I saw exactly what she meant. Because people were going to look at me and think *amputee*. (126)

Izzy goes home and begins readjusting her life to being different from other people. She and Rosamunde have become friends in school and out of school. Rosamunde becomes too protective, and Izzy must ask her to stop clingging. Rosamunde stops; Izzy and she understand each other, and for the first time in many months, life begins to seem normal for Izzy.

This novel, although dealing primarily with adjustment to a life change due to an accident, addresses relationships, friendship, honesty, parent-child relationship, and inner self-perception. Isobel "Izzy" Lingard and Rosamunde Webber grow to accept each other on individual merit—not individual body image.

Wersba, B. (1990). *Fat: A Love Story*. New York: Dell. 156 pp. (ISBN: 0–440–20537–9). HS.

This novel is for mature adolescent readers. The protagonist is a mature 16-year-old who eventually moves in with, then marries, an older man. It is about her constant bouts with dieting, eating, and being overweight. The tone is flippant, often sarcastic. Rita Formica feels badly about her body and, outwardly, deals with her heaviness in a cavalier fashion, while inwardly she is totally frustrated. "To be fat is a signal to other people that you have no control, no pride, and this is the message that they get about you right away" (12). She gets a job working at Arnold's Cheesecake. Arnold, the owner, is older (32 years old), and they become fast friends. This friendship, over the time span of the novel, turns into love. It is a mature love. Arnold accepts Rita for who she is, without regard for her physical shape. Rita begins to lose weight—not because she is trying, but because she begins to understand that being overweight does not mean that an obese person is totally ugly in a universe of beautiful people. With Arnold's support, friendship, and love, Rita understands that there is more to life than food. There is loving and being loved as a person—not as an object.

Barbara Wersba offers the older adolescent reader characters and situations that are real, identifiable, and honest. The novel offers insight into the multifaceted concerns of growing up into a mature, caring young adult.

Williams-Garcia, R. (1988). *Blue Tights*. New York: Bantam Books. 138 pp. (ISBN: 0–553–28293–X). MS, HS.

All Joyce Collins wants to do is dance. She wants to be a ballet dancer on pointe wearing pink chiffon and satin slippers. Her body has grown beyond what she considers the requirements of a ballet dancer, who, she thinks, should be slender, devoid of hips and breasts. She feels that the dance mistress, Ms. Sobol, doesn't like her because Joyce has a "big butt." A dancer cannot have a big butt and dance. She feels that Ms. Sobol picks on her during dance instruction. Later Joyce realizes that Ms. Sobol (who knows that Joyce has the inner passion and sense of music to become a fine dancer) "doesn't hate me. She just wants me to be good" (94). Joyce has to discover this inner quality herself. Until Joyce recognizes this, she considers herself a social misfit. She will not look at her reflection in the dance mirrors. She flaunts her womanly body for all the wrong reasons. She wants to be loved and love. She wants to be accepted by her peers for their reasons—not hers. She dresses so that all her attributes are obvious to others. Her mother tells her, "We always go looking for someone to love us. We forget to love ourselves first" (116). She accepts who she is—a 15-year-old girl—and what she is— an African American dancer. At the close of the novel, Joyce's "focus remained in the mirror at something wonderful opening up before her eyes" (138).

Wolff, V. E. (1988). *Probably Still Nick Swansen*. New York: Scholastic. 175 pp. (ISBN: 0–590–43146–3). MS, HS.

Nick Swansen, age 16, invites Shana to the prom. She was a member of his special class in room 19 and has recently been sent "up" to regular classes. Nick is eagerly awaiting the day when he will have his "going up party" like Shana. He speaks to her in the halls after she leaves the class, but he misses seeing her every day. She accepts his invitation, and he begins preparations for the big event. He teaches himself to dance, he reads up on prom etiquette, and he works extra hours to earn the money for tickets, flowers, and the after-prom cruise. Shana does not show up. He is mortified. Right up to the minute that the dance is over, he pictures Shana showing up with stories of car trouble, family emergencies, and acceptable reasons for being so late. While he is waiting for Shana, Nick overhears two chaperoning parents talking about students who have special needs. "No son of mine's gonna sit with the droolers. It'd be a handicap. You put a kid with the droolers, he'll end up a drooler" (65).

Throughout the novel, the term "drooler" is often repeated. Nick's image of himself as a person is diminished. He refers to himself as a "jerk. A moron. Double triple stupid jerk" (90). Through the use of flashback, Wolff makes it all too apparent that students with special needs are referred to as "dummies," "jerks," and "droolers" by parents and—often to their faces—by other students. Nick questions his worth as a person: "he wished he could have no color and no shape and no weight, he'd be invisible and just walk around and nobody would know he was there" (125).

Shana finally tells Nick why she didn't show up. Through a series of unfortunate circumstances and frustrations, Shana told her parents that Nick had called and canceled their date. Nick and Shana's friendship is rekindled only after each opens up and talks about what each is feeling.

Readers of this novel will come to appreciate and understand feelings and perceptions from another's point of view. The author presents the story and doesn't become preachy or involved. The reader comes to understand "other people" after seeing life through Nick's eyes.

Nonfiction Works and Poetry Collections

Agard, J. (Ed.). (1990). *Life Doesn't Frighten Me at All.* New York: Henry Holt. 95 pp. (ISBN: 0–8050–1237–0). MS, HS.

John Agard has compiled poems from poets who reflect multicultural backgrounds. The topics addressed range from that awful zit that erupts just before an important date to having to recite in front of a class filled with "smarter people than myself." Body image and self-perception are addressed throughout the text. So many topics will provide moments for exchange of ideas. The illustrations are wonderful. Teens and adults will enjoy every entry and every illustration. Each visit to the text will produce new insight and understanding.

Beckelman, L. (1994). *Body Blues.* New York: Macmillan. 48 pp. (ISBN: 0–382–24743–4). MS, HS.

This title is a part of the Hotline series, which includes these topics: anger, body blues, boredom, depression, envy, grief, loneliness, stress. Its audience is the young female and male adolescent. It offers a discussion of body image and how it affects self-esteem. Beckelman provides a frank discussion about body development and ideas to consider for young teens who feel unhappy with their appearance. The book offers suggestions for overcoming a negative body image by keeping journals, reading suggested novels, and watching certain television programs and specific movies for young people—both male and female. The book is honest and directly addresses the many issues of the young, burgeoning adolescent body and the inner concerns dealing with rampant physical change.

Canfield, J., M. V. Hansen, and K. Kirberger. (Eds.). (1997). *Chicken Soup for the Teenage Soul.* Deerfield Beach, FL: Health Communications. 354 pp. (ISBN: 1–55874–463–0). MS, HS.

The *Chicken Soup* texts have become almost a household word. The compilation offers insight into relationships, friendship, family, love and kindness, learning, tough decisions, making a difference and going for your dreams. The entries are sad, glad, humorous, serious, and sometimes wacky. Readers of all ages can digest feelings and thoughts that will make life more livable and understandable. The text is all about sharing feelings and ideas. It can be read from cover to cover or in a haphazard fashion—which so often is how teens feel. It's a wonderful text for generating discussion and/or written responses for journal or diary entries.

Lewis, S. (1996). *A Totally Alien Life-Form: Teenagers*. New York: New Press. 363 pp. (ISBN: 1–56584–282–0). MS, HS, Adult (A).

Sydney Lewis presents a series of vignettes of teenagers from all socioeconomic levels, from all geographic areas, and of diverse ages. This is a readable book. Older adolescents will enjoy reading sections of interest and discover how other teens think similarly. The older teenage reader will also discover how other teens of different cultures and geographic localities think differently—and that that's okay. Parents, teachers, counselors, and clergy, among others, will find that this text offers the inner thoughts, feelings, and fears that teens have but are reluctant to voice. It will also jog memories of adolescence for the adult reader. Too often, we forget what we felt as teens. Lewis's book reminds us.

Medearis, A. S. (1995). *Skin Deep and Other Teenage Reflections*. Illustrations by Michael Bryant. New York: Macmillan. 48 pp. (ISBN: 0–02–765980–1). MS, HS, A.

This short, well-illustrated collection of poems addresses feelings and thoughts of teenagers. For example, "Jigsaw" (7) deals with trying so hard for self-discovery that the narrator seems to have lost himself/herself. The poems offer wonderful opportunities for open discussion. Most of the illustrations present sketches of African Americans; however, topics concern all teens, from the very young to the more mature.

Pratt, J. (1995). *For Real: The Uncensored Truth about America's Teenagers*. New York: Hyperion. 317 pp. (ISBN: 0–7868–8064–3). MS, HS, A.

In her "Not a Boring Introduction" (xi), Jane Pratt offers reasons why she compiled this book: for parents and teachers (and adults in general) to understand teenagers and what they are going through; and for kids who want to know what other kids are thinking about and doing. This is a "pick up and read" book. It need not be read from cover to cover—but once begun, it might be. Pratt presents stories from teens. These teens have had different experiences; they are from everywhere. They range from ages 14 to 19. Pratt doesn't get in the way. She does include entries from journals that she has been keeping most of her life. This, she hopes, reaffirms the point that adults were once teens. She wants adults to remember that. She also wants teens to realize that adults were once their age and had similar feelings, thoughts, and fears. This text offers a bridge between kids and adults. It is readable, not at all condescending toward young readers. It is not adult bashing. It offers a starting place for mature, honest, open, mutual discussion of ideas, thoughts, and feelings.

Yep, L. (Ed.). (1993). *American Dragons: Twenty-five Asian American Voices*. New York: HarperCollins. 236 pp. (ISBN: 0–06–440603–2). MS, HS.

Each short story deals with how Americans of Asian descent assimilate their own culture along with American culture. Authors, who are themselves of Asian descent, present poems, nonfiction scenarios, and ancestral stories that speak to Asian Americans and to the general population. All young people will see something of themselves in the struggle to find an identity that isn't generic. For example, Austin in "Stoplight" wonders what it would be like to "live with white skin, with white parents in this white world. It must be strange, that's for sure" (16). The stories deal with dating non-Asian persons, physical differences, and having to deal with demands from conflicting cultures. The characters are likable, realistic, and identifiable. Readers might realize that everyone (regardless of cultural heritage) has similar anxieties and obstacles to overcome.

REFERENCES

Agard, J. (Ed.). (1990). *Life Doesn't Frighten Me at All*. New York: Henry Holt.

American Association of University Women Educational Foundation. (1991). *Shortchanging Girls, Shortchanging America: A Call to Action*. Washington, DC: American Association of University Women.

American Association of University Women Educational Foundation. (1993). *Hostile Hallways: The AAUW Survey on Sexual Harassment in Amer-*

ica's Schools. Washington, DC: American Association of University Women.

Bauer, J. (1992). *Squashed*. New York: Bantam Doubleday Dell.

Beckelman, L. (1994). *Body Blues*. New York: Macmillan.

Canadian Teachers' Federation. (1990). *A Cappella: A Report on the Realities, Concerns, Expectations and Barriers Experienced by Adolescent Women in Canada*. Ottawa: TTF.

Canfield, J., M. V. Hansen, K. Kirberger. (Eds.). (1997). *Chicken Soup for the Teenage Soul*. Deerfield Beach, FL: Health Communications.

Carroll, R. (1997). *Sugar in the Raw: Voices of Young Black Girls in America* New York: Crown Trade Paperbacks.

Cofer, J. O. (1995). *An Island Like You: Stories of the Barrio*. New York: Orchard Books.

Cole, B. (1987). *The Goats*. New York: Farrar, Straus & Giroux.

Crutcher, C. (1993). *Staying Fat for Sarah Byrnes*. New York: Bantam Doubleday Dell.

Crutcher, C. (1995). *Ironman*. New York: Greenwillow Books.

Ferris, J. (1994). *Invincible Summer*. New York: HarperCollins; Farrar, Straus & Giroux.

Feuer, E. (1990). *Paper Doll*. New York: Farrar, Straus & Giroux.

Jackson, D. (1996). "Acting Hard." In J. Salisbury and D. Jackson (Eds.), *Challenging Macho Values: Practical Ways of Working with Adolescent Boys*. Washington, DC: Falmer Press.

Janover, C. (1988). *Josh: A Boy with Dyslexia*. Burlington, VT: Waterfront Books.

Kerr, M. E. (1972). *Dinky Hocker Shoots Smack!* New York: Dell.

Lee, L. (1994). *Stella: On the Edge of Popularity*. Chicago: Polychrome.

Lewis, S. (1996). *A Totally Alien Life-Form: Teenagers*. New York: New Press.

Mazer, N. F. (1993). *Out of Control*. New York: Morrow Junior Books.

Medearis, A. S. (1995). *Skin Deep and Other Teenage Reflections*. Illustrations by Michael Bryant. New York: Macmillan.

Mellin, L. M., C. E. Irwin and S. Scully. (1992). "Prevalence of Disordered Eating in Girls: A Survey of Middle Class Children." *Journal of the American Dietetic Association* 92: 851–853.

Moore, D. D. (1993). "Body Image and Eating Behavior in Adolescents." *Journal of the American College of Nutrition* 12: 505–510.

Newman, L. (1986). "Slipping through the Cracks." In *Good Enough to Eat*. Ithaca, NY: Firebrand Books.

Newman, L. (1994). *Fat Chance*. New York: Putnam's Sons.

Orenstein, P. (1994). *School Girls: Young Women, Self-Esteem, and the Confidence Gap*. New York: Doubleday.

Paulsen, G. (1993). *The Boy Who Owned the School*. New York: Dell.

Pipher, M. (1994). *Reviving Ophelia: Saving the Selves of Adolescent Girls.* New York: Ballantine Books.

Pitts, P. (1986). *For a Good Time, Don't Call Claudia.* New York: Avon Books.

Pratt, J. (1995). *For Real: The Uncensored Truth about America's Teenagers.* New York: Hyperion.

Salisbury, J., and D. Jackson. (1996). *Challenging Macho Values: Practical Ways of Working with Adolescent Boys.* Washington, DC: Falmer Press.

Voight, C. (1986). *Izzy, Willy-Nilly.* New York: Fawcett Juniper.

Wersba, B. (1990). *Fat: A Love Story.* New York: Dell.

Wilhelm, J. (1997). *"You Gotta BE the Book": Teaching Engaged and Reflective Reading with Adolescents.* New York: Teachers College Press.

Williams-Garcia, R. (1988). *Blue Tights.* New York: Bantam Books.

Wolff, V. E. (1988). *Probably Still Nick Swansen.* New York: Scholastic.

Yep, L. (Ed.). (1993). *American Dragons: Twenty-five Asian American Voices.* New York: HarperCollins.

CHAPTER THREE

Society's Impact on Adolescents and Their Sexuality

Elizabeth L. Watts and LaShawnda Eggelletion

The two of us grew up together in two-parent, middle-class African American homes in South Florida during the 1970s and 1980s. We were fortunate to have parents who stressed education, community activities, and a strong sense of self. We often discuss how we had time to grow up, time to be children. We participated in youth groups and were active in church and school activities. We were immersed in schools, activities, communities, and homes where we "belonged."

Our coming of age was a time of crushes on boys, dating in groups, giggling about our new loves, and reading the young adult books rumored to be hot on campus. We voraciously read one such novel, *Forever* by Judy Blume, which helped us answer the questions we had about sex. We had supportive mothers, who were usually open to talking with us about our changing bodies and increasing hormones. They made sure we attended teen sexuality workshops, sponsored by community organizations, every year of our adolescence. We learned about how rushing into sex and being uninformed about its risks could ruin our chances for a bright future. Our sexual awareness along with the sense of belonging we felt at home and in the community grounded our decisions not to have sex during adolescence.

Our years in school settings, as an educator and mental health counselor, respectively, have shown us that many of today's adolescents do not come from families and communities where they feel a sense of belonging. These adolescents may seek a sense of belonging through sexual activity. In 1990, an estimated 54 percent of students grades nine through twelve said they had had sex, 40 percent by ninth grade and 72 percent by twelfth grade ("Smells Like Teen Spirit," 1992, 38).

Adolescents coming of age attempt to understand who they are individually and in relation to others. Part of adolescence is developing and coming to terms with sexual identity, which involves behaviors and attitudes. Adolescents' perceptions of sexuality are influenced by society's views as portrayed by the media, in their community, by their peers, and at home. These external influences are compounded by adolescents' changing bodies and growing curiosity about physical and emotional intimacy.

The purpose of this chapter is to discuss young adult literature as a vehicle for helping adolescents understand sexual identity and how it relates to their growing sense of self. In an ode to Judy Blume, La-Shawnda Eggelletion, a mental health counselor working with adolescents, paints two vivid portraits: (1) how young adult literature played a part in her sexual identity development and (2) how contemporary teens face difficult issues in developing sexual identity. Then, we address young adult literature as a way for adolescents to explore issues related to their sexuality, such as decisions about sex and contraception.

LASHAWNDA'S ODE TO JUDY BLUME: MY MEMORIES

On a hot summer's day in 1981, three young adolescent girls huddle over pillows on the floor; novels in hand, they exchange giggles and awkward glances. All three girls appear engrossed in a story of a teenager named Margaret, who uses her diary to express her everyday questions and curiosities about the wonders of her emerging sexual development. Each diary entry begins, "Are you there God? It's me Margaret." She pours out her woes, wishes, and tales of adolescent confusion in her diary, searching for answers about her hormonal urges, her changing body, and her questions about sex.

The girls huddling on the floor that summer understand Margaret's questions, concerns, and dilemmas, brought on by endless hormones and boys. They rush through the pages, wanting to know if Margaret ever escapes the wretched problems of puberty. Each new page generates discussion, wonder, and learning among the girls. After the girls finish the novel, they praise its author, Judy Blume, and wonder how someone "so old" understands them so well. They walk out into the warm day, armed with new knowledge and confidence that their sexual development is not the end of the world, but the beginning of a new day.

It is now 1998, and outside the windows of my office I see another group of adolescent girls. They seem to share the same glances I shared with my friends during that wonderful summer of '81, but the laughter is gone. I struggle to listen for conversations based on innocent curiosities and naive woes about sex and boys. Instead, these adolescent girls weave stories of more serious social issues, such as pregnancy, abortion, and dating violence. These adolescents appear burdened by their sexuality, as if it had infected them with some strange, incurable disease.

I know a few of their stories; three of the girls are clients that I counsel on a weekly basis. They come to me with innocent faces, adult bodies, and adult tales of sex at their boyfriends' houses. They are not curious about if or when they will have sex; instead they are seeking knowledge about how to "do it" better. They bring in the latest *Cosmopolitan* magazine, quoting articles like "How to Satisfy Your Man Every Time." They laugh when I tell them there is more to relationships than sex, but never fail to listen when I tell them what that might be.

The adolescent girls I counsel remind me of how lucky my friends and I were to be afforded the luxury of growing up slowly and exploring our sexuality without the burdens of knowing "how to satisfy your man every time." We looked to writers of young adult novels, such as Judy Blume, to tell us information our mothers would not. Today, adolescents look to more sophisticated literature to relate and normalize their reality.

I wish that I could give the adolescents outside my window the innocence and laughter of my yesterday. However, this would require that I ignore the fact that their sexual behaviors and attitudes have been molded in the context of a different era. They reflect a world burdened with serious social issues affecting every facet of their development. The news and school hallways are filled with stories of teen pregnancy, abandoned babies, and date rape. Thankfully, what remains constant between my adolescent world and their own is the wonderful fact that young adult literature is still embraced as a tool and/or guide for adolescents to explore their sexual questions and curiosities, no matter how sophisticated or naive today's adolescents may seem.

LIKE SISTERS ON THE HOMEFRONT

Adolescents may benefit from reading *Like Sisters on the Homefront* (1995), a young adult novel by Rita Williams-Garcia that explores decisions about sex and the consequences of teen pregnancy.

Scenario

Gayle, a 14-year-old African American girl, lives in Jamaica Queens, New York, with her 9-month-old infant, Jose, her older brother, and her widowed mother. She has just completed the eighth grade when she finds out she is pregnant again. The father of her first baby is a married Puerto Rican man with whom she had liaisons in her mother's home. He wants her to put the baby up for adoption, but she refuses. When Gayle's mother, Ruth, learns of this second pregnancy from a teenage boy named Troy, she takes Gayle to an abortion clinic. As Gayle and her mother sit in the waiting room, surrounded by other pregnant young women, an adoption counselor enters; Gayle considers adoption but gives in to her mother's vehement demand and goes through with the abortion.

Gayle and her mother argue about Gayle's sexual promiscuity and pregnancies from two different males. At her wits' end, Ruth sends Gayle and the baby to Georgia to live with her brother, Luther. Luther is a preacher who lives on the family's ancestral land, once a plantation.

Gayle and her infant son, Jose, arrive at Uncle Luther's country home outside of Columbus, Georgia. Gayle soon learns that her uncle, the reverend, is not pleased with her situation, but he takes her in as a favor to his sister. Like Gayle's mother, Uncle Luther refuses to hear Gayle's back talk. Gayle meets Uncle Luther's wife, whom she calls Miss Auntie, and his daughter, Cookie. Miss Auntie tells Gayle that Jose is no one's responsibility but hers. Gayle must take Jose with her wherever she goes. She is expected to help out around the house and to take care of Great, her frail and senile great-grandmother who lives in an upstairs bedroom.

Upset, Gayle decides she will do whatever she can to get back to Jamaica Queens. She hates her surroundings, the country home, the chores, the responsibility, but most of all her goody-two-shoes cousin, Cookie; Cookie is Gayle's exact opposite. Cookie is 16-years-old, a virgin, and a dutiful daughter. She is involved in her church youth group, plays gospel music in her car, and is a star singer in her church choir. Cookie loves her home and family, delights in taking care of Great, and tries to befriend "lost Cousin Gayle."

Through a series of girl talks, trips to the mall, and church gatherings, Cookie and Gayle's relationship and the polarity of their sexual attitudes and behaviors are revealed to the reader. When Gayle finds out Cookie is still a virgin, she asks if Cookie has at least gone to second or third base with a guy. Cookie has only kissed a boy once and found it disgusting. She will keep her virginity until marriage because, to her, being a Christian warrants that. Gayle believes Cookie's feelings will not last long: "You know, Cook, you wastin' away. Don't even know what you missing. But find a boy who knows all the moves, all the talk, and forget it. You be dropping your drawers before you know it. That's how Jose's daddy got me" (68). Gayle thinks of sex as no big deal, while Cookie believes sex is a sacred, matrimonial institution.

Adolescence confronts Cookie with hormonal urges and decisions about sex. Cookie meets Stacey, an 18-year-old college student, and goes on her first date with him. After the date, she has an inner conflict about her sexual desires toward him. She questions her chastity in the context of her Christian beliefs, turning to her mother, not Gayle, for guidance. Gayle could hardly talk to her mother about such matters; she cannot understand why Cookie would even consider involving Miss Auntie. Cookie asks Gayle if she ever considers what life would be like without Jose, suggesting that she could have finished school and met someone nice. Cookie ignores Gayle's reply: "Cookie, stop watching those commercials! If I didn't have Jose I wouldn't be thinking 'bout no college or sailing 'cross the seven seas. And for meeting someone 'nice,' I'd rather smell a guy coming than get tripped up by a 'nice' game" (126).

Cookie falls in love with Stacey, who is in her every thought. When a well-known female gospel singer performs a solo at Uncle Luther's church, Cookie steps in during the solo to impress Stacey, only to be drowned out by the singer. Miss Auntie and Uncle Luther punish Cookie for her behavior. Stacey comes to the house to see Cookie, only to be barred by Uncle Luther, who thinks Stacey has his daughter under a spell. Cookie retreats to her room in depression and anger.

While Cookie is preoccupied with her love interest, Gayle gradually learns to enjoy her stay at Uncle Luther's home. Gayle becomes a valuable member of the household, helping Miss Auntie with chores while accepting responsibility for Jose's needs. She continues to care for Great and learns family history from her. Gayle becomes Great's companion and the one responsible for passing on the oral family history Great tells her before dying.

Upset about not being allowed to see Stacey, Cookie receives visitors at the house before Great's funeral only with her mother's coercion. She decides to sneak away to see Stacey after the visitors leave and asks Gayle to lie to Uncle Luther and Miss Auntie: "Tell them I'm sick and I want to go to bed early. Leave the back door unlatched and put my robe in the pantry so I can slip it on. If Daddy or Mommy come downstairs, I'll just say I wanted a snack" (160). Gayle agrees and finds out that Cookie wants to sneak away to surprise Stacey and have sex with him. Later that night, Gayle confronts Cookie as she leaves the house, "Thought you was saved, Cookie" (163). She stands between Cookie and the car, only to be knocked down by Cookie, who is determined to lose her virginity to Stacey that night. Gayle pleads with Cookie, "Let me save you, Cuz" (164), and they walk back into the house together. Gayle decides to save herself by finishing school and remaining at Uncle Luther's home, joined by her mother and brother.

Mental Health Counselor's Response

Like Sisters on the Homefront is a young adult novel that realistically presents several social issues that influence an adolescent's sexual behavior and attitude. The social issues presented are adolescent pregnancy, single-parent families, difficulties in communication between parents and adolescents, and the lack of nonjudgmental role models to guide adolescents at the beginning of their sexual development. This young adult novel illustrates the impact of each of these important social issues on adolescent females through the lives of two young characters, Gayle and Cookie. Both characters encounter one of the most challenging and confusing tasks faced during adolescence: development of sexual identity.

The author portrays Gayle as a sexually promiscuous teenager who rejects her mother's authority. Underlying this outward behavior and sexual risk taking is a single female–headed household, where communication and guidance related to the responsibilities and choices of an emerging sexual identity are not discussed. Gayle also lacks a clear role in her family and community. She does not belong to any community youth organizations and has not developed a positive peer group with which she may interact. Several social issues that have a negative cumulative effect on Gayle's sexual development and behaviors are portrayed, including these: being raised in a single female–headed household; having no established role in family or community; and the absence of parental communication and guidance about sexuality.

Gayle's attitude as reflected in her surface appearance realistically demonstrates her unsuccessful negotiation of an emerging sexual identity. She has a nonchalant attitude about sex; this attitude exemplifies her emotional immaturity and lack of inner focus. She has yet to understand or discover that her sexuality is an important expression of her physical and emotional being.

The "sex is no big deal" attitude that Gayle exhibits resembles the attitude of many of the adolescent mothers I counsel. These young mothers are suffering from lost childhoods. Their emotional and cognitive development has not advanced to the level of their physical maturity. These adolescent mothers at one time found themselves in adult situations with males who viewed them as more mature than they were. For example, the majority of adolescent mothers with whom I work have been impregnated by males over the age of 19. As one adolescent stated, "Most guys, they look at me and all they see is that I got that 25-year-old body. . . . They don't never ask me my age, so I guess it don't matter if I'm only a teenager" (Tina, age 15). Mixed messages that your age and emotional maturity are not important as long as your body looks old enough create confusion among adolescents who are constantly struggling to be noticed and valued. They soon learn to structure their identities around their outward sexual appearance and do not seek essential knowledge to build their inner self-esteem, future goals, communication skills, and knowledge of sexuality, such as facts about conception, contraception, and sexually transmitted diseases.

Gayle's sexual affair with an older married man may be linked to an environment that lacks, at the very least, structure and clear roles. Without clear and consistent family structure and guidance toward assuming healthy, productive roles, adolescents tend to lack inner focus and self-confidence. Seeking a clear identity, adolescents will struggle to create their own surrogate family structure through boyfriends, girlfriends, gangs, or other groups.

When counseling, I often encounter adolescent females who look forward to having babies in hopes of achieving a traditional family structure of father, mother, and child and a role as a mother. These adolescent females have sexual affairs with older men, who often have no intentions of developing a serious, long-term relationship. In fact, approximately 70 percent of the adolescent mothers I counsel, who are impregnated by adult males, have stated that they only dated these men one to three months before they discovered they were pregnant. Unfortunately, these adolescent girls are often confronted with the reality of taking on the difficult role of being young single mothers. Thus, they find themselves mirroring the original single-parent family in which they live, one they had hoped to escape.

The positive consequences of providing an adolescent with age-appropriate roles to explore is demonstrated in the initial strong ego we witness in Cookie's character. Cookie uses her Christian beliefs and her gospel singing as the foundation for her decision not to become sexually active before marriage. Her role in the church and Christian beliefs are enough to keep her focused on building positive self-esteem and future goals, until she experiences a sudden sexual awakening. This emerging sexual identity and her overwhelming feelings for Stacey present a healthy challenge to her already established belief system. This challenge is met with punitive actions on the part of her parents, instead of a realistic discussion that it is normal to question established beliefs in the face of the excitement about a new love. The consequences of Cookie's parents' using punitive actions rather than communication is a short period of rebellion and confusion, when Cookie isolates herself from the family and plots a late-night escape to sleep with Stacey.

Many parents who have worked diligently to instill values and encourage goals for their adolescents fail to meet the challenge of maintaining open communication as their children search to develop a sexual identity. Parents must keep in mind that their adolescents are faced daily with the task of balancing the opinions of their peers with those of their parents. If parents do not have a consistent, caring, nonjudgmental attitude during the normal time of adolescents' sexual exploration and curiosity, problems are likely to escalate. When parents discuss sexual issues with their adolescent offspring, providing cautionary words about sex without specifics is sure to build adolescent curiosity rather than hinder it. Also, discussions that are limited to "Don't have sex until you are married" create a barrier to the kind of communication that is essential for understanding adolescents' sexual behavior, knowledge, and attitudes.

Though Cookie and Gayle encounter different challenges as they begin to develop their sexual identities, both find resolution within their existing family structure. Gayle's problems of sexual promiscuity, lack of a clear social role, and need for a strong male role model are all resolved when she settles into her uncle's home. Her aunt gives her responsibilities and the role as caretaker for her great-grandmother. In addition, Gayle's previously identified role as an adolescent mother is validated when family members acknowledge the importance of her taking full responsibility for raising her own child. Learning to value her role as a mother and establishing a new role as her great-grandmother's caretaker help to fill a void in Gayle's life. Filling this void dramatically changes her attitude toward herself and others. Perhaps it is this change in attitude about her self-worth that gives Gayle the strength and caring to help her cousin Cookie avoid the same mistakes Gayle made when exploring her own sexuality.

Ironically, Cookie, who is portrayed as a goody-two-shoes, is prevented from making an impulsive, life-altering decision to lose her virginity to Stacey, her new boyfriend, by the advice of her cousin, sex-is-no-big-deal Gayle. This literary twist of fate is quite authentic in its message that a peer's opinion is sometimes much more powerful and convincing than that of a parent or other adult. Teens often feel more comfortable discussing their ideas and questions about sex with peers because they receive validation that their questions and actions are normal and acceptable. Thus, whenever a peer objects to their behavior, teens are more likely to take a second look at their thoughts and actions.

Having parents reach out to extended family members for help with their adolescent offspring is certainly a reasonable and believable solution in the context of *Like Sisters on the Homefront*. However, it is not a favorable option for some parents. Some parents believe their children are their problem and that other family members should not become involved. Other parents do not have extended family to turn to when they need someone who is willing and able to structure an environment for a rebellious adolescent. The cultural importance of an extended family structure is not a universal concept. It is important to understand that parents who ask for help with their adolescent offspring are not demonstrating weakness or poor parenting. There are times when even the most educated and patient parents are challenged by their adolescent's emerging sexual behaviors, curiosity, or attitudes. At the very least, a family member, friend, counselor, or community member may offer a supportive ear and fresh perspective on the problem at hand.

In summary, *Like Sisters on the Homefront* presents itself as a learning tool for adolescents, parents, family members, and the community. Adolescents and their parents need support and education about the normal and necessary adolescent process of developing a sexual identity. Adolescents need a basic foundation in understanding their roles, goals for the future, importance of positive attitude toward self and others, and factual knowledge of their biological development. Overall, the most effective tool in helping any adolescent with developing a healthy sexual attitude and behavior is that of open, honest, factual, and nonjudgmental communication.

TOO SOON FOR JEFF

Adolescents may explore their questions about the effects of teen pregnancy by reading *Too Soon for Jeff* (1994), a young adult novel by Marilyn Reynolds, written from a teen father's perspective.

Scenario

Jeff Browning, a 17-year-old senior, struggles with decisions about his future after learning that his girlfriend, Christy, is pregnant. Jeff is reared in a single-parent home by his divorced mother. Christy comes from a two-parent Hispanic family. Her father is the dictator of the household, while her mother is docile.

Jeff and Christy live in a suburb of Los Angeles and attend Hamilton High, where they are both on the debate team. They have been together since Christy's freshman year. Just when Jeff is about to break off their relationship, Christy announces that she is four months pregnant, with his baby. This baffles Jeff because he and Christy always used a contraceptive when they had sex. In fact, Jeff tells readers about his decisions to use contraception: "Always I'd used condoms. That was something I was very careful about, even the first time, when I was fifteen and fumbling all over the place. But a few months ago, when Christy said she'd gone on the pill because of being irregular or something, well . . . it was a lot easier. And we didn't worry about AIDS, or other diseases, because we were only with each other," (16–17). Jeff reminds Christy that she told him the pill was 99 percent effective. She replies, "Maybe I forgot to take it sometimes. . . . I don't know. All I know is, I went to the clinic and we're going to have a baby" (14). While Jeff is outraged and believes they are too young to start a family, Christy cites the fact that "lots of people still in high school have babies" (15) and refers to Phillip and Susan, a high school couple with a baby. Jeff points out that Phillip works at a fast-food place, Susan complains about the baby's needs, and Susan and Phillip have all but quit school. Jeff maintains that he will not give up going to college next year for anyone, even though Christy says he could work more hours at the Fitness Club, his after-school job.

Jeff offers to take her to an abortion clinic. When Christy replies, "You want to kill our baby?" the conversation shifts back to their plans after high school. Jeff reminds Christy of her intentions to become an audiologist and that teen mothers do not attend college. Christy believes that some teen mothers do and thinks that she and Jeff will receive financial and moral support from their parents. Jeff tells Christy that she is dreaming and that their parents, especially her father, will be extremely upset about the pregnancy.

Jeff sees Christy in debate class, and she ignores him. He confronts her about the pregnancy, telling her it is not too late to have an abortion. Christy stands her ground, insisting that she will not have an abortion.

Christy tells Jeff that even though he does not love her anymore, they have a responsibility to their baby. Jeff believes they have a responsibility to themselves to pursue college and their careers. At home, Jeff makes a list of pros and cons of Christy having an abortion, dividing his list into "Reasons not to have an abortion" and "Reasons to have an abortion" (37). His "Reasons to have an abortion" list includes: "It's too soon to have a baby because you and I both have to finish school. It's not murder! It doesn't have a brain yet—it's a mass of cells, that's all. Why should we pay for the rest of our lives for some stupid mix-up with birth control pills?" (37). He gives the list to Christy, who ignores him after reading it.

Christy's parents arrive at Jeff's house that night, just after he discusses the pregnancy with his mother. Mr. Calderon, Christy's father, demands Jeff and Christy legitimize the baby by getting married. Jeff refuses, saying he is not ready to marry anyone. Christy's father slaps her and refuses to let her return home.

Christy resides at Jeff's house for a few months. During this time, Jeff's peers at Hamilton High learn he is the father of Christy's baby, and most members of the debate team stop talking to him. Jeff's home life is also unstable because he cannot get along with his mother. He stays with his mother's brother, Steve, who is a father figure to him. Steve talks with Jeff about adoption as an option for Christy.

When Jeff approaches Christy about adoption, he says that they cannot take care of the child and should give it to parents who can. Christy adamantly opposes the idea, telling Jeff she wants no information about adoption. Jeff continues to raise questions about the consequences of having the baby asking how they'll support it and what about college. When Christy replies that she does not care about college right now, Jeff reiterates his self-interest: "Okay, Christy. Okay. But I'm not in this with you. I'm not going to play house with you. I'm going to live my life" (91). When he blurts out that he does not want to be with her, Christy moves back to her parents' house. Jeff feels tied down and boxed in by Christy's pregnancy. His only desire is to attend college on a debate scholarship, taking no part in his baby's life. The baby is Christy's responsibility.

Jeff gets accepted at Brooker University on a debate scholarship. He goes to his favorite restaurant to celebrate with his mother, his uncle Steve, and Stacy, a teenage neighbor. They chatter excitedly about Jeff's new adventure when Barb, the restaurant owner, saunters over to their table with her infant granddaughter, Rosie, on her arm. She talks with them about Jeff's scholarship, mentioning her daughter Emmy, who wanted to go away to college but who got pregnant with Rosie: " 'Yep, Emmy had plans to be the big college girl up north, away from home, living in a dormitory,' Barb says, laughing that hoarse laugh again. 'Now Rosie's her roommate and Emmy's taking classes at that glorified high school called Hamilton Heights City College,' she says, then walks back to the counter, still carrying the little girl" (115–116). The mood changes at the table, and Jeff feels boxed in again, thinking that Christy's pregnancy is not his fault and that he will not let it ruin his life.

Back at Hamilton High, the school nurse, Mrs. Gould, calls Jeff down to her office to talk about his role as a father. Mrs. Gould tells Jeff that Christy now attends the Teen Mothers Program for her academic classes and for education about physical and financial issues related to her pregnancy. Mrs. Gould encourages Jeff to go to weekly teen dad meetings at the Teen Mothers Program site. Jeff vents about Christy's pregnancy, her refusal of abortion, and how his peers treat him at school. Mrs. Gould informs him about his custodial rights and his financial obligations to the baby. Jeff leaves her office with the situation on his mind and has trouble concentrating in his afternoon classes.

After graduation, Jeff must make key choices between his interests and those of his baby. Christy goes into premature labor in the thirty-first week of her pregnancy. At the hospital, the doctor tells Christy's parents and Jeff that Christy's water broke, posing a risk of infection to the unborn baby. She must stay in the hospital, carrying the baby for a few more weeks so that his lungs may develop completely.

In Christy's thirty-third week, Jeff is about to travel to New Orleans to compete in the National Debate Tournament with the Hamilton High Debate Team. On the morning of his departure, the hospital informs him that Christy must have a cesarean section that afternoon in order to reduce her blood pressure. Jeff's plane is scheduled to leave for New Orleans at eleven that morning. He goes through an inner struggle of whether or not to let down his debate team or to miss the birth of his son. Jeff decides to forgo his trip to the National Debate Tournament in New Orleans and drives to the hospital with his mother for his son's birth.

Jeff and Christy have a baby boy, who must spend time in the neonatal intensive care unit. When released from the hospital, Christy and the baby, Ethan, reside at her parents' house. On the night Jeff leaves for college, he visits Ethan; Jeff argues with Christy, whose father wants her to quit school and take care of the baby. Christy believes it is unfair that she must stay behind and care for Ethan while Jeff goes away to college. She tells Jeff her feelings about the pregnancy: "I was so stupid! I thought you would love me more when I was pregnant with your baby, and that we'd live together at your house where people talk nice to each other!" (179). When Christy says she regrets Jeff fathering her child, he reminds her that she decided to make him a father and must live with her decision.

Christy returns to school while Jeff completes his first semester of college in Texas. Thinking his son may forget him, Jeff leaves Brooker University and returns home to be a part of Ethan's life on a daily basis. He enrolls in Hamilton Heights City College and works at the Fitness Club. He and Christy have a cordial relationship. Jeff cares for Ethan a few days per week; he has no qualms about missing school when his son is ill and requires a doctor's visit. Jeff believes he can be a good father to Ethan, teaching him about the facts of life so Ethan can avoid teen fatherhood.

Mental Health Counselor's Response

The young adult novel *Too Soon for Jeff* realistically shows young adults how quickly their dreams for a successful future can be destroyed by an unplanned pregnancy. This literature brings to life the story of two adolescents, Jeff and Christy, who have different plans for escaping their environments. Jeff plans on pursuing a college education, while Christy, who wants to be an audiologist, plans to pursue a life with Jeff. Christy gets pregnant with the hope that she can leave the turmoil of her dysfunctional home and live in the comfort of Jeff's stable home. Unfortunately, she does not share her plans with Jeff, and they are both faced with handling the responsibilities of a baby versus pursuing their dreams as young adults.

Too Soon for Jeff gives an authentic account of how adolescent males are often faced with the circumstances of unwanted pregnancy and given very little choice over how the matter can be resolved. In the 1990s, where a woman's right to choose is still a controversial issue, a man's right to choose, or in Jeff's case, an adolescent boy's right to choose, is almost never considered. When Christy finds out that she is pregnant, she gives no consideration to Jeff's feelings or his honest assessment that he is unwilling and financially unable to care for a child. Christy ignores his feelings and thinks less about Jeff's needs and those of her baby than her own fantasies of escape from her family life. Even when

Jeff suggests adoption as a viable alternative to abortion, Christy does not consider his rights and opinions as the father of their child. Jeff is given little time to consider his role as a father and absolutely no choice in becoming one, once the baby is created.

This young adult novel does an excellent job of demonstrating the confusion, anger, and rejection of the father role when adolescent males are not given the time and consideration they deserve in a matter that affects their future and their child's well-being. There are many adolescent females like Christy who believe that their boyfriends will embrace the idea of an unplanned pregnancy. Christy's decision to plan a pregnancy to escape her home environment shows her lack of communication with Jeff and a lack of concern about his future. It also demonstrates the fact that many adolescents are not given the support they need to solve difficult problems they face in the home. Perhaps if Christy were given less dramatic solutions to coping with her problems at home, she would have explored these options before considering pregnancy.

Another issue to consider in this novel is how Jeff makes a conscious choice in not using condoms with his sexual partner. This decision leaves him powerless to protect himself from sexually transmitted diseases and teen fatherhood. All too often, I encounter adolescent males and females who, after maintaining a steady relationship like Christy and Jeff's, decide that they do not need to use condoms. They tell me, "It's a trust thing." While adolescents' need to trust is understandable, it does not account for the fact that their partners are young and human, and therefore capable of cheating on them. Perhaps *Too Soon for Jeff* and similar young adult novels can help to illustrate to adolescents the real-life consequences of engaging in blind trust in sexual relationships.

Although the resolutions depicted in this novel are noble, they are not believable from a clinical standpoint. Given Jeff's anger at Christy's decision to have the baby, and his clear focus toward his future in college, it is difficult to believe he would give up a scholarship to return home to go to college at the local institution. It would be more reasonable to understand Jeff returning home during the summers in an attempt at forming a relationship with his child. If his relationship with Christy were portrayed as one of caring and kindness, Jeff's resolution would be much more believable. However, Christy continues until the end of the novel to alienate Jeff and blame him for her conscious decision to have the baby. Christy's final response of anger, self-pity, and deferment of responsibility is the most authentic portion of the resolution in this book. Her response mirrors that of female adolescents I have counseled postpregnancy, who are faced with the reality that having a baby far from guarantees them a stable life in a boyfriend's home.

Issues such as a man's rights in choosing whether to care for an unwanted or unplanned child and the unrealistic and desperate attempts of adolescent females to escape dysfunctional families through pregnancy are not easily resolved. The United States has yet to create an open forum that dares to deal with the frustrations and anger that many males face when they are given little choice over their rights to become fathers. We certainly have no problem debating the issue when it pertains to women. Given these circumstances, it is important that parents educate themselves and their adolescent male offspring about the rights and responsibilities of fatherhood. Perhaps adolescent males' awareness of the fact that they will be held accountable for their child's needs, no matter how unprepared they find themselves, will help them to understand the importance of wearing condoms during all sexual encounters. Finally, it is crucial that counselors, parents, and other community members take the time to interact with adolescents experiencing turmoil in their homes. Perhaps adolescents can be offered alternatives to having babies "too soon."

BABY BE-BOP

Adolescents may explore the emotions and issues surrounding teen homosexuality by reading *Baby Be-Bop* (1995), a young adult novel by Francesca Lia Block, written from the point of view of an adolescent male.

Scenario

Dirk, who is in high school, lives with his grandmother, Fifi, in Hollywood, California. His parents are deceased. Dirk believes he is homosexual but does not know how to admit it to others. Dirk sees his grandmother's gay friends, Martin and Merlin, as frail, frightened, and sad. He does not want to be like them; instead, he "want[s] to be strong and to love someone who [is] strong; he want[s] to meet any gaze, to laugh under the brightest sunlight and never hide" (6). He wants to tell Fifi about his sexual orientation, but he does not want to crush her hopes of having great-grandchildren.

Dirk decides that his homosexual feelings are just a phase and resolves to keep silent about them. Then he meets Pup, a vibrant and mischievous boy who attends his school. They become friends, and Dirk develops feelings for Pup. Dirk and Pup spend time together at Fifi's house during lunch on school days, and on weekends. Dirk enjoys their friendship, but he is afraid that his homosexual feelings will be discovered. He wonders if his feelings for Pup are mutual and must confront these emotions when Pup becomes involved with a girl at school.

After a day of surfing, Pup and Dirk hitchhike; two girls from their school, Tracey and Nancy give them a ride. Tracey drives them to her mother's house; Pup sits next to Tracey while Dirk sits in the backseat with Nancy. Tracey's mother is out of town, and the two couples climb into a Jacuzzi in Tracey's backyard. When Pup leans over and kisses Tracey, Dirk follows his lead, kissing Nancy nonchalantly. Dirk becomes preoccupied by watching Pup and Tracey kiss and pet one another. Pup gazes at Dirk, whose heart beats more rapidly: "Dirk knew then that Pup loved him too. But mixed with Pup's love was fear and soon it was just fear sucking the love away" (26). Dirk and Pup continue their friendship, but Pup does not spend as much time with Dirk as he used to.

When Pup tells Dirk that he is seeing Tracey, Dirk decides he must confess his homosexual feelings for Pup and invites him over that afternoon. In Dirk's room, the two boys smoke marijuana. Dirk thinks this will make his confession easier. He begins sharing his secret: "I just wanted to tell you. I've been pretending my whole life. I'm so sick of it. You're my best friend" (31). Pup stops him:

"Don't even say it, Dirk," said Pup.
Dirk started to reach out his hand but drew it back. He started to open his mouth to explain but Pup whispered, "Please don't. I can't handle it, man."
He got up and pushed his hair out of his eyes. "I love you, Dirk," Pup said. "But I can't handle it."
And before Dirk knew it, Pup was gone. (31)

Dirk sees himself as a scared child in love with Pup; he hates himself. He cuts his hair into a Mohawk, imitating a punk rocker he saw at a club. He dresses in all black clothes and big boots, and this becomes his normal attire. Students at his school believe he and Pup are no longer friends because of Dirk's Mohawk and punk clothes.

On Dirk's sixteenth birthday, Fifi gives him her red-and-white 1955 Pontiac convertible; the crowning glory of the car is a golden lamp hood ornament. Fifi says that the ornament is a family heirloom that comes off the car and that Dirk can tell his story to it, talk to it about Pup, or tell it any secrets he has. Dirk believes he has no story and that "if he did no one would want to hear it. He would be laughed at, maybe attacked" (36). Dirk concludes it is better to be dead inside, with no story at all. He goes to punk rock clubs and engages in slam dancing, hurling himself into the crowd and submitting to its control. At a club, he provokes some skinheads by shouting obscenities at them. One skinhead calls him a "faggot," and this brings Dirk's secret to the forefront of his consciousness: "Dirk felt they had looked inside of him to his most terrible secret and it shocked him so much that he lost all the quiet strength he had been trying to build for as long as he could remember" (45). The skinheads beat Dirk senseless, and he wants to die. Bruised and bloody, he manages to drive himself home. He removes the lamp Fifi gave him from the hood and goes inside the house.

Collapsing on his bed in immense pain, Dirk cries out to the lamp, "Tell me a story that will make me want to live, because right now I don't want to live. Help me" (49). He shuts his eyes and then awakens to find a woman in the corner of the room, whom he later learns is his deceased great-grandmother. She tells him the story of her life, of how she was shut away in her aunt's home and verbally abused by her aunt, and how a man, Dirk's great-grandfather, came to save her. In the course of that night, Dirk also talks to his deceased parents, learning their life stories. He tells them he is gay, and his father replies, "I know you are, buddy" (86). Dirk's father refers to notable men in history who were homosexual and tells Dirk not to be afraid of himself. Dirk's parents urge him to tell them what has happened in his life since they died. Dirk talks about the night his parents died, his life at Fifi's, and about Pup Lambert. His parents leave him, and a mysterious man relates the story of Duck, a teenage boy, who gains the courage to tell others about his homosexuality.

Dirk wakes up in a hospital room with Fifi at his side. She says he has been in the hospital for some time and that they have been telling each other stories, "Past present future. Body mind soul" (106). Fifi knows Dirk's secret; she loves him and knows his homosexuality is not just a phase. Dirk gains the will to live. He believes that stories can set us free when we share them.

Mental Health Counselor's Response

The turmoil of an adolescent male's sexual identity development is well portrayed in *Baby Be-Bop*. This novel deals with the difficult and controversial issue of a gay adolescent's struggle to understand his emerging sexuality. Though homosexuality should not be considered a social problem in and of itself, the inevitable confusion and feelings of rejection and self-hate that surface as a result of society's intolerance of gay and lesbian persons is definitely an issue. From a clinical perspective, significant stress and thoughts of suicide often occur when adolescents consider the possibility that they are homosexual. In fact, homosexual adolescents of both sexes are two to six times more likely to attempt suicide than are heterosexual adolescents (Berman and Jobes, 1994).

The main character in the novel, Dirk, is faced with the difficult question of whether others will accept him despite the fact that he is gay. This question becomes even more involved when he falls in love with his best friend, Pup. Dirk feels that he is at risk of losing everyone he loves because of his sexuality. His struggle to hold back his sexual identity leads him into a dangerous and violent confrontation with a group of skinheads. He is forced to face society's intolerance of his homosexual identity and becomes a victim to his circumstances. It is through this tragic event, marked with violence and hate, that Dirk is forced to a resolution.

Dirk's resolution is one of telling his story and listening to the stories of others. This is a realistic and believable resolution to a very difficult problem. In fact, telling one's problems to someone who is willing to listen and not judge is the basis of any therapeutic interaction. The book's resolution demonstrates for young adults the importance of turning to those who have consistently listened, despite any fears of rejection.

There are times when adolescents, as well as adults, discover that the majority of humans have had some personal experience with rejection or fear of judgment. Parents, teachers, and community members must reach deep inside for their own stories and the strength to listen whenever they encounter an adolescent who needs to share a secret. We may all benefit from sharing our stories with a young person who has yet to understand that moving through struggle and pain only makes us stronger.

"MY SWEET SIXTEENTH"

Adolescents may explore issues surrounding teen pregnancy by reading the short story "My Sweet Sixteenth" (1993) by Brenda Wilkinson, in *Join In: Multiethnic Short Stories* (edited by Don R. Gallo).

Scenario

Monique is an African American 17-year-old from Brooklyn. She meets Carla at a summer church camp at Jersey State College; the girls are roommates. Carla notices Monique's picture of a little girl and asks who she is. Monique says it is her goddaughter, but Carla mentions a striking resemblance between the little girl and Monique. Monique admits that the little girl is her daughter; she explains that her mother said not to tell anyone at the church camp about the baby because people might look down on Monique. The day she turned 16, Monique had her daughter, Maya, after trying to hide the pregnancy. Monique and Maya's father still communicate, but they broke up before Maya's birth because they did not agree on a solution to the pregnancy. Monique was sure she was pregnant after two or three months. Her boyfriend wanted the baby, but Monique wanted an abortion. She hid her pregnancy from her family while saving her allowance to finance the abortion. No one besides her boyfriend, Robert, and her friend Verna knew about her pregnancy. An abortion in a safe, clean clinic would cost at least two hundred dollars. She knew she would be getting about five hundred dollars for her birthday from relatives, and she decided to wait until after her sweet 16 birthday party to have the abortion. Carla asks if Monique was worried about getting "pregnanter and pregnanter" (131), and Monique says she was preoccupied with having enough money for the abortion.

Monique received more than enough money for the abortion, two hours into her sweet 16 party. However, Monique began feeling sick and went to her room on the third floor of the house, isolated from the other bedrooms. She fended off her mother by saying she had a stomachache. After Monique asked her friend Verna to stay with her, Monique's mother left the room. Verna held Monique's hand during the labor pains. Suddenly Monique's water broke, and Verna wanted to get help. Monique talked her out of it; Verna delivered the baby.

Verna got some warm milk and water from Monique's mother, keeping the birth a secret. Verna fed the baby with drops of warm milk and water, and the girls wrapped the baby in towels. The next morning they took the baby to the hospital in a big shopping bag, saying they found her on the way to school. Monique's plan was to give Maya up for adoption, but she fainted in front of the receptionist's desk at the hospital.

Monique woke up in a hospital bed. Verna refused to admit Monique was the baby's mother. Monique admitted the truth, and the hospital staff called her parents. Her mother was extremely upset but agreed to let Monique give Maya up for adoption. Verna informed Robert, the baby's father, about the birth. He was excited that his wish had come true, and he spread the news to the neighborhood. Then Monique's mother decided against the adoption because people would speak badly of Monique and Robert for giving up their baby.

Monique says that Robert arrived at the hospital wanting to take Maya home: "He was all worked up, claiming he would take care of her on his own if necessary" (139). Monique became attached to Maya and decided to keep her. Monique now lives at home with her parents and grandmother, who help her take care of Maya. Monique tells Carla, "I just need to concentrate on getting myself out of high school. And I hope Robbie continues to do the same" (139). Monique's mother worries that her daughter will have another child during adolescence. Monique says that she will not have another child while a teenager and that she feels blessed to have a family that supports her. Carla points out that Monique's family situation is not normal for the average teenage girl with a baby. Monique agrees and believes there are few happy endings for teenage mothers.

Mental Health Counselor's Response

Some parents and teachers may read "My Sweet Sixteenth" and think, "This kind of thing never happens." Some adolescent girls may read this story and say, "This happened to me." In fact, it was my personal experience of helping to deliver the baby of a 17-year-old friend during my own adolescence that peaked my personal interest in counseling adolescent mothers. Monique's story of giving birth to a baby without her parents' knowledge of her pregnancy is very real. It happens more often than we as parents, counselors, teachers, and professionals would dare to imagine.

The two most challenging problems presented in "My Sweet Sixteenth" are adolescents' fear of communicating with their parents and their lack of factual knowledge about sexuality—the development of their bodies, the process of conception, sexually transmitted diseases, and decisions about having sex. Monique hides her pregnancy from her parents out of fear of what they may say or do. She also holds on to the hope that she will save enough money for an abortion before the baby is born. Monique does not stop to consider the dangers of not telling her parents about the pregnancy, such as the health risk to herself and the baby. She also has no understanding of the fact that she will be well into her third trimester of pregnancy before she saves enough money for an abortion.

Monique's fear of communicating with her parents, as well as her obvious lack of sexual knowledge, may have stemmed from a home where the topic was not up for discussion. Some parents may believe that their adolescent offspring have learned all they need to know from the health class they took in high school. Other parents may believe that discussing and educating their adolescents about sex will make them want to go out and "do it." Whatever the reason for delay in parent-child communication about sex, adolescents like Monique are made to suffer the consequences.

Ironically, Monique finds the solution to her pregnancy when her family offers their full support in caring for her child. This resolution is believable; many families I counsel do not take the time to stress prevention of teen pregnancy but offer their full support around the birth of a child. Perhaps if Monique had been more aware of this support through other situations in her life, she may have been more comfortable in facing her parents with her pregnancy.

While Monique's parents should be commended for their noble support of their daughter and grandchild, questions still remain about their educating Monique about her sexuality. No adolescent should feel compelled to withhold such important information for as long as Monique does. The only way for parents and teachers to ensure that they are not encouraging adolescents to withhold information is to create several opportunities for adolescents to communicate openly and honestly about their emerging sexuality.

QUESTIONS AND ANSWERS

Teen Sexuality: Watts and Eggelletion Address Implications for Secondary School

Working in public school settings, we have opportunities to speak with secondary school teachers and principals about the implications of teen sexuality for the secondary school. Some voice the concern that students who do not have parents to talk to about sexual questions and issues turn to their teachers and other adults in the school as their confidants. For example, one middle school peer counseling coordinator discussed how her students regularly ask her questions about sexual jargon they hear from their peers; students tell her they would rather confide in her than their parents. One secondary school principal expressed concern for kids in her school who were homosexual or confused about their gender, commenting that they seemed to be alone and "lost in the crowd." She felt they needed someone to talk to but was not sure how to approach the issue. The principals and teachers I talked to agreed that teens need a forum for discussing the social issues they face when developing a sexual identity.

Drawing on my experiences as a former teacher of English at the high school level, and my current work with teachers and administrators, I ask LaShawnda about the implications of adolescent sexuality for the secondary school. She provides answers as a mental health counselor who works with adolescents daily in a counseling center at a high school and in the community.

Is sex foremost in the minds of adolescents?

No. For most adolescents, sex is the number-two issue. Family issues, such as divorce, parental approval, or abuse are usually foremost in their minds. I have found that adolescents from more stable backgrounds tend to have more room for thinking about and exploring sex. The most important issue for adolescents is being accepted. If they do not feel accepted at home, they will seek acceptance through sex. Adolescents are not crazy, hormone-driven people, but sex definitely impacts their lives. In other words, adolescents' sexual behaviors and attitudes grow out of whether or not they feel a sense of belonging at home.

How important is it for teachers to consider adolescents' growing sexual awareness?

I think it is important for teachers to consider adolescents' growing sexual awareness when considering student behavior: a student acting out in class; girls dressing inappropriately; a student trying to impress a new student in the class. Teachers should speak with students in a caring, not a condescending, manner. For example, if a girl dresses inappropriately, her teacher should discuss this with her, but not in a reprimanding way. Some adolescent girls think dressing in short skirts, tight pants, or revealing tops is sexy and will get boys' attention, because that is what they see in the media. The teachers should talk with the adolescent girl about the fact that there are other ways to show beauty.

Do you think teachers should explore young adult literature about sexuality with their students?

Definitely. Young adult literature is relevant to their students' age, maturation, and social development. Since adolescents may be dealing with several issues portrayed in this literature, exploring it with the students may create discussion and provoke thought about social issues affecting adolescent development. If teachers want to generate a love of literature in their students, young adult literature is a place to begin. There is more of a chance for students to connect with it. Adolescents can see themselves in young adult literature, and besides, not everybody can relate to Faulkner.

Should teachers explore literature about homosexual characters with their students?

Yes, so that homosexual adolescents can feel included, and so that heterosexual adolescents can better understand the struggles that their homosexual classmates are likely to experience. Homosexual adolescents go through various emotions. Their dating world is different; they have to feel out other members of the same sex to find out if they are homosexual. They run the risk of being beaten up or being labeled a social outcast because of their sexual orientation. Some people approach the subject of homosexuality by being too sensitive, but teachers cannot afford to do that. Usually nobody talks about adolescent homosexuality in school; homosexual adolescents, or those suffering from gender confusion, are left on their own with no clear guidance or understanding of their situation. These adolescents may feel isolated. They already feel singled out because during adolescence all teens have that "I" perspective, almost paranoia about their actions. Literature about homosexual teen issues should be taught as a matter of fact, like teaching any other sexual issue, such as experimenting with sex. If teachers teach literature about teen homosexuality this way, without focusing on it like a red flag, the students may not. Kids pick up on our attitudes about issues.

Do you think it is valuable for teachers and librarians to have young adult literature about homosexual teens, or teens who are experiencing gender confusion, on their bookshelves?

I think it is valuable and necessary because it deals with diversity, real issues that at least one adolescent in a teacher's class is going through on a daily basis. It should also be available for adolescents to read because they may gain an understanding of this issue by reading about it; it may develop tolerance for teen homosexuality.

I also think it is important for teens to read this type of literature because I do not think there is a family in America that does not have a close connection to a member or friend who is homosexual. I do not think middle school students are ready for direct attention to this literature in the classroom, but at the high school level, where sexual experimentation reaches its height, this type of literature is definitely needed. So many teenagers are homophobic because they do not understand homosexuality; they usually reflect the beliefs about homosexuality that they see in the media. Fortunately, now teens are seeing very real people who are gay.

How might teachers encourage students to read young adult literature about teen sexuality in middle school and high school?

In middle school, teachers can use the library as a vehicle. They may work with the librarian to create displays about social issues related to adolescents' sexual behaviors and attitudes. Rather than explicit reading and discussion of this type of literature in class, teachers and librarians may encourage student awareness of these issues with displays intended to ask, "Have you thought about this lately?" They might do this with a display of young adult literature, reference books, and other resources on teen sexuality and make these materials available for student exploration.

In high school, teachers may encourage the reading of young adult literature on teen sexuality not only in an English class, but through a life management class that incorporates health, time management skills, and parenting skills. Usually students are given regular life management textbooks that are less than interesting to adolescent readers. Teachers could have different small groups in the class read certain young adult literature based upon topics the class is studying. Teachers could have small groups of students lead discussions about the social issues in their assigned young adult text and how these issues are relevant to the students' lives. This is a way for students to get information about particular aspects of their sexuality, such as their changing bodies and their decisions about engaging in sex. However, teachers have to be prepared for what they hear in large group and small group discussions about this literature. Teachers have to anticipate the fact that at least one of the students in the class will currently be dealing with the sexual issue they are discussing. Teachers also have to be careful of student opinions that the literature and discussion may evoke; in addition, teachers must be conscious not to promote their opinions about sexual attitudes and behaviors but, rather, to approach this issue as a concerned and trusted adult facilitating an open forum for adolescents.

RECOMMENDED READINGS

Because adolescent sexuality is an issue that is, by its nature, controversial to many adults, the recommendations that follow each text listed below can be used only in a broad sense. The recommended readership that is noted after each entry is provided as a comment on the readability of the text; that is, it is used to indicate whether or not a middle school or high school reader (and, in some cases, an adult reader) should be able to make sense of the book.

Fiction Works

Young Adult Literature

Bauer, M. D. (Ed.). (1994). *Am I Blue? Coming Out from the Silence.* New York: HarperTrophy. 273 pp. (ISBN: 0–06–440587–7). Middle School (MS), High School (HS).

This collection of sixteen short stories by notable authors, such as Lois Lowry, M. E. Kerr, and Francesca Lia Block, addresses gay and lesbian issues.

Block, F. L. (1997). *Baby Be-Bop.* New York: HarperTrophy. 106 pp. (ISBN: 0–06–447176–4). MS, HS.

Dirk must face his homosexual feelings and the consequences of suppressing them.

Blume, J. (1970). *Are You There God? It's Me, Margaret.* New York: Bantam Doubleday Dell. 149 pp. (ISBN: 0–440–40419–3). MS.

Eleven and going on 12, Margaret uses her diary to talk about her questions about growing up, boys, and her sexuality.

Blume, J. (1975). *Forever.* New York: Pocket Books. 220 pp. (ISBN: 0–671–69530–4). MS, HS.

Katherine and Michael believe their love will last forever. The excitement of first sex and first love seem overwhelming. (Some explicit language and situations may offend readers.)

Garden, N. (1982). *Annie on My Mind*. New York: HarperCollins. 234 pp. (ISBN: 0–374–40414–3). MS, HS.

This novel is about an adolescent girl who falls in love and experiences confusion about love and sex.

Head, A. (1967). *Mr. and Mrs. Bo Jo Jones*. New York: Penguin. 189 pp. (ISBN: 0–451–16319–2). MS, HS.

Two young people are forced to get married when they find out they will have a baby. They learn the love they shared in high school cannot hold their marriage together.

Kaye, G. (1992). *Someone Else's Baby*. New York: Fawcett Juniper. 140 pp. (ISBN: 0–449–70457–2). MS, HS.

Seventeen-year-old Terry is pregnant and does not know who is the father of her baby. She must choose between keeping her baby and adoption.

Kerr, M. E. (1994). *Deliver Us from Evie*. New York: HarperTrophy. 177 pp. (ISBN: 0–06–447128–4). MS, HS.

This novel is about an 18-year-old girl who lives on a farm with her family in a small Missouri town. She is forced to confront her homosexual feelings when she meets a beautiful girl at a party and to face the consequences of her family and the town learning of her secret.

Klein, N. (1977). *It's OK If You Don't Love Me*. New York: Ballantine Books. 255 pp. (ISBN: 0–449–70236–7). MS, HS.

Near the end of high school, Jody meets Lyle, an 18-year-old virgin. She struggles with her sexual feelings for him and the reappearance of her ex-boyfriend.

Reynolds, M. (1994). *Too Soon for Jeff*. Buena Park, CA: Morning Glory Press. 222 pp. (ISBN: 0–930934–91–1). MS, HS.

A high school senior must choose between his own dreams and the needs of his unborn child.

Roberts, T. (Ed.). (1997). *Am I the Last Virgin? Ten African American Reflections on Sex and Love.* New York: Simon & Schuster. 145 pp. (ISBN: 0–689–81254–X). MS, HS.

This is a collection of personal stories by young African American women. Stories deal with virginity, rape, decisions about sex, sexual abuse, pregnancy, and AIDS. Contains a list of resources on sexual issues. (Some controversial language and situations may offend some readers.)

Steptoe, J. (1976). *Marcia.* New York: Penguin. 69 pp. (ISBN: 0–14–034669–4). MS.

Fourteen-year-old Marcia tells the story of how she grows up in the midst of confusion about her place in the world and her choices about sex.

Ward, L. (1997). *Choosing: A Novel for Teenage Girls.* Austin, TX: Plain View Press. 171 pp. (ISBN: 0–911051–92–9). MS, HS.

This novel is about an adolescent girl and the choices she must make about sex. The author gives the reader the option to make choices for the main character and then turn to the appropriate section that tells the consequences of choices the reader makes for the main character. (Some language and situations may offend some readers.)

Wilkinson, B. (1993). "My Sweet Sixteenth." In D. R. Gallo (Ed.), *Join In: Multiethnic Short Stories.* New York: Bantam Doubleday Dell, 128–140. (ISBN: 0–440–21957–4). MS, HS.

An adolescent female tells her story of teen pregnancy and a birthday gift that was a surprise.

Williams-Garcia, R. (1995). *Like Sisters on the Homefront.* New York: Lodestar. 165 pp. (ISBN: 0–525–67465–9). MS, HS.

A 14-year-old African American mother from Jamaica Queens, New York, learns to understand herself after being sent to live with her uncle in Georgia. Her 16-year-old female cousin struggles with decisions about sex.

Zindel, P. (1969). *My Darling, My Hamburger*. New York: Bantam Books. 122 pp. (ISBN: 0–553–27324–8). MS, HS.

Going into their senior year, two couples are caught between their fears about intimacy and their sexual desires. One couple deals with pregnancy and abortion.

Nonfiction Works

Bass, E., and K. Kaufman. (1996). *Free Your Mind: The Book for Gay, Lesbian, and Bisexual Youth—and Their Allies*. New York: Harper-Collins. 417 pp. (ISBN: 0–06–095104–4). MS, HS, Adult (A).

This is a practical guide for homosexual and bisexual youth and their families, counselors, teachers, and friends. It talks about the lives of homosexual and bisexual youth and how to deal with homosexuality and bisexuality.

Basso, M. J. (1997). *The Underground Guide to Teenage Sexuality*. Minneapolis: Fairview Press. 230 pp. (ISBN: 1–55749–034–7). MS, HS.

This is a handbook that answers teens' questions about health and sexuality.

Bell, R. (1987). *Changing Bodies, Changing Lives*. New York: Vintage Books. 254 pp. (ISBN: 0–394–75541–3). MS, HS.

This guide for adolescents discusses issues of adolescence, such as sexual awareness, substance abuse, and relationships.

Bode, J., and S. Mack. (1994). *Heartbreak and Roses: Real Life Stories of Troubled Love*. New York: Delacorte. 158 pp. (ISBN: 0–385–32068–X). MS, HS, A.

This is a collection of interviews with a group of teens, telling their stories of obsession, confusion, and sometimes violence as they attempt to establish love relationships. (Some language and situations may offend some readers.)

Coles, R. (1997). *The Youngest Parents.* New York: W. W. Norton. 223 pp. (ISBN: 0–393–04082–8). MS, HS, A.

This book, for parents and those who serve young adults, and for adolescents, too, chronicles the lives of teen parents.

Ford, M. T. (1995). *The Voices of AIDS: Twelve Unforgettable People Talk about How AIDS Has Changed Their Lives.* New York: William Morrow. 225 pp. (ISBN: 0–688–05323–8). MS, HS.

This is a collection of interviews of twelve people touched by AIDS. The book contains a list of resources on HIV and AIDS.

Harrison, M. (1995). *The Preteen's First Book about Love, Sex, and AIDS.* Washington, DC: American Psychiatric Press. 97 pp. (ISBN: 0–88048–698–8). MS.

This guide for preteens addresses puberty, parental concerns about adolescent sexuality, stages of teen sex, homosexuality, sexually transmitted diseases, and abstinence.

Johnson, E. W. (1988). *Love and Sex in Plain Language.* 4th ed. New York: Bantam Books. 207 pp. (ISBN: 0–553–27473–2). MS, HS.

This book describes the development of sexual characteristics in boys and girls; explains the physiology of intercourse, pregnancy, and birth; and discusses homosexuality, masturbation, contraception, and venereal disease.

Journal of Adolescent Health. New York: Elsevier Science. HS, A.

This journal, published monthly in two volumes, deals with issues of adolescent health.

Kelly, G. F. (1993). *Sex and Sense: A Contemporary Guide for Teen-agers.* Rev. ed. Hauppauge, NY: Barron's Educational Series. 262 pp. (ISBN: 0–8120–1446–4). MS, HS.

This is a comprehensive book for young adults on social, physical, and emotional aspects of sexuality. The author emphasizes personal responsibility.

Lauerson, N. H., and E. Stukane. (1993). *You're in Charge: A Teenage Girl's Guide to Sex and Her Body*. New York: Ballantine Books. 345 pp. (ISBN: 0–449–90464–4). MS, HS.

This book provides information for teen girls about puberty, sex, birth control, boys' bodies, and sexually transmitted diseases.

Madaras, L. (1988). *The What's Happening to My Body Book for Boys*. New York: Newmarket Press. 251 pp. (ISBN: 0–937858–99–4). MS, HS.

Suitable for 9- to 15-year-old boys, this book covers questions many have about puberty.

Madaras, L. (1988). *The What's Happening to My Body Book for Girls*. New York: Newmarket Press. 269 pp. (ISBN: 0–937858–98–6). MS, HS.

Suitable for 9- to 15-year-old girls, this book covers questions girls may have about puberty.

McCoy, K., and C. Wibbelsman. (1992). *The New Teenage Body Book*. New York: Putnam Publishing Group. 286 pp. (ISBN: 0–399–51725–1). MS, HS.

This guide answers questions teens may have about puberty and sexuality.

McCoy, K., and C. Wibbelsman. (1996). *Life Happens: A Teenager's Guide to Friends, Failure, Sexuality, Love, Rejection, Addiction, Peer Pressure, Families, Loss, Depression, Change, and Other Challenges of Living*. New York: Berkley Publishing Group. 213 pp. (ISBN: 0–399–51987–4). MS, HS.

This is a comprehensive guide for young adults about several issues they face during adolescence.

Solin, S. (1996). *The* Seventeen *Guide to Sex and Your Body*. New York: Simon & Schuster. 129 pp. (ISBN: 0–689–80795–3). MS, HS.

This guide for adolescent girls answers questions about the female body and sex. It also provides lists of resources for teens.

Sparks, B. (Ed.). (1992). *It Happened to Nancy: By an Anonymous Teenager.* New York: Avon Flare. 241 pp. (ISBN 0–380–77315–5). MS, HS.

This diary, a true story, tells experiences of an anonymous female narrator. The diary begins at the end of her fourteenth year and ends shortly after her sixteenth birthday. She is date-raped and contracts AIDS from the encounter. The diary also includes discussion about friends, a boyfriend, school, shuttling between divorced parents, and physical and emotional pain. (Some controversial language and situations may offend some readers.)

Thompson, S. (1995). *Going All the Way: Teenage Girls' Tales of Sex, Romance, and Pregnancy.* New York: Hill & Wang. 340 pp. (ISBN: 0–8090–1599–4). MS, HS.

This book, for parents and those serving young adults, discloses girls' experiences with love, sex, birth control, and motherhood.

Videos

Children's Television Workshop. (1992). *What Kids Want to Know about Sex and Growing Up.* Pacific Arts Video. Directed by Ozzie Alfonso. Produced by Terri Randall. (ISBN: 1–56111–182–1). MS.

Created for children 8 to 12, this video addresses the physical and emotional aspects of puberty and sexual issues.

National Family Health Center. (1993). *How to Talk to Your Kids about Sex, Love, and Responsibility.* MS, HS.

This video provides a factual background for parents to talk with their children about sex, love, and responsibility.

Web Sites

http://www.ala.org/teenhoopla/

This is the Web site of the American Library Association's new "Teen Hoopla." For 12- to 18-year-olds, the site provides information on all aspects of adolescent life. (MS, HS)

http://www.educ.indiana.edu/cas/adol/risk.html

This is the site of the Adolescence Directory On-Line, an electronic guide on adolescent issues. It is a service of the Center for Adolescent Studies at Indiana University. (MS, HS, A)

http://www.notmenotnow.org/

This site deals with issues of teen abstinence. (MS, HS, A)

http://www.plannedparenthood.org

This is the site of Planned Parenthood and is filled with resources for parents, adolescents, and those serving young adults. The agenda can be described in political terms as pro-choice. (MS, HS, A)

http://www.rci.rutgers.edu/~sxetc

This is the Web site of *SEX, etc.*, a newsletter about sexuality, written by teens for teens. (MS, HS)

REFERENCES

Berman, A., and D. A. Jobes. (1994). *Adolescent Suicide: Assessment and Prevention*. Washington, DC: American Psychological Association.

Block, F. L. (1995). *Baby Be-Bop*. New York: HarperTrophy.

Reynolds, M. (1994). *Too Soon for Jeff*. Buena Park, CA: Morning Glory Press.

"Smells Like Teen Spirit." (1992). *The Village Voice* 37 (14): 37–38+.

Wilkinson, B. (1993). "My Sweet Sixteenth." In D. R. Gallo (Ed.), *Join In: Multiethnic Short Stories*. New York: Bantam Doubleday Dell, 128–140.

Williams-Garcia, R. (1995). *Like Sisters on the Homefront*. New York: Lodestar.

CHAPTER FOUR

Adolescent Rape

Gail P. Gregg and Maureen Kenny

As adolescents navigate through society testing their new quasi-adult independence, they are often exposed to incidents of personal violation that cause them to feel insignificant as human beings. Adolescents who are molested, sexually abused, or raped usually feel disgraced and devoid of personal integrity, and oftentimes choose silence rather than exposing their humiliation to others.

Living in the twilight of the twentieth century, where myths and metaphors have lost the power to shape and animate their lives, sexually abused adolescents hear the cracking of old certainties. Yet they remain silent, afraid to speak out for fear of being defined as inferior, with shame being placed on them rather than on the offender. Oftentimes, concealment is victims' only alternative. Victims never tell their stories for fear that they will not be believed, that the incident may be minimized, or that they may be blamed for what happened.

If it is true that human beings are defined by their stories and that students learn through stories, it is reasonable to surmise that literature featuring protagonists who are victims of abuse may be an effective way to help adolescents who have been personally violated. By carefully reading and reflecting on literature depicting abusive relationships and situations, adolescents who have suffered similar transgressions can tap into domains of experience ordinarily obscured, ignored, or unspoken. While it is true that words do not move mountains, if sexually abused teens are able to see themselves in some of the literature they read, they may be able to break their silence and begin the healing process.

Though personal violations are many and varied, we have chosen to center our discussion on rape of female adolescents by males as a focus for this chapter. As common as they are disturbing, sexual assaults are on the rise. Large numbers of female adolescents are being forced into sexual intercourse against their will; often the male perpetrators are acquaintances or supposed friends. Young women seem especially at risk because males assume that they will not fight back and that the females can be intimidated into silence. The statistical vulnerability of minority women to the violence of rape has increased as well (Salholz, 1990).

Rape is a serious life event that leads to both immediate distress and long-term effects for the victim. The abused adolescent can suffer a wide range of emotional and behavioral effects, including depression, anxiety, deficits in self-esteem, and substance abuse or other self-destructive behaviors (e.g., suicide or prostitution). Additionally, some victims repress the memory of sexual abuse. These issues relate directly to young adults as they seek to manifest and maintain an identity in today's hostile world.

RAPE IN FOUR FICTION BOOKS FOR YOUNG ADULTS

There are several novels that high school teachers could use in the classroom to stimulate discussion on the issue of rape and the adolescent. R. Peck's *Are You in the House Alone?* (1979) deals realistically with the stalking and rape of an eleventh-grade girl. The rapist is a boy from one of the most prominent families in Connecticut. After the rape, the victim faces the realities of a legal system filled with laws that are stacked against the victim and in favor of the criminal. Unfortunately, Peck's book is sometimes difficult for teachers to find because it has been criticized for being too realistic and on the basis of "community standards" has been removed from the shelves of many classrooms and libraries.

A. Corman's *Prized Possessions* (1991) is an excellent novel to use with adolescents. This novel focuses on Elizabeth Mason, a talented, outgoing, and beautiful young woman who is raped by the star of the tennis team during her first week of school at a prestigious northeastern college. This novel also looks at how the rape affects the two families and the institution involved. The victim's parents struggle for justice within the legal system while fighting the challenges to the safe and affluent life that they have built for themselves and their family. The family of the rapist must also face challenges to their lifestyle and assumed value system. They choose to not only cover up, but to diminish the significance of the actions of their son. The university must weigh the need to alert students and their families that the crime of rape has occurred on campus against the effects of negative publicity and loss of prestige as a secure environment for students.

A third novel that would work well with this topic is R. White's *Weeping Willow* (1992). Set in the Appalachian Mountains, this novel, which was named one of the ALA Best Books for Young Adults (1993) and included among the IRA Young Adults' Choices books (1994), tells the story of a young female protagonist, Tiny, who is raped by her stepfather. The local minister exacerbates the situation when he turns the episode into gossip. Tiny is left to rely on a make-believe friend in order to restore her self-esteem.

W. Lamb's *She's Come Undone* (1992) is a realistic portrayal of the life of Dolores Price; the novel covers a forty-year period. The story takes Dolores from a child living in a small town, to a rape in adolescence, through an attempt at college, to time spent in a mental institution, to her release and subsequent attempts at forging a life of her own. Unlike the previous three novels, this particular work gives the reader a glimpse at what happens to the adolescent rape victim after the teen years and into adulthood.

Dolores's teenage years are similar to those of many adolescent readers. Her parents' divorce comes at a time when she is navigating her way through adolescence and most needs their support. Her body is changing, her feelings are confused, and she needs someone to care for her and guide her through this difficult time in life. Unsure about why her parents are divorcing, Dolores is angry with her father for his departure and subsequent remarriage. Preoccupied with her own grief—the heartache of losing a child, the reality of her husband's unfaithfulness, and the loss of her husband and marriage—Dolores's mother is emotionally unavailable to her daughter. Eventually, the mother's hospitalization and confinement to an institution leaves her daughter in the temporary care of a less-than-loving grandmother.

At a critical point in her development, adolescence, Dolores has her innocence stolen. She becomes a victim of rape; the incident causes a host of difficulties and ultimately leads her to attempt to take her own life. True, Dolores Price had a difficult childhood, but it was Jack Speight, the man who rapes her, who causes her to "come undone."

The author does an excellent job of setting the stage for the rape to occur. Dolores is the perfect prey for the rapist. She is suffering from an overwhelming sense of loss, brought on by the departure of her father, about whom she fantasizes, and by the subsequent divorce of her parents. Because of the divorce, she also must endure the loss of her childhood home. She has to leave her best friend and move into a home with a grandmother, whom she despises, and a mother (recently released from a mental institution) who is seldom available to her. Neither love, nor attention, nor supervision is provided for Dolores. As she works to establish a network of friends in her new school, enter Jack Speight, the perfect object of Dolores's fantasies. He is a young, attractive, personable disc jockey. He drives a convertible sports car and lives with his wife in the apartment above Dolores. He takes advantage of Dolores's low self-esteem, spending time chatting and teasing her with his smile, giving her rides to and from school, and generally making her feel good about herself. Since her father's departure, Dolores has longed for male attention. Unfortunately, the male attention she yearns for is provided by a charismatic rapist.

After he explains that two incidents in which he fondled Dolores are just his way of fooling around, Jack forcibly rapes Dolores. He immediately threatens to kill himself and his wife if Dolores tells anyone about what happened. Dolores's immediate response after the rape is to bathe, in an effort to not only wash away the blood from the rape, but to wash away the shame that overwhelms her. She feels dirty and blames herself for what has occurred. Unable to confide in her grandmother, and because her mother is again unavailable, Dolores confides in a friendly neighbor. The neighbor immediately brings the rape to the attention of Dolores's mother.

Upon being told of the rape, Dolores's mother chooses not to press charges again Speight. She asks Dolores to pretend the rape never took place. Dolores's grandmother treats the teen as if she is a dangerous stranger. She acknowledges the rape only once, using the phrase "that business with him" (120). She begins to indulge Dolores, "not as a victim, but as someone on whose good side she felt safer" (120). After one brief session with a psychiatrist, Dolores refuses to continue treatment and begins to suffer the consequences of her silence. She becomes depressed, develops an eating disorder that causes her to balloon up to 257 pounds, is angry, bitter, and once again, all alone. Disgusted with herself, she takes on a false identity to meet the demands of the outside world. In letters to her future college roommate, she portrays herself as a beautiful, happy high school senior who has a boyfriend and comes from a loving family. Years later, when she is finally married, she grieves when her insensitive and selfish husband demands that she have an abortion; nevertheless, she depicts herself as a happy housewife with a loving husband in her letters home to her grandmother.

As a result of the rape, Dolores suffers greatly from a lack of self-esteem, causing her grave difficulties with interpersonal and intimate relationships. The rape also had deleterious effects on Dolores's sex life. In a moment of confusion, Dolores, who knows she is heterosexual, engages in a sexual encounter with a woman because the woman is the first person who accepts her the way she is, all 257 pounds of her. The shame and self-loathing she feels after this incident cause her to flee college in the middle of the night.

After her flight from college and subsequent suicide attempt, Dolores spends the next seven years in a mental institution, four years as a resident and three as an outpatient. After those years, she marries a man who is later fired from his high school teaching job for sexually molesting one of his teenage students. The book ends with Dolores realizing that while Jack Speight undid her as a teenager, she almost succeeded in undoing herself as an adult. With luck, and with the love of a new, healthy husband, she can transcend some of the damage of the terrible incidents that had befallen her during the first part of her life.

While this well-written novel covers a much broader time span than the typical adolescent novel, it is nonetheless appropriate for use with teenagers. Written, surprisingly enough, by a male, *She's Come Undone* recounts a teenager's touching and often devastating journey into adulthood. Despite going through the worst possible violation of self, Dolores finally opens up thanks to the care of a sensitive professional and to self-recognition and acceptance of what she was during childhood and adolescence: a victim. Rising above her past, Dolores leaves her fantasy world and joins the real world by establishing a meaningful relationship and a family of her own. *She's Come Undone* is a novel that can provide adolescents faced with similar circumstances a mirror in which view themselves and begin the process of breaking their silence.

THE VICTIM SPEAKS

The following are the actual comments of a rape victim who recorded her thoughts after reading *She's Come Undone*. Minor editing, primarily of punctuation and grammar, was undertaken only to enhance clarity of ideas.

At first I didn't know what to write. I was at a loss and supposed that it had to do with my story and emotions mingling with those in the book, as well as having to give my rape more thought than maybe I ever had before. Actually, I think reading the book may have helped me. At the very least, it allowed me to see things clearer. It doesn't matter that what happened to me occurred thirty-eight years ago. Even with my less than sterling memory and, oftentimes, lack of retention of details, the day of my rape stands out vividly in my mind. Allow me to briefly recap that day.

My girlfriend and I were 16. She was spending the night with me. It was just before midnight, and we probably shouldn't have been out driving around at that hour. We were taking advantage of my dad—Mom was out of town, visiting up north. We had been home earlier, but an older guy— probably 21 or so—whom I had a crush on called and asked if we would pick him up at work and give him a ride home, which we did. I now realize that this older boy was just using me, but at the time, I was flattered with his attention.

After we took him home, a car pulled alongside of us and began attempting to run us off the road. I quickly turned onto a side street to avoid being run off the road, but the offending car followed and eventually succeeded in forcing me off the road and to a stop. Everything happened very quickly from this point. I remember looking frantically for lights in any of the houses in this neighborhood, but there was none. A man got out of the car, and as I tried to drive away, he grabbed my steering wheel with one hand while displaying a knife at my throat with the other. He pulled open the door of the car, pushed me aside, and drove to a deserted area near a lake. Threatening us with a knife, he forced my girlfriend to climb into the trunk of the car. Something inside of me told me to stay quiet and calm, and somehow, that became the most important thing in my life to do. I didn't want to upset this man who I figured must be crazy. As he repeatedly passed the knife back and forth past my throat, he pulled down my underwear and raped me. When he finished, he acted as if nothing had happened and calmly released my girlfriend from the trunk. Though our conversation was minimal, I tried to keep him calm by speaking in a very soft voice as we drove back to where his car was parked. I am sure that when I recounted this part of the story to the police, they misconstrued its meaning and thought that my actions were very mature, when in fact, I was scared to death and had difficulty finding my voice.

After his departure, my girlfriend and I did not know what to do. It was late; everything was closed. We found a phone at a bowling alley and called the police. I had no idea that I looked a mess or that I was covered with blood. There's a gap in my memory here—my only recollection is that I felt dirty. The next thing I knew, I was at a hospital and my brother, a police officer at the time, and my dad, a prison guard, were there. I was questioned by the police and told that I could not discuss the events of that evening with my girlfriend.

My father and brother never asked me what happened that night. They impressed upon me, however, that I should not ever tell my mother about this incident. They made me think that if my mother were told, she would be the victim, not me. To this day, my father and brother have never discussed the events of that evening with me, and my mother was never told that I had been raped.

The rapist was apprehended very quickly. He was a young man, about 25 years old; he was married and had two children. Although I don't remember too much about it, a trial was held, and the rapist was convicted and given a five-year prison term. I know that my brother knew when the rapist was released from prison, but he never discussed with me what else he knew about the case.

Even though Dolores's rape was not by a stranger, there were many similarities between her story and mine. Her mother chose not to tell her father, insisting that Dolores needed to pretend that the rape never happened. That's sort of the way it was with me. I was not to tell my mother, and I felt that since my brother and dad never spoke about it with me that maybe they wanted to pretend that my rape never happened. This is one of the things that angers me the most. I had been violated—a serious crime against me had taken place—and nobody wanted to talk about it; they just wanted to sweep it under the carpet and pretend it didn't happen. Although I knew better, I got the feeling that everyone involved thought that the rape was my fault—that I must have been doing something wrong, like being out at midnight or the way I dressed, acted, or looked. Society at the time had a feeling that there must have been something the girl was doing wrong to get raped in the first place. I was encouraged by the police to just ignore what happened and not file charges, which convinced me that I must have done something to cause this event to happen. This was just like Dolores in the book; she felt that it must have been her fault she got raped because she fantasized about Jack Speight and let him take her to and from school. To this day, I am sure that charges were only filed because my family was in law enforcement.

Like Dolores, who felt guilty for what she had done, I began thinking that maybe I shouldn't have been out riding in a car that late at night. Rather than engaging in self-destruction like Dolores, I just became silent on the issue. I knew that remaining silent was wrong, but there really wasn't anybody available who would talk about the rape. After the rape, a brief article about it appeared in the paper. For some reason, a family friend asked me if I was the unnamed party in the article, and I denied knowing anything about it. This denial lasted for many years—indeed, I began to pretend that it didn't really happen.

Several years after the rape, I spoke to my sister about being a rape victim. She may have already known that I had been raped, but never admitted knowing. We only spoke of it once, and the subject has never come up again. To this day, I have never discussed my rape with family members, and as a matter of fact, had dismissed it from my mind until reading *She's Come Undone*. Am I like Dolores? I don't think so, yet there are some similarities. We were both victims. She directed her anger at herself; I directed mine at others and at a system that treats the victim as the perpetrator. Both of us are also victims of silence. My silence has just recently been broken, and I have been able to discuss my rape with close friends such as one of the authors of this chapter. I guess that friends are more open and understanding than family. Dolores broke her silence with people outside her family, as well.

Both Dolores and I expressed fear of the rapist returning. I was fearful that the rapist would come looking for me after he was released from prison. Though I didn't know the exact date that he was being released, I calculated the approximate date in my head and feared that he would try and find me. Dolores had nightmares about Jack and feared that he would come back into her life and hurt her.

Although I had completely forgotten about it until I read the book, my girlfriend from that night—not an immensely stable person anyway—tried to commit suicide a few years after the incident. I often have wondered how that night affected her. We never discussed it! Once again, silence!

My silence lasted thirty-eight years. Reading *She's Come Undone* began to bring everything into focus for me. Feelings that I hadn't experienced in years reemerged. The writing that followed, and which I have contributed to this chapter, was truly cathartic. I began to reflect on the events of that long-ago night as I read the book, and the veil of silence began to lift.

VIEWS OF THE CLINICIAN

Many teenagers will experience rape during their adolescence. Statistics reflect that 683,000 women are raped every year. Half, or 341,500, of these women are under 18 years of age and 16 percent are younger than 12 years of age (Langan and Harlow, 1994). The experience of such a trauma leaves emotional scars that may remain far beyond adolescence. These victims are likely to blame themselves for what happened, or believe that they should have been able to prevent it. Feelings of shame and anger, and a sense of being violated both physically and spiritually, emerge for many of these victims. These feelings often lead to silence on their part. They are too embarrassed to share their trauma with others and often go through life carrying their burden alone. Other times, victims may confide in family members, who turn out to be nonsupportive and at times even encourage silence "in the best interest of the victim." Society also can contribute to the shame felt by rape victims. Often the victim is blamed for what she wore, where she was, or who she was out with at the time of the incident.

Using literature for bibliotherapy, as an adjunct to treatment with a trained mental health professional, can be very helpful for rape victims. Literature can provide affirmation, support, and validation of the victim's feelings. The victim may feel uncomfortable discussing aspects of her rape and can talk about it from behind the shield of a fictitious character's rape. She may have questions that she feels self-conscious about asking the professional. Reading similar accounts, or educational information about the healing process that needs to occur following the rape, may help alleviate some of the discomfort. Literature addressing the common feelings and aftermath of being raped may also help to "normalize" the victim's feelings. The reader sees that she is not the only one who has suffered and may feel relieved.

Understanding and relating to other victims may be cathartic as well. Reading accounts of other rape victims may lift the sense of isolation that many victims possess. It should be noted, however, that at times reading others' accounts may make the reader feel angry, terrified, and grief stricken. These strong feelings need to be addressed in concomitant therapy. The therapist can help the adolescent understand that many feelings may arise after a rape and that they are all part of the healing process.

Literature can also help the victim of a rape realize that it was not her fault. In *She's Come Undone*, Dolores continually blames herself for what happened. She recalls all the afternoons she rode in Jack's car with him and all the nights she touched herself while thinking about him. The victim who relates her story in this chapter, above, shares similar self-blame. She states, "Society at the time had a feeling that there must have been something the girl was doing wrong to get raped in the first place." She blamed herself for being out at midnight, driving around. She says, "we probably shouldn't have been out."

Neither Dolores nor the victim who tells her story in this chapter receives treatment for her emotional wounds after being raped. Dolores's mother makes a few feeble attempts to take her to a psychiatrist after the rape, but when Dolores refuses, her mother does not press the issue, choosing to assist Dolores by buying her food and thus enhancing her eating disorder. In fact, the mother's own guilt over not protecting her daughter leads her to allow Dolores to do whatever she desires, which is basically to eat and watch television in her bedroom. Though the mother's reaction is typical of many mothers of rape victims, her lack of emotional support following her daughter's rape contributed to Dolores's eventual nervous breakdown. Mrs. Price believed she was doing what was best for her daughter by giving her what she wanted, food. However, her treatment of Dolores actually constitutes neglect because she did not get Dolores the medical or psychological treatment she needed.

Many mothers, due to their own feelings of guilt and denial, are unable to assist their daughters in the healing process after the rape. In some ways, for them to acknowledge the rape is to acknowledge their own part in letting it happen. Additionally, they must now come to terms with their own ideas about rape victims and apply these to their own daughters. In the story told in this chapter, the victim's father does not assist her in the healing process, nor does he allow her mother any involvement. The victim is thus denied both professional treatment and family support. Instead, she is encouraged to be silent about her rape. The victim is left wondering if her family blames her.

From a clinical perspective, several aspects of Dolores's treatment are unusual. In general, the description of the place where Dolores is sent for inpatient treatment is indicative of the time. The novel is set in the early 1970s, and patients in private psychiatric hospitals were probably treated somewhat better than in state hospitals. The medical treatment, however, was standardized; included were many psychotropic medications, mostly tranquilizers, and group and individual therapy. The reader must keep in mind that Dolores's treatment is not for rape per se, but for her subsequent emotional breakdown and attempt at suicide. It can be assumed that her suicide attempt might have been the result of her not ever coming to terms with being raped. Once again, the silence issue rears its ugly head; it could have been responsible for Dolores's death, had she been successful in her suicide attempt.

Although Dolores is treated by several different doctors while in the hospital, her most notable and longest stay in therapy is with Dr. Shaw. He is described as a good-looking, outdoor-nature type. She quickly develops a crush on him and fantasizes about him at night while alone in her bed. Her feelings toward Dr. Shaw are considered normal in the psychotherapy field; they are commonly referred to as "transference." Often when a patient spends as much as four to five hours a week alone with his or her doctor, discussing the most intimate details of his or her life, the patient may develop sexual feelings toward the doctor.

Through therapy, Dr. Shaw explores Dolores's relationships with others, including her mother and father. Reluctantly, Dolores begins a highly unusual type of regression therapy suggested by Dr. Shaw. In this therapy, Dr. Shaw attempts to get Dolores to relive her life symbolically, with him as her mother. To accomplish this feat, he "gives birth" to her in a pool on the grounds of the hospital. Slowly, she begins to grow up; he provides all the love and care that a mother would typically bestow on a child. Discussion often centers around the emotional and physical changes that Dolores is undergoing during the treatment. Dr. Shaw frequently swims with her in the pool and tells her that he loves her. This type of treatment is extremely unorthodox and controversial; it has great potential for blurring the boundaries between patient and doctor. Although the author does a good job in making Dolores's treatment believable, there is no evidence that this type of treatment actually exists. Historically, unusual therapies were taking place in California in the 1970s. This may be the genesis of what the author describes as Dr. Shaw's explanation to Dolores that he has spoken to a doctor in California who has had success with such a treatment. Dr. Shaw further contends that he must convince "the Freudians" at the institute (Freudianism was the dominant therapeutic orientation of the time) that the regressive treatment could be tried with her.

A patient like Dolores could easily be misled by Dr. Shaw's statements that he loved her, especially when she does not believe that anyone loves her. Nevertheless, the basic premise for the approach used by Dr. Shaw is understandable: He wants Dolores to relive her life, this time with a much more healthy outcome; she can now speak about the past and someone will listen—she need not be silent anymore.

The idea of reliving one's past is common in therapy. Specifically, therapy with rape victims combines both a cathartic experience and a psychoeducational approach. First, the victim must begin to feel safe talking about what happened to her and getting in touch with her feelings. In Dolores's case, the predominant feeling is the anger that she has misdirected at herself. Oftentimes the feelings are not expressed at the time of the rape due to the enforced silence. The therapist also educates the victim to understand that it was not her fault and works toward eliminating the self-blame that is common among rape victims.

She's Come Undone can be a starting point for breaking the silence of rape victims. These individuals often have a lot to say but are forced into being silent. An adolescent who has been raped may begin the healing process by relating to the victim, Dolores. Through reading about someone else who has been raped, rape victims can begin to erase the feelings of isolation and loneliness and begin to speak about the event, relative at first to the protagonist and then relative to themselves.

ISSUES AND IMPLICATIONS FOR THE CLASSROOM

The use of literature featuring the issue of rape is well suited to the developmental and intellectual characteristics and interests of adolescents —both male and female—in today's classrooms. The events of any of the novels mentioned in this chapter could happen anytime and anywhere; the protagonist could be any adolescent student in any school. Literature theorist Louise Rosenblatt (1976) explains that the use of this type of literature "may bring into play and be related to profoundly personal needs and preoccupations" of adolescent students, which makes it "a powerful educational force" because it is "out of these basic needs and attitudes that behavior springs" (182).

Some teachers and students may be hesitant to use literature featuring a protagonist such as Dolores because doing so means possibly having to facilitate a discussion of rape. A focus on the character, Dolores, and her experience as portrayed in the book may help defuse uneasiness. Failure to discuss this topic within the parameters that the literature provides could send the message that rape is an experience that is too horrible for words, too horrible to discuss. Students who have been victims of rape or other forms of abuse may think that, by implication, they, too, are therefore horrible. Discussion of a literary incident of rape, on the other hand, can be transformative for a student who is a victim of rape, as well as educational for students who have not suffered such a cruel violation. The rape victim gains a chance to see her experience and herself through the often compassionate eyes of other readers; this view can help to eliminate the shame and secrecy that keep rape victims isolated. Perhaps through this type of literature, adolescent rape victims will understand that they can speak out and, through their telling, alleviate their guilt and the shame that comes with it.

RECOMMENDED READINGS

Because adolescent rape is an issue that is, by its nature, controversial to many adults, the recommendations incorporated in the entries below can be used only in a broad sense. The recommended readership that is noted in the young adult literature entries is provided as a comment on the readability of the text; that is, it is used to indicate whether or not a middle school or high school reader should be able to make sense of the book.

Fiction Works

Young Adult Literature

Allende, I. (1982). The *House of the Spirits*. New York: Bantam Books. 433 pp. (ISBN: 0–553–25865–6). High School (HS).

A historical novel dealing with the class struggles of families. For one family in particular, these struggles are made even more difficult by an incident of rape.

Angelou, M. (1996). *I Know Why the Caged Bird Sings*. New York: Bantam Doubleday Dell. 334 pp. (ISBN: 0–553–38001–X). Middle School (MS), HS.

Maya Angelou explores her growing up, including being raped as a youngster, which ultimately causes her to remain silent for many years.

McKinley, R. (1994). *Deerskin*. New York: Ace Books. 320 pp. (ISBN: 0–441–00069–X). MS, HS.

After the queen dies, the king begins to pay more attention to his daughter and eventually rapes her; she leaves the palace to live in the wild as a new person, Deerskin.

Naylor, G. (1983). *The Women of Brewster Place*. New York: Penguin USA. 192 pp. (ISBN: 0–14–006690–X). MS, HS.

The story of seven different women, one of whom suffers one of the most brutal rapes in literature.

Tamar, E. (1993). *Fair Game*. New York: Harcourt Brace. 272 pp. (ISBN: 0–15–227065–5). MS, HS.

Cara, a mildly retarded teenage girl, is gang-raped by popular athletes. The girlfriend of one of the athletes blames Cara for getting the boys in trouble.

Tan, A. (1989). *The Joy Luck Club*. New York: Ballantine Books. 288 pp. (ISBN: 0–8041–0630–4). HS.

A wealthy man forces An-Mei's mother to be his concubine by dishonoring her through rape.

Walker, A. (1998). *The Color Purple*. New York: Washington Square Press. 204 pp. (ISBN: 0–671–01907–4). HS.

An exquisitely written portrayal of a young rape victim's letters to God, written as her attempt to come to terms with who she is, despite how she is treated by others. This is a moving, powerful story of both unthinkable injustice and triumph over adversity.

Nonfiction Works

Resources for Teachers and Other Adults

Bass, E., and L. Davis. (1993). *Beginning to Heal*. New York: Harperperennial Library. 144 pp. (ISBN: 0–06–096927–X). A.

This short paperback is designed to help rape victims through the healing process. The authors encourage readers to move through the book at their own pace; if a chapter is too powerful at the moment, the reader is encouraged to skip it and return to it later. The authors present cases in which women of all races, cultures, and sexual orientations share their stories of sexual abuse that occurred during their childhood. This book tells readers that they are not alone. It assures readers who are victims of sexual abuse that what has happened to them and their feelings about the events have been experienced by others and that there are ways to move beyond the pain.

Gil, E. (1988). *Outgrowing the Pain: A Book for and about Adults Abused as Children*. New York: Dell. 96 pp. (ISBN: 0–440–50006–0). A.

This is a short book addressing the feelings that may emerge as a result of being a survivor of childhood sexual abuse. The information is presented in an easy-to-read style, using photographs to depict various emotions. This book may help sexually abused adolescents normalize their feelings and may assist them in understanding the emotional changes that they experience.

Koss, M., and M. Harvey. (1991). *The Rape Victim.* 2nd ed. Thousand Oaks, CA: Sage. 288 pp. (ISBN: 0–8039–3894–2). A.

This nonfiction book relates the stories of several rape victims. The authors share important information about how victims and their families can help each other through this trauma.

Ledray, L. (1995). *Recovering from Rape.* New York: Owlet. 88 pp. (ISBN: 0–8050–2928–1). A.

An excellent guide relevant to the immediate aftermath of rape; includes chapters on dealing with doctors, police, the legal system, emotional recovery, and the long-term consequences of rape.

Web Site

http://pubweb.new.edu

See this site for a bibliography of books about rape and its victims, along with a twenty-four-hour hotline and information on reporting rape.

REFERENCES

Corman, A. (1991). *Prized Possessions.* New York: Simon & Schuster.
Lamb, W. (1992). *She's Come Undone.* New York: Pocket Books.
Langan, P., and C. Harlow. (1994). *Child Rape Victims.* Washington, DC: Bureau of Justice Statistics.
Peck, R. (1979). *Are You in the House Alone?* New York: Dell.
Rosenblatt, L. (1976). *Literature as Exploration.* New York: Noble & Noble.
Salholz, E. (1990). "Women under Assault." *Newsweek* (July 16), 21, 23–24.
White, R. (1992). *Weeping Willow.* New York: Farrar, Straus & Giroux.

CHAPTER FIVE

Sports in the Life of Today's Adolescents

Pamela S. Carroll and Steven B. Chandler

INTRODUCTION

"Sports"—the word may conjure up an image of an extra-large football player crashing into others as they struggle to push a ball down the field, or a slender tennis player wiping sweat from his face while squinting into the intense sun during a summer match. The word may prompt a vision of a diminutive gymnast stretching her perfectly defined muscles before gracefully approaching the balance beam, or a confident rock climber patiently stretching her chalked hands across the face of a cliff.

Along with visual images of particular kinds of sporting activities, it is likely that the word "sports" evokes some type of feeling. The successful athletes among us may feel comfortable with the word, while those of us who participate with only moderate success may experience a prick of interest and connection. If we have tried but failed at sports, or have seen our glory replaced by the skills of younger athletes, we may feel threatened or defeated by the word. Those who have no interest in sports may feel like protesting—or yawning.

Despite a multitude of conceptions and attitudes about them, few aspects of contemporary life are so ubiquitous as sports. Today's sports stars are elevated to the status of heroes and heroines; advertisers take advantage of the positive association of sports with fun in order to sell all kinds of products, from soft drinks to underwear. Many families plan weekends around participating in or attending sporting events, watching sports on television, or using video games as surrogates for participation in wrestling matches, downhill ski events, cars races, or myriad other sports. Except when there is the threat of a players' strike, we count on hearing about the Super Bowl, the Kentucky Derby, the Master's Golf Tournament, Wimbledon, and the World Series on national news; we can follow local high school runners during cross-country season and compare young swimmers' times by reading our local newspapers. Many of us join health clubs in order to become more physically active; many join community teams for recreation and social purposes. When we want outlandish new kinds of challenges, we can tune in to ESPN-2 to find extreme sports, such as acrobatic skydiving, to engage our attention, or visit a bookstore to flip through magazines on topics that range from scuba diving to karate.

It is no wonder that sports, which have an important role in our society at large, are an important feature in the lives of many adolescents. In the pages that follow, we have created a short story as a means of addressing issues that are central to the questions, What characteristics of adolescents' participation in sports have an important impact on adolescents' social, emotional, and physical development? and, How accurately are these characteristics portrayed in sports-oriented books for young adults? In order to work toward answers, we have approached these questions from our different professional backgrounds and identities, but with a shared interest in sports and fitness.

We have taken the liberty of borrowing, or transporting, Ben, Al, and other Sturbridge citizens from Rich Wallace's fine novel *Wrestling Sturbridge* (1996) to use as characters in our story. In *Wrestling Sturbridge*, Ben is a high school senior who lives in Sturbridge, Pennsylvania. The town is known for two things: its cinder block factory, where most of its men work, and its high school wrestlers. Ben is a talented wrestler; the only person in the state who can beat him in his weight category is his teammate, Al. Ben knows that his life should not revolve around wrestling, but he does not have the vision he needs to seek other options. He is a mediocre student who might have a chance for a college wrestling scholarship, but his coach is not involved with the futures of the wrestlers; the coach cares only about their performance while they are members of his team. Ben has a girlfriend, Kim, who tries to help him see that there is a world beyond the gym and the town of Sturbridge; she is a runner who has set her sights on a productive future, with the help of supportive parents. Al is suspended from the team for vandalizing the school one night when he is drunk; Ben suddenly has an opportunity to establish himself as the best wrestler in the state, but he is unable to beat

Al once Al returns to the team. Ben realizes, at the end of the season, that he has two choices: He can become an adult who works at the cinder block factory and who lives vicariously through the success of younger wrestlers, or he can leave wrestling and Sturbridge in order to build a life for himself, on his own terms.

We have created another character, sports psychologist Dan Palmer, to add to the cast created by the novel's author. In our story, it is Dan who helps Ben and others understand some of the complexities of sports participation. We hope that the story will illuminate, for our readers, many of the interrelated social, emotional, and physical development issues of sports participation among adolescents.

Following the story, we address common questions related to adolescents' participation in sports and propose answers to those questions. The chapter closes with an annotated bibliography of nonfiction and fiction books to help adults and teens further explore issues that are raised within the chapter. Although it is far from complete as a listing of sports-oriented books for young adults, our list does provide a variety of titles in four broad categories: fiction that uses sports as a key element in a story (many of these books involve athletes and sporting events; the best, however, are not focused solely on the sport, but on the people who are involved in some way with the sport or athletes); nonfiction, including a sampling of how-to books that explain rules, moves, and regulations of sports; biographies and autobiographies of successful athletes, including stars like 1994 Olympic figure skater Nancy Kerrigan and more obscure figures like Ted Lewin, a teenage professional wrestler; and expositions on sports in America.

FIRST, A STORY

Things that still matter . . .
leaving Sturbridge

loving Kim

Jesus and Elvis

Things that don't . . .
pinning Al

whoever's pumping gas

cinder blocks

I took the five bucks Dad gave me for gas and made a slow pass through town. The little kids who were at the arcade last night were all home watching cartoons this morning. Kim and I had plans to get together for a picnic. I had the feeling she had something else on her mind; exactly what I wasn't sure. She wanted to talk to me, so we were going to cruise around then have a picnic.

When I pulled into the lot of the gas station, I didn't see Jody, just the owner inside and no one at the pumps. He got up and came out when I pulled up.

"What'll it be, sport?" he asked as he spit tobacco at the trash can next to the pump.

"Five regular," I told him. "Jody's got the day off?"

"She got all her days off from here on, sport. Decided to pack up her kid and move to Pittsburgh. Gettin' away from that no good husband of hers. 'Bout damn time if you ask me. They friends of yours?"

"Yeah, kinda." So she left town. I guess that takes care of that. I won't have to wonder about what might have been with her anymore. Guess I was right to stick with Kim. Can't see myself with a kid right now anyway.

I cruised into Kim's driveway and honked the horn. She came out after about a minute, carrying a blanket and wearing her tight Calvin Klein jeans and a little black crop-top with "DKNY" across the front. It bounced up and down as she jogged the few steps from the house to the car. No doubt about it, Kim looked hot. She jumped in and slid over beside me, and we headed for McDonald's for our drive-through picnic supplies.

It was a beautiful day—warm and sunny—a touch of spring in the air. Kim wanted to ride out to the Gaines Farm to watch the ponies run. We saw them in the fall, and it'd be fun to see how much they'd grown over the winter. The Gaines Farm was one of her favorite places. Mine too, I guess. So much grace and energy in those ponies. Just like her.

We found a sunny spot on the slope above the pasture. The grass was a beautiful newly grown green, and a few wildflowers had popped up in the sunshine. She spread the blanket, and we got down to the burger business as we watched the ponies playing in the field below. They were chasing each other around and braying at each other. They still had gangly looking stick legs, but they were growing, getting fast. In a few months they'd be running with their mother.

I stretched out on the blanket and pulled Kim down onto me so we could get down to our other business. She gave the coolest kisses, soft and wet, with a kinda suction at the end. She could kiss me on the neck, and I would feel that suction down below. I ran my hands along the warm skin under the back of her little black shirt. The sun felt great steaming through her top onto her smooth skin. She let my hands travel up and down her back and along the length of her thighs.

Her hair kept falling into our mouths, so I rolled her over and got on top of her and started kissing her face and neck. She liked that, so I moved my hand up the interstate from thigh land toward New York City. She caught my wrist on the way up and tried to pushed it down a little, but not enough to stop the journey, so I went on up and settled it right there. Kim tried to push me up and off her with a weak little move and moaned something like "Ben, don't," but the move barely budged me. I reversed her hand off my wrist and pulled her arm away from her chest. She was pushing me hard, but I outweigh her a good twenty pounds. Next she tried to knee me down below, but I slipped off her. Then, out of the blue, she slaps me hard across the face and just goes ballistic slapping and scratching and screaming at me. I had to duck in under her arms, too close for her to hit me, before I could get her under control. By the time I got her arms down, she was all pouting and crying, and she turned her head every time I tried to kiss her. This was no fun, so I let her up.

Kim sat up on the blanket, holding her knees to her chest like I had hurt her. Wiping big tears from her eyes, she stared, red-faced and tired, at the horses down below.

"What's your deal, Kim? What are you crying about?"

"You hurt me, Ben. I'd like to go home now."

"Look, Kim, that couldn't have hurt much. I barely touched you."

She glared at me, starting to cry again. "You don't know how strong you are, Ben. I'm not one of your brawling buddies."

"C'mon, Kim. You know I like you. I wouldn't hurt you."

"You just did, Ben. Look at my wrists. I'm gonna have a bruise on my arm."

"Yeah, well that was a pretty good slap, too, lady."

"You deserved it. Haven't you ever heard you don't hit a lady?"

"Hey, well . . ." She started to stand up, and I grabbed her wrist again, then let it go when I realized that was a bad idea.

"Look, Kim, I was just playing around. It didn't matter."

"It mattered to me, Ben. Take me home. Nothing matters to you but wrestling. You don't respect anyone who can't pin you. You need to learn to respect people whether they're stronger than you or not."

"C'mon, Kim, I respect you. You're my ummm, my . . ."

"Oh yeah? Well, if you respect me, then take me home."

I was really ticked off and dropped Kim off at home, like she'd asked me to. I didn't even stop the car engine when I said good-bye to her. She stopped my breath when she got out of the car and turned back toward me just long enough to say, "You need help, Ben. You really do. If you don't care about anything but wrestling, fine. But don't count on me to wait around here until you realize that there is more to life than sweaty mats and powerful holds."

I was still thinking about that scene with Kim, playing it back over and over in my head, when Coach called the team in for a meeting. He congratulated us for winning state and, along with the boosters' president, presented each of us with a plaque engraved with "Sturbridge Wrestling—Pennsylvania State Champions" and our name and weight class. Then Coach introduced us to Dr. Dan Palmer, an old college buddy of his who was now a professor and consulting sports psychologist at Pennsylvania State University. If people look like their dogs, then this guy's gotta have a greyhound. He was tall and thin and gaunt. Dr. Palmer explained to us what a sports psychologist was: someone with a doctoral degree who had studied psychology, counseling, and the psychology of sports. He described how his own background as a marathoner had inspired him to study how the mind of the athlete could be trained along with the body to contribute to the highest level of performance in sports. He told us about some the courses he had taken in his graduate studies at Florida State University and some of the counseling he did in his internship as the academic counselor for athletes at Auburn University. He also told us about some of the clients he has now, how they are mostly pro athletes for teams in Pittsburgh, Philadelphia, and Baltimore. Dr. Palmer had us fill out a bunch of questionnaires about our sports and life goals, how we reacted to different situations, how we handled stress, and even some stuff about our personality and diet. We all had to make an appointment with him to talk about our answers the following week.

When I arrived for my appointment, I really didn't know what to expect. What would a sports psychologist say about me?

"Hi, Ben. I'm Dan Palmer," he said, extending his hand as he stood up and met me when I came into his office.

"Hi, Dr. Palmer. Nice to meet you," I said as I shook his hand and sat down in the large overstuffed chair in front of his desk. He sat down in a chair beside me with a folder full of my questionnaires.

"We're going to talk about your questionnaire in a few minutes, but first let's talk about the season. How'd you do?" he began.

"Hey, we won state, you know."

"Right. I know that. But what I really wanted to know is how *you* did this season."

I knew what he wanted to know, and I felt lousy about telling him. But I figured, what the heck—he knows it, and I know it, and everyone else knows it, too. "Well, I'm in a tough spot this year. Al's in my weight class, and he's the best wrestler in the state. I'm too light to wrestle in a heavier group, and if I move down, I have to go against Hatcher, and he's the best in that weight class, too. So what can I tell you, Doc? I basically rode the bench except for the one match when Al got suspended for pissin' on the radiators."

"Yeah. I'll be talking to him about that soon, too. Who'd you wrestle in your match for the league championship?" Dr. Palmer asked.

"Arnie Keifer, from Laurelton High."

"How'd you do?"

"I won. Pinned him in fifteen seconds. Even got the 'Most Outstanding Wrestler' trophy."

"So, Ben, you said Al's the best wrestler in state. Who's second best?"

"Well, that'd be Keifer, I guess."

"But you just told me that you pinned him in fifteen seconds." He paused a minute, looking at me, to let that soak in, I guess. Then he asked me again, "Who's the second best wrestler in the entire state of Pennsylvania?"

"I never thought of it that way. I guess you mean me, huh?"

"Yeah," he said, grinning at me. "So, Ben, who'd you wrestle against just about every day this season?" he asked, still grinning.

"You mean Al?"

"Coach tells me you almost pinned him, too."

"Yeah, but close only counts in horseshoes and hand grenades, you know."

"So they say. How close did you get?"

"Eight to seven. Couldn't pin him, though. But I sure gave it all I had."

"He's always beaten you?"

"Yeah, ever since freshman year. He used to hammer me easy."

"But now you're only one point apart? What gives? Are you getting a lot better, or is he getting worse?"

"I guess I must be getting better. So what are you getting at here, Doc?"

"Well, let's see if I'm hearing what you're telling me. You're the second best wrestler in the state, and you're getting better, while the number-one guy is sittin' still."

He had a point. I'd never looked at it that way before.

"Do you think any colleges would be interested in the up-and-coming number-two wrestler in the state?"

The lights were starting to go on in my head about how this sports psychology stuff worked. This guy was trying to help me here. "Yeah, Doc. I guess so. I never looked at it like that."

Dr. Palmer got up and walked over to his desk and sat on the edge. "What'd you say you and me and Coach get together later this week and write a few letters to college wrestling coaches about you? Do you think we could sell 'em on a kid like you?"

"That'd be great! Sure!" Maybe I could get a scholarship. I can't believe I'd never thought of that before now. I just sat there, smiling to myself for a minute.

Dr. Palmer folded his arms, rested his chin in his hand, and looked down at me with something close to a frown. I wasn't sure what was up, but something wasn't right. He picked up the folder with my questionnaires and sat back down in the chair.

"There was another thing I wanted to hear about. Something about you punching out a priest?"

So that was it. Coach told him? The guys? Did that matter?

"He's a reverend, and yeah, I punched him." I looked him in the eyes and added, "And I'd probably do it again, all things considered."

"Oh? Tell me about it."

"We were coaching kids at the Y's youth soccer camp, basic stuff for little kids. The whole idea is that the kids get to play and have fun, so they'll want to get into soccer, you know. Anyway, things were going great until the championship, when my team and his team were going for it at the end of the game. When it was time to play the subs, to let them have their shot at it, I put mine in, but what did he do? Left in his best players and made the rest ride the bench. He won the game, but he cheated the kids. I couldn't let that go. When the game was over, we got into it a little, that's all."

"So you punched him."

"Yeah. He pissed me off." Now I was the one who was frowning.

"I see. How do you feel about it now?" he asked.

"I'm not happy about it. I know he's a reverend and all, but, hey, he was wrong."

"That's interesting," Dr. Palmer said thoughtfully. "You did the right thing in standing up for the kids, but you chose a poor way to do it. Young children do have different motives for playing sports than adolescents and adults. You were right to want everyone to get to play and have some fun. Sounds like I need to conduct a coaching clinic at the Y for the parents and volunteer coaches. It's pretty common for adults—coaches and fans, and especially parents—to impose their desire to win on children's chances to play. Two of the most common reasons kids give for quitting a sport are that it isn't any fun anymore and that it gets too competitive." He smiled a little bit at me and added, "I guess they don't teach 'em that in seminary, either!" I was beginning to like this guy again.

"I understand why you were angry, Ben, but I still don't understand why you had to hit him."

He was pickin' at me again, so I thought I'd feed him a line this time.

"You're right. I should have pinned him to the ground and sat on his chest!"

He lifted an eyebrow at me and said, "You know better, Ben. That's a real problem some athletes face. Violence is hurting all aspects of the game. Sports train the body to be strong and quick. And in sports like wrestling, you learn aggressive skills to dominate an opponent. But those skills have no place off the mat."

I got the point. I'd heard this before, from Kim, and I knew he was right.

"If you were coaching that soccer game again, right when you started getting angry, what could you do to stop the action and express what you felt?"

"Maybe take a time-out, call him over, and remind him why we play the game and why I put my subs in, and give him a chance to put his in so we could finish the game fair and square."

"Now you're thinking!" He smiled a full smile at me then nodded to Coach, who was leaning in the door of the outer office. "Looks like my next appointment's here. You're doing great, Ben. I'd like to talk with you again tomorrow. Two items for you to work on: one, think of a couple of other things you might do to assert yourself when you're upset besides getting physical; and two, be ready to discuss what you want to major in next year in college."

"Okay, Doc. Thanks for the talk. I'll see you tomorrow."

"See you then, Ben. Coach! Come on in!"

"Coach Dave . . . Big Dave! How long has it been? Have I not seen you since we were at FSU?" Dr. Palmer asked as Coach settled in for his round in the overstuffed chair.

"About ten years, I guess. Feels like we ought to still be in school ourselves, some days. Other times, it seems like a hundred years ago. But you look great, Dan."

"Thanks, Dave. I know what you mean about time. But how's it going here, in the present?"

"Great! Just won state, you know. 'Course Sturbridge is a little more like Sturburg, or Stircrazy. But we're winning, and everybody here loves wrestling."

"So town's a little slow?"

"Everybody who's anybody gets a satellite dish and a six-pack just to pass the time. Kids can't wait to leave once they get old enough."

"I grew up in the same kinda town. There's fifty thousand people there now. I can hardly find my way around when I go home. . . . This place has potential. . . . You heard me talking to Ben?"

"Just a little. About the reverend who he punched 'cause the guy wouldn't let the little kids play?"

"Yeah. You know, I don't think Ben realizes you did the same thing to him, keeping him on the bench all season."

"Hey, bud, my job's to win, and Al's undefeated in the state. He's a sure winner."

"But you could have wrestled both of 'em. You woulda had two undefeated kids at 135 pounds. Ridin' the bench sure didn't do much for Ben's future."

"Look, Dan, that's the way the sport works. Somebody wins and somebody loses. You know the story: Only the strong survive."

"You been watching the pros too much, Dave. A high school coach's job is to grow kids into adults. To give them the tools they need to have the best life they can. Sports is just a way to get them to where they need to go."

"That sounds nice, but you know how coaching is, Dan. If I don't win, I get fired."

"From what the principal tells me, you might get fired anyway. He seems to think you're missing the point."

"What'd that peckerwood say?"

"Hey, man, his job is to run the school. Yours is to support him. He's talking about poor control, hazing on your team, drunk kids breaking into the school—pissin' on radiators! He's talking about old ladies calling him in the middle of the night saying they've been mooned from the team bus."

Coach sunk in the chair and looked distressed.

"What's your team's grade average?" Dan asked.

"Hell if I know. That's the teachers' job."

"That's something else you're missing, Dave. Your job is to get these kids through high school and into college—whether they wrestle there or not. Your job is to see to it that they graduate with the ability to succeed at the next level. To watch 'em graduate there and bring that diploma back here and open up a business in this community. You're building a town here, Coach, one kid at a time. Your job is growing people."

"You always were one to look at the big picture, Dan. What should we do?"

"We're going to set up an academic program for the team—for all the sports here—to begin with. If a kid doesn't study, he doesn't wrestle—no pass, no play. You're gonna track the kids to college, boast about your graduation rate, and build your alumni base. Grow some really good kids for this town. You do that, and you'll be here 'til someone hires you away from 'em to do the same thing for their town."

"You're gonna help me set this up, right?"

"Sure, man, that's what I'm here for. Let's plan out the details, then we'll sell it to the boosters—open their eyes and watch it roll."

"You think the boosters will buy it?"

"Sure. That's what school is for. They can't *not* buy it. Shoot, we'll even ask them to pay for it!"

"Dan the Man! I knew there was some reason I liked you. Let's give it a shot."

"Great. Let's get together in the morning and start on it. Right now, I want to talk to you a bit about Al."

"Al? He's set. He'll get a scholarship offer for sure . . . unless you know something I don't. What'd he do now?"

"Nothing yet. It's what he's gonna do that we need to talk about."

"Okay, Mr. Crystal Ball, what do you see for him?"

"Reminds me a little of a ballplayer from over in Springfield. Good athlete. Big drinker. Went off to college never losing a game, then fell apart when he got away from home. You know Al's gonna get his butt kicked in college, and not just in wrestling. He's gonna be a freshman facing the best college talent. All he really knows how to do is get drunk and screw up. He doesn't know how to study. He doesn't even train like an athlete. He has just been lucky so far. His luck is bound to run out, though. And soon. You figure it out. If he doesn't change, he'll get creamed on the mats and he'll also flunk out the first year. The way he is now, he'll hate college. He'll quit and come back to Sturbridge, where he's everybody's hero. Five years from now, he'll be wrestling cinder blocks and downin' two six-packs a day."

Coach looked like he was ready to yell at Dan and stood up as if he were going to leave the office, but suddenly he stood still for a minute, then spoke.

"Pretty bleak picture, but I guess you're right. I hadn't really thought of it like that before. All right, Mr. Sunshine, what's our plan to save this one?"

"Glad you asked. First off, Al's just part of the problem. I'll start with a specific evaluation with him, and then do some one-to-one work. What we really have to do is address the alcohol culture of the team and this town. You know alcohol is a diuretic and that it can cause dehydration. That cuts into the body fluids and can hurt performance. So even if you ignore the fact that drinking lots of beer makes your wrestlers act like idiots, you have to admit that alcohol is bad for them as athletes. We'll start with a dietary intervention. Get 'em eating lots of carbohydrates, low amounts of fat, and lots of fiber . . . and no alcohol, especially during season. Once the kids are convinced it will help them win, they'll eat it up."

Dan feigned a snicker at his pun, then continued. "We'll work on 'em and see if we can't get some of the diet to rub off at home, too."

"Dan, they're kids. They're drinkin' because there's nothing for 'em to do in this town but drive around and look at each other."

"Ah yes, Grasshopper, but in every crisis, there is opportunity. How can we benefit from their boredom?"

"Hell if I know. Open a gas station? Charge 'em by the mile?"

"Not a bad idea . . . but we're the sports guys, remember? Who runs that video arcade downtown?"

"One of the boosters. Mostly young kids hang out there, though."

"Never too young to start. Do you think we could get them to add a gym floor to the place, put up a couple of hoops? Maybe we could get a youth league going with the Y, come up with some recreational outlets for 'em. Any of the boosters on the city commission?"

"The mayor's a booster. Most of the commission. Hell, we've got four hundred boosters."

"Let's get 'em together with some of the urban planning faculty from Penn State. Maybe they can help us find some grant money for a community development program."

"Sounds like a long-term project."

"Yeah. You'll probably win state again before we're done."

"Hey, buddy, I'm gonna win state again next year."

"Then we better get busy!"

QUESTIONS AND ANSWERS

We believe that the following questions and answers will help adults who work with adolescents understand more fully the significance of sports in the lives of many teens. We would like to see sports continue to attract the interest of children once they are adolescents, and to see adolescents who participate in sports activities have the support of adults who balance goals of record-setting performances and stardom with goals of health, fitness, and fun.

What can we learn from a sports psychologist?

Complementing physical conditioning and the seemingly endless hours of practice, the mental preparedness of an athlete is a crucial ingredient for optimal performance. Recognizing this necessity has lead to investigation of the psychological dimensions of sports and to the training of qualified professionals to administer sports psychology–based techniques. Professional organizations, such as the Association for the Advancement of Applied Sport Psychology, set criteria for the certification of such professionals. Those criteria generally include the following: a doctoral degree with specific course work in sports psychology, exercise science, and research methodology; training, and a supervised internship, in counseling; and knowledge of the biological, cognitive-affective, social, and individual basis of sports behavior. Sports psychologists are employed as consultants by sports organizations and individual athletes to facilitate mental readiness. Through our fictitious sports psychologist, Dr. Dan Palmer, we depict an actual work setting and demonstrate how sports psychologist might approach a counseling problem.

Who is primarily responsible for adolescents' participation in sports?

The influence of significant others, a person or persons the opinion of whom the child or adolescent values, may have an important effect on sports participation. The significant other may strongly influence the attitudes, values, and behaviors the young athlete chooses to adopt. Examples include the nuclear family (father, mother, siblings), the peer group, coaches, school or community personnel, and the mass media.

Family influences appear to be the best indicator of sports participation. Parents tend to pass along attitudes to their offspring regarding sports. If parents believe a particular activity is more appropriate for a female and another activity is for a male, the young female may adopt this attitude. A home environment that models, supports, and provides incentives for young girls' participation in sports makes such participation more attractive. Fathers appear to be the most important significant other in deciding which sports are appropriate for daughters, and girls are more affected by lack of support of fathers than are boys. Daughters of athletic parents often select the sport of their mothers. When this is not the case, the female athlete is often surrounded by siblings or other relatives, usually older ones, with sports-related interests.

Sports-related young adult literature is replete with examples of the influence of family members and significant others on participation in sports. Fathers, brothers, mothers, uncles, girlfriends, boyfriends, and coaches either encourage, allow, or disapprove of adolescents' participation in sports, and examples of each of these tendencies can be found in young adult books.

Often, adolescents have family members or significant others who provide encouragement and guidance by example and nurturing. Kim's parents encourage her to continue running track because she enjoys it, in *Wrestling Sturbridge*. Sun's father realizes that his daughter needs his help to learn basketball skills just as much as her brother needs him, in Will Weaver's "Stealing for Girls" (1995). Dean's coach and mentor, Jack Trant, who is a father figure, pushes Dean to define himself exclusively as a baseball player, in Randy Powell's *Dean Duffy* (1995). Valerie's father encourages her to learn to scuba dive so that they can dive together in Virginia Euwer Wolff's "Brownian Motion" (1995).

In Chris Crutcher's *Ironman* (1995), it is not a family member, but a teacher, Mr. Nakatani ("Mr. Nak"), who becomes Bo Brewster's strongest supporter. Mr. Nak is in charge of the anger management class that Bo is forced to attend after he is kicked off the football team and fights with his English teacher. Bo believes that no adult can be trusted, and he uses his abusive father as convincing evidence. However, Mr. Nak helps him realize that it is Bo whom Bo is most afraid to trust. With Mr. Nak's help, Bo is able to figure out how to "get away from the monster that lived *inside* [him]" (145).

Families and significant others who are not involved directly in adolescents' sports activities may, nevertheless, offer moderate support or tacit permission for adolescents to participate in sports. In *Wrestling Sturbridge*, Ben's parents, unlike most of the town, do not attend all of his matches, but they do not object to his team membership. Mrs. Cowan seems happy to be the chauffeur who drives her daughter and a friend to the racquetball court, in Norma Fox Mazer's "Cutthroat" (1995). Rollo's father is angered when Rollo and two friends attack Valerie, but he does not associate the violence with the kind of abuse Rollo is known for as a football star in Norma Fox Mazer's *Out of Control* (1993). In David Klass's *California Blue* (1994), John's father, a former football hero who still holds records at John's school, is sarcastic about John's failure to win cross-country meets. He finally shows some support for his son and teaches him that "the secret to always winning is not to let yourself lose" (188). All of the children's parents are too busy to coach them but are happy to see the "Misfits" form a soccer team in Bill Wallace's *Never Say Quit* (1993).

Families and others, may, on the other hand, only grudgingly allow or even vehemently deny adolescents the opportunity to participate in sports activities. George and Monty's mother forbids the boys to visit their uncle, who runs a gym where boxers are trained, in Chris Lynch's *Shadow Boxer* (1993). Her father refuses to let Cat wear pants instead of her dress when she wants to defend her title as fastest runner in her school in Zilpha K. Snyder's historical novel *Cat Running* (1994). Sonny's aunt is openly hostile toward basketball coaches and boosters, and many of the players, in Jay Bennett's *The Squared Circle* (1995). Peter's mother wants him to concentrate solely on becoming a prize-winning pianist; she is disturbed when Peter becomes enchanted with running, after he watches Kevin sprint by his house every afternoon, in Jim Naughton's "Joyriding" (1995). In Graham Salisbury's "Shark Bait," (1995), David Ford and Johnny Blas are teammates who row a Koa-wood racing canoe as members of the Kai Opua Canoe Club. Each has to deal with an abusive father who, for his own reasons, fiercely objects to his son's being part of the team competition.

Why do children and adolescents participate in sports?

Playfulness appears to be a fundamental aspect of human nature. It expresses itself particularly in childhood and adolescence, where it provides pleasures associated with movement, enhances exploration of the environment, develops the mind and body, establishes the value of achievement, and, in some cases, assists in socialization. Children and adolescents engage in sports, ritualized forms of play, because they enjoy some or all of the following: learning and improving skills; making and being with friends; improving health, strength, and fitness; being a part of a team or group; engaging in competition; having fun. It is important to realize that the benefits differ for each child, adolescent, and adult; it is also important to realize that as groups, children, adolescents, and adults derive different benefits from participation in sports.

Early success and reinforcement of emerging competencies in sports is critical for children if they are going to continue to participate in sports. Adults must uphold a code that insists that we reward effort, rather than focus on outcomes (winning or losing), when working with child athletes. As adults, we must remember that outcomes are more important to us than they are to adolescents and that a focus on winning and losing may actually be punitive to children. In our story, Dr. Palmer talks to Ben about an incident, mentioned in *Wrestling Sturbridge*, in which Ben punched a reverend who was coaching an opposing soccer team. Ben explains that the reverend cared more about winning a game than he cared about the feelings of the less-skilled players on the young soccer team. Ben is angry because the reverend-coach violated the code.

How are girls and women portrayed in sports-related young adult literature?

Women and girls are usually portrayed positively in young adult literature; however, females are typically supportive or minor characters, not protagonists. In *Wrestling Sturbridge*, Kim is intelligent, articulate, and athletic. Her guidance has a positive impact on Ben. Sissy, the feminist professor in Bennett's *The Squared Circle* (1995) supports and challenges Sonny, sometimes sarcastically, as she nurtures her unsophisticated cousin. Authors occasionally contrast a strong female figure against weaker males. For example, George and Monty's mother in Lynch's *Shadow Boxer* (1993) is an impressive symbol of rectitude cast against some sorry male characters (a dead boxer father, a gym junky uncle, a pervert building supervisor, and an abusive neighbor).

A role conflict between being feminine and being a female athlete, which results in fear of success, seems to drive fewer females from sports in literature than it does in reality. The females in Mazer's "Cutthroat" (1995) appear to be well satisfied with their athleticism and competitiveness. Kim in *Wrestling Sturbridge* apparently loves running. However, in reality, adolescence represents a time when many females quit sports. This decline may be due partially to females' reduced competency in skill execution; as they grow rapidly during early adolescence, they often experience loss of coordination, for example. Some may leave sports because of their desire to assume more ideals of femininity; others may become involved in relationships with significant others who view sports participation as inappropriate for females.

Perhaps recent media attention to women's athletics, including basketball, softball, gymnastics, swimming, speed skating, ice hockey, running, and other sports, will gradually begin to change stereotypes and misconceptions about women athletes and women's sports. Perhaps, too, it is time for more writers to follow the leads of Zilpha Snyder and Norma Fox Mazer, who feature female athletes as protagonists in their books and stories.

What should adolescents expect from the adults who work with them in sports?

Adults provide guidance and coaching to young people in sports for a variety of reasons. Previous or current positive participation in sports, love of sports, a desire to interact with and contribute to the development of youth, employment opportunities, and fun are among motives often cited. While professional organizations often set guidelines and conduct certification programs for those who wish to coach youth, not all adults obtain adequate training or provide proper leadership. As such, adolescents and parents should expect to see a range of coaching behaviors that are sometimes less than effective or desirable. There are obvious examples of poor coaching behavior in Lynch's *Iceman* (1994), where Eric is allowed to be a truculent ice hockey player, and in Bennett's *The Squared Circle* (1995), in which the star player, Sonny, is pressured to put practice time above academics and to speak at press conferences, where he feels intimidated and out of place. More subtle is the treatment Dean receives in Powell's novel *Dean Duffy* (1995). Dean is recruited by Dick Drago to try out for a spot on a new baseball team at an expensive, elite private college. Drago offers Dean a one-semester scholarship with the understanding that the scholarship will be extended if Dean is able to contribute to the team's success. The offer sounds generous to Dean, at first, since Dean had quit playing baseball several months earlier, following a disastrous senior season in high school. However, he soon realizes that Drago is interested solely in his performance as a pitcher. Drago assumes that Dean's academics and social life will take care of themselves; he sees Dean as an athlete, not as a person.

The Youth Sports Task Force of the National Association for Sport and Physical Education has prepared a Bill of Rights for Young Athletes to help adults provide quality programs for youth. In the bill, the task force states that it is reasonable for young athletes to expect the following rights:

to participate in sport,

to participate at a level commensurate with their maturity and ability,

to have qualified adult leadership,

to play as a child and not as an adult,

to share in the leadership and decision making of their sport participation,

to participate in safe and healthy environments,

to receive proper preparation for participation in sport,

to have an equal opportunity to strive for success,

to be treated with dignity,

to have fun. (Marten and Seefeldt, 1979)

In our story earlier in the chapter, we used Dr. Palmer's conversation with Coach Dave to elaborate on what can happen if the adult who is in a leadership role does not fulfill all of the obligations of his position. Qualified coaches of children and adolescents must strive to understand the children and teens with whom they work. They must organize and conduct efficient practices, and be able to introduce and reinforce the basic skills and strategies of the particular sport. Coaches must also keep the activities fun. Leaders cannot be those who abuse the power of their positions or endanger in any way the children who are under their supervision. For a full discussion of the relationship between male coaches and adolescent male athletes, see Chapter Seven.

Is violence necessarily a part of sports participation? Does violence in sports carry over into violence in other aspects of life?

Another very significant issue in sports-related young adult literature is the portrayal of violence in sports. The ritualization of violent warlike behavior in sports and the use of sports as entertainment have an ancient history. A delicate balance exists between the rules of a sport, which are intended to control play, and the knowledge that violent behavior is a lucrative commodity that draws many spectators. Confrontational sports like wrestling and boxing are the most violent because the objective of those sports is the incapacitation of the opponent. In some sports, such as football and ice hockey, the objective seems to have become almost as much the incapacitation of an opponent as in the more traditionally violent sports.

Violence refers specifically to the physical component of aggression. Aggression consists of inflicting an adverse physical, verbal, or gestural stimulus upon another participant. In sports, aggression encompasses a wide array of behaviors displayed by players, coaches, and spectators. In most cases, aggression in sports is instrumental, that is, aimed at achieving a goal associated with the lawful conduct of the game. At other times, however, aggression may be hostile, in which case the athlete performs an act to willfully inflict pain upon another. The mixed message regarding violence in sports threatens to undermine the entire institution of sports and is often portrayed realistically in sports-related young adult literature. The skills employed in a sport often spill over into the non-sports social behaviors of the characters. The violent struggle two boys have with abusive fathers in Salisbury's "Shark Bait" (1995) and the after-hours fistfight Sonny has with a player who feels threatened when Sonny becomes the dominant player in Bennett's *The Squared Circle* (1995) are examples of the violence of sports becoming part of the athletes' lives beyond their sports. Surprisingly, sports-related young adult literature only marginally addresses the complex issues of instrumental versus hostile aggression in sports and the value of character development through fair play. Because we found little attention to this issue in the young adult books we read, we chose to elaborate the idea in our story; Ben's counseling session with Dr. Palmer addresses it.

Violence displayed by athletes is essentially a learned behavior. If violent behavior is rewarded when it is displayed, it is likely to increase in frequency. With regard to game rules, if the expected reward for violent play is greater than the punishment for the violation, the athlete is likely to be violent when the meaning placed on the game's outcome (winning at any cost) outweighs the value of fair play. Violence in sports may also increase when athletes become frustrated by losing, when they are not playing well, or when they perceive unfairness in the competition. Such violent acts do not appear to have a cathartic effect, as some suggest, but actually appear to lead to more violence (Chandler, Johnson, and Riggs, 1998).

The issue of whether athletes are more violent than nonathletes outside the sports setting is implied in the fiction portion of this chapter. Media portrayals of the violent acts of athletes, such as Mike Tyson's infamous biting of Evander Holyfield's ear during a 1997 heavyweight championship bout, heighten the expectation of violent behavior. Nevertheless, these instances represent rare behaviors of a small number of athletes. Some evidence does suggest, though, that athletes are more likely than nonathletes to resort to physical acts when faced with a confrontation. It is easy to assume, as we attempted to allow in our portrayal of Kim and Ben's picnic confrontation, that aggressive skills learned in sports may be applied to nonsports situations. In this regard, coaching that reinforces the value of fairness, appropriately punishes breaches of fair play, and teaches social skills that encourage altruism are critical to minimizing violence among athletes.

What immediate and lifetime fitness benefits can adolescents who are active in sports expect?

Participation in sports generally imparts physical fitness benefits. However, it must be stressed that participation in sports poses an inherent risk of injury that athletes, parents, and coaches must all acknowledge. Further, the developmental aspects of adolescence present specific risks. Every prudent effort should be made to condition the athlete to perform well and participate safely. The fitness benefits derived from well-structured sports participation can be considerable, depending on the existing fitness level of the adolescent when training begins. In general, novice participants are least conditioned and therefore have the greatest potential for improvement before they attain peak condition. Effective programs are structured to provide gradual, progressive increases in effort; the increases in effort are then met by subsequent improvements in fitness, as the body adjusts to the newly imposed demands. The body adjusts to the specific demands placed on it; training that requires strength results in strength development, and training that requires endurance results in improvements in endurance.

The intended goal of sports conditioning is to heighten performance in sports. It does not necessarily confer lifetime benefits or a high level of general well-being. Further, since the body responds to the demands placed on it, improvements achieved as a result of training will gradually recede toward pretraining levels if training efforts are stopped. Sports that offer lifelong fitness benefits are those that afford lifetime participation opportunities. Organized school and community-based programs that feature team sports for youth experience a rapid decline in participation as adolescents reach adulthood. Programs that emphasize physical conditioning for the sake of fitness, on the other hand, have broad age appeal and remain popular among active adults throughout their lives.

Sports-related young adult literature often features elements of high-level performance. One of the most profoundly invigorating feelings experienced by the human body occurs as a transient state in high-level physical performance. The feeling is referred to among sports psychologists as "flow". Flow is a point in performance, practice, or training when the physical, cognitive, and affective dimensions of a skill synchronize to provide the athlete with a sensation of infallibility. This state of flow generally results in a peak performance; it is a state that athletes strive to achieve. Kim experiences this endorphin-charged condition in her amazingly graceful training run through the cemetery with Ben in *Wrestling Sturbridge* (Wallace, 1996, 117–119). In their effort to convey this phenomenon to readers, authors at times portray characters who seem to defy reality. Eric's highly intense, protracted training runs hint at exaggeration in *Iceman* (Lynch, 1994). Describing his training run, Eric says, "I don't jog this, or cruise, I run. I run every step as if it's the last leg of the 4×100 meter relay. When I'm done, I'm always spent, legs like overdone pasta, my brain humming like an air conditioner. More than hockey, my run runs me down, nice. That's peace. That's what peace is" (16).

CONCLUSION

Coming of age through the vehicle of sports seems to be the prevailing theme of young adult writers of sports-related literature. Sports have long been viewed by society as capable of imparting positive values (citizenship, cooperation, teamwork, etc.) to participants, and they certainly are. However, two points must be emphasized. First, the transmission of positive values through sports is not automatic. The experiences of participants must be carefully planned and successfully orchestrated by responsible coaches, teachers, parents, or other significant persons for meaningful, appropriate socialization to occur. Second, sports are equally capable of transmitting inappropriate values, often due to the failure to plan experiences properly or because inappropriate values are stressed by those in a position to influence the adolescent. An overemphasis on competition, hostile aggression, and selfishness are examples of the results. Coaches, teachers, parents, and other adults who work with adolescents must ask themselves if they are more committed to helping children and adolescents become expert athletes or well-rounded human beings. They must honestly assess whether they will treat winning as the only worthy reward or whether they will help children and adolescents accept winning as an additional reward for participation in sports activity. Children and adolescents have different needs and respond to different kinds of encouragement. Young children usually participate in sports activities first because they want to have fun, and second because they enjoy developing skills. Adolescents may be more motivated to participate by a desire to foster relationships, gain recognition, and define themselves through sports activities. These age groups do, however, have one thing in common: When competition becomes more important than cooperation and when winning is the only goal that counts, sports activities lose their appeal. Children and adolescents walk away from sports at that point. Coaches, teachers, parents, and other adults who are willing to *teach* children and adolescents about sports must be willing to *learn* from the children and teens, as well.

RECOMMENDED READINGS

Fiction Works

Bennett, J. (1995). *The Squared Circle*. New York: Scholastic. 288 pp. (ISBN: 0–590–48671–3). High School (HS).

This novel is one that sophisticated high school readers are likely to enjoy. It describes Sonny Youngblood's freshman year as a college basketball star, one who has been heavily recruited to play for Southern Illinois University, a team that is in contention for the national championship. Bennett presents a troubling picture of athletics, in which love of the game counts for little but desire to win counts for everything. The press, coaches, and boosters, including Sonny's uncle, are portrayed as contributors to the unbalanced situation. Sonny's only escape from college basketball is the time he spends with his cousin, Sissy, an art professor; even his place in her life becomes questionable when she crawls into bed with him one night. Sonny cuts off part of his right hand, rendering himself unable to play at the college level any longer. Readers are left to wonder, with Sonny and Sissy, about whether or not the "accident" was actually intentional—Sonny's way of removing himself from the pressures of the sport.

Bloor, E. (1997). *Tangerine*. New York: HarperCollins. 304 pp. (ISBN: 0–152–01246–X). Middle School (MS).

Paul, a seventh-grader, is legally blind, but when he moves to a small and odd community in Tangerine County, Florida, he begins to see his world, including his wicked older brother, Erik, accurately. Paul makes a good group of friends and becomes a soccer star when he changes schools (his first school is almost completely swallowed by a sinkhole). Erik, who is a football star in a region that continues to celebrate football even when a local player is killed by a lightning strike, eventually becomes so violent that he self-destructs before Paul's eyes. Finally Paul realizes and forces his parents to admit that Erik is responsible for the fact that he has been legally blind since he was 5 years old.

Christopher, M. (1991). *The Basket Counts*. New York: Little, Brown. 84 pp. (ISBN: 0–316–14076–7). MS.

This short novel is included because it is one of fifty-three (to date) in an action-sports series written by Matt Christopher. Many young readers may learn that reading can be fun if they enter it through one of Christopher's quick, clean books. In this one, a new kid wants to become part of the school team; the only problem is that he is African American, and none of the other players are. After the other players accept him as a team member, they go on to win more games than any other team in their league.

Crutcher, C. (1995). *Ironman*. New York: Greenwillow. 181 pp. (ISBN: 0–688–13503–X). MS, HS.

Chris Crutcher is one of today's most popular writers for adolescents. In all six of his previous novels and one collection of short stories, he uses sports as a vehicle for examining the lives of adolescents who have to struggle with serious problems, like physical and emotional abuse, physical handicaps, and dysfunctional adults. And for each of the books, he has won an American Library Association Best Book for Young Readers award. *Ironman* follows well in Crutcher's tradition. In this novel, Bo Brewster has taken as much from an unreasonable, controlling father, and has gotten in as much trouble at school, as he can endure; he turns from team sports to training for the Ironman Triathlon. Bo vents his frustrations through training, and also by writing a series of letters to television talk-show host Larry King. He learns to defuse anger and frustration while growing closer to Shelly, whom he meets while attending a required anger management class at school. In the class, he is influenced by the strength of Mr. Nak. Bo finishes his story with the assurance that he will not lead a "desperate life" like his father's—and with the assurance that he and Shelly, who plans on becoming an American Gladiator, will be able to reach their dreams.

Gallo, D. (Ed.). (1995). *Ultimate Sports*. New York: Delacorte. 333 pp. (ISBN: 0–385–32152–X). MS, HS.

This collection of short stories is one of our favorite choices; we recommend it particularly for teen readers who are overwhelmed by the length of novels and for adults who would like a quick introduction to the fiction of some of today's best writers for young adults. Gallo is the editor of several fine collections of young adult short stories. In *Ultimate Sports*, he has gathered "Stealing for Girls" by Will Weaver, "Brownian Motion" by Virginia Euwer Wolff, "Cutthroat" by Norma Fox Mazer, "Fury" by T. Ernesto Bethancourt, and several other engaging stories by writers such as Thomas Dygard, Chris Crutcher, and Chris Lynch. Because of the variety of topics addressed by the authors and the differences in their artistic styles, almost every reader will find at least one story to sink into when reading this outstanding collection.

Klass, D. (1994). *California Blue*. New York: Scholastic. 199 pp. (ISBN: 0–590–46689–5). MS, HS.

This novel is much more than a sports story. It comments on the environment, unbalanced family relationships, the betrayal of friends, and the importance of trusting the strength of one's convictions. John is a runner who turns to the sport as an escape from the realities of his father's newly diagnosed leukemia and other complications in his life. He has found a rare breed of butterfly on the land owned by the local lumber company—a discovery that is likely to halt lumber operations and thus put the plant that supports his town out of business; during the discovery, he comes to feel betrayed by almost all of the adults in his life, except one teacher. Anyone who has poured energy into the performance of a sport in order to work through anger, fear, or frustration is likely to understand the role of sports in John's life. The book is reminiscent of Cynthia Voigt's popular, but slightly dated, *The Runner* (1985).

Korman, G. (1997). *Running Back Conversion: I Was Barry Sanders*. New York: Hyperion. 84 pp. (IBSN: 0–7868–1237–0). MS.

This is a book that we recommend for young athletes or sports fans who are unskilled or unmotivated readers. Like the others in the Monday Night Football Club series, the novel engages the young adolescent reader in the fantasy of a young fan who magically trades places with his football hero. (Other titles feature John Elway, Dan Marino, and Junior Seau.) Although the concept may seem silly to adults, Korman, a talented writer of other fiction for young people, does an excellent job of creating a funny, intriguing, wholesome story. In addition to the fiction, the book includes two statements written by Barry Sanders himself. In the opening statement, Sanders encourages children to read; in the second, he asks for support for the United Negro College Fund. The book also includes coupons for National Football League shirts, caps, and other souvenirs, as well as toll-free telephone numbers for ordering the merchandise.

Lynch, C. (1993). *Shadow Boxer*. New York: HarperTrophy. 215 pp. (ISBN: 0–06–447112–8). MS.

George, who is 14 years old, is the protector of his younger brother, Monty, and is his mother's helper. He is determined to prevent Monty from following in the footsteps of their father, who died five years ago after suffering for years with the physical residue of a lifetime of boxing. The problem is that Monty is exceptionally talented as a boxer, and he is urged on by his uncle Archie, who still owns a gym for boxers. George, with far more maturity than many teens, struggles with the realization that Monty must decide for himself to give up boxing. The final scene of the book is a poignant one in which Monty wins a fight with George, yet understands, in a moment, how much his brother has sacrificed in order to be the man of the family. Both are finally able to walk away from boxing.

Lynch, C. (1994). *Iceman*. New York: HarperCollins. 181 pp. (ISBN: 0–06–023340–0). MS.

Written by one of the most popular of today's young adult novelists, *Iceman* is the story of Eric, a high school ice hockey player. Eric plays hockey like an animal; during games, he pays no attention to opponents' safety or ways that he might assist his own teammates. His father encourages him to live up to his nicknames, "Animal" and "Iceman," and is proud of his fearless play. His brother, Duane, sees that Eric is fueled by frustration and confusion, rather than love of the sport. On the verge of quitting the game that has taken control of his personality, Eric finally learns that if he controls his play, his finesse will make him as successful as his violence. Eric is a complex character; he is, for example, inexplicably drawn to a funeral home and the secretive mortician; he will appeal particularly to middle school readers who are struggling to find their own places in the world.

Mazer, N. F. (1993). *Out of Control*. New York: Avon Flare. 218 pp. (ISBN: 0–380–71347–0). MS, HS.

Valerie, who is an unusually serious and artistic high school student living with her eccentric father, is the victim of sexual molestation in the hallway at her school. The attackers are three friends: Rollo, the narrator, whose nickname is "Mr. Stomp" because of the way he plays football; Candy, who is the president of the student senate; and Brig, who is "Mr. Star Pitcher" and the president of the Honor Society. The boys convince themselves that they have done nothing wrong and that Valerie deserves to be harassed because she does not go along with their games. Valerie is terrorized by them and by the actions of the school principal, who tries to cover up the situation rather than punish the boys with more than a suspension. Finally, Valerie finds that she is not the only victim of their cruel games and harassment. As Valerie regains some sense of power, Rollo begins to feel guilt; he follows Valerie around and tries to befriend her. She does not reciprocate. Finally, Rollo realizes that he must separate himself from Candy and Brig and begin to make decisions for himself.

Powell, R. (1995). *Dean Duffy*. New York: Farrar, Straus & Giroux. 170 pp. (ISBN: 0–374–31754–2). MS, HS.

Although he has just graduated from high school, Dean is washed up as a baseball pitcher. He has little direction for his future, but is offered a second chance to play college baseball by a friend of his coach and mentor, Jack Trant. The offer includes a limited scholarship to an elite private college; the scholarship will be renewed if Dean performs well as a baseball player. Jack wants Dean to give himself another chance, because Jack had become used to living vicariously through Dean's successes. Dean, however, does not know whether or not he is willing to dedicate his life, again, to the dream of baseball stardom. He confronts questions about his own past and meets others his age, including an unwed teen mother and a drug-abusing former classmate, who teach him to consider the consequences of his actions carefully. The novel ends with delicious and aggravating ambiguity: The reader is not told what Dean decides to do about the scholarship offer.

Snyder, Z. K. (1994). *Cat Running*. New York: Bantam Books. 168 pp. (ISBN: 0–440–41152–1). MS.

Set in California during the Great Depression, when the Dust Bowl had driven farm families to California in search of land to work, this is a novel in which sixth grader Cat Kinsey comes face-to-face with her own prejudices and eventually transcends them. She is a talented runner but chooses not to participate in the school's field-day races because her father refuses to let her wear pants instead of her dress. To her surprise, the race is won by a barefoot new boy, an "Okie." Through an interesting turn of events, Cat befriends the boy's little sister. Finally, she and the boy have to use their running skill to find a doctor and save the little girl's life. This is an ideal book to use in an interdisciplinary unit on the Dust Bowl or in a unit that focuses on accepting people regardless of their circumstances. Middle school readers might be intrigued by the idea of a young female athlete from a past era.

Wallace, B. (1993). *Never Say Quit*. New York: Pocket Books. 184 pp. (ISBN: 0–671–88264–3). MS.

Young adolescents will enjoy this amusing story of an unusual group of sixth graders, the Misfits, who form a soccer team. In gathering enough people to field a team, the Misfits themselves start discriminating against some who want to join, unconsciously using money, looks, and intelligence as criteria. Once they realize that the spirit to play is the only real criterion for team membership, they have the challenge of finding a coach. They finally have to settle for their former elementary school principal, a man who turned to alcohol when his wife left him and who needs a reason to enjoy living again. The team never becomes a soccer powerhouse, but they do improve. More important, they learn what it takes to work together by following the coach's rules, which require them to study together, to spend the night at each other's houses, and to learn all they can about their teammates' families. Wallace, a former elementary school principal and physical education teacher, clearly understands young adolescents.

Wallace, R. (1996). *Wrestling Sturbridge*. New York: Alfred A. Knopf. 133 pp. (ISBN: 0–679–87803–3). MS, HS.

This novel is the story of how Ben, the second best 135-pound wrestler in the state of Pennsylvania, begins to examine his life to discover what is important to him. In an environment in which winning wrestlers are local heroes for their lifetimes and in which high school graduates typically become workers in the cinder block factory, Ben realizes that there should be more to life than what he finds in Sturbridge. He struggles to find the support and direction he needs at the same time that he works to prove his talent and determination as a wrestler.

Nonfiction Works

How-To Books

Fox, A. (1992). *Kayaking*. Minneapolis, MN: Lerner. 48 pp. (ISBN: 0–8225–2482–1). MS, HS.

Written for young adolescents, this book is a solid introduction to the sport of kayaking. Fox gives attention to the benefits of learning with a group, proper clothing and equipment, safety tips and warnings, and trip-planning hints. He speaks directly to children and young teens who are interested in learning not only what kayaking is, but how to have fun doing it. Color photos and boxes of special information about contests, stars, hazards to avoid, and so on add interest.

O'Shea, F. (1989). *Advanced Windsurfing*. Harrisburg, PA: Stackpole Books. 127 pp. (ISBN: 0–8117–2303–8). MS, HS.

The author, who is a professional windsurfer, sports consultant, and journalist, presents readers with a brief history of windsurfing, with a focus on stars, competitions, and evolving equipment. In the remainder of the book, he describes proper equipment; methods for getting started; how to pay attention to dangers of weather, tides, currents, and other surfers; how to perform tricks; and different kinds of competition. The book includes a glossary of terms associated with the sport that avoids trendy jargon and seems up-to-date. Color photographs and diagrams enhance written descriptions of maneuvers. The tone is straightforward; adolescents who are seriously interested in the sport will appreciate the safety tips and the no-nonsense style in which the information is presented.

Sprague, K., and C. Sprague. (1991). *Weight and Strength Training for Kids and Teenagers*. Los Angeles: Jeremy P. Tarcher. 142 pp. (ISBN: 0–87477–643–0). MS, HS.

This book is coauthored by Ken Sprague, founder of the original Gold's Gym, and his 11-year-old son, Chris. The former presents information that addresses parents' concerns about weight training for young people in a responsible way. His advice is based on research that he felt compelled to do when he worried that his own son could injure himself by lifting too much, too soon. Every few pages, there is an insert from

Chris, in which he speaks directly to adolescent readers with encouragement and training tips. Photographs and diagrams enhance discussions of ways to begin weight training, proper equipment, the use of spotters, differences between males and females in terms of exercises and expected body changes, and other topics.

Stone, J., and R. Meyer. (Eds.). (1995). *Aikido in America*. Berkeley, CA: Frog, Ltd. 330 pp. (ISBN: 1–883319–27–7). MS, HS.

This book is a history of the growth in America of the martial art aikido, which originated in Japan. It is told in conversational style from the perspectives of fourteen American aikido artists: four who studied in Japan and one who studied with founder Ueshiba (grouped under the heading "The Disciples"); three who are master teachers (grouped under the heading "The Teachers"); and six who are among the first generation of American-trained aikidoists (grouped under the heading "The Innovators"). Their stories are told in their own voices—one is a former police officer whose language is sprinkled with four-letter words, and another is the director of a female sports program at a federal women's prison who describes her path to self-understanding through aikido. Regardless of their individual voices, the contributors' goals are consistent; each explains how he or she strives to "make aikido an American art, and interpret the message of aikido in a way that makes sense to Americans without distorting or watering-down" its spiritual dimensions (14).

Autobiographies and Biographies

Boga, S. (1992). *Cyclists: How the World's Most Daring Riders Train and Compete*. Harrisburg, PA: Stackpole Books. 225 pp. (ISBN: 0–8117–2413–1). HS.

The first and largest section of this book is the result of the author's interviews with eight prominent cyclists. It includes, for example, a chapter titled "Eric Heiden: Rebel with a Cause," about the five-time Olympic gold medalist in speed skating who used cycling for cross-training, then became a professional cyclist in order to put himself through medical school, and a chapter titled "Martha Kennedy: Iditabiker," about a former winner of the women's expert class at the National Off-Road Bicycling Association nationals who recalls a 210-mile race over the ice and snow of Alaska. All of the profile chapters are intriguing in different ways; all provide rich insights into cycling that could only come from those who have devoted large parts of their lives to their versions of the sport. Adolescents who are interested in mountain biking, road cycling, triathlons, and other competitions that involve bicycles will enjoy the athletes' profiles and the last section of this book, which is a handbook of resources about training, injuries and recovery, nutrition, and safety. The book concludes with a brief illustrated history of bicycles and a glossary of terms associated with cycling.

Coffey, W., and F. Bondy. (1994). *Dreams of Gold: The Nancy Kerrigan Story*. New York: St. Martin's Press. 180 pp. (ISBN: 0–312–95399–2). MS, HS.

This is the account of Nancy Kerrigan's rise to top levels of figure skating, despite obstacles such as her mother's gradual blindness and the incident that shocked the sports world: the physical attack on Kerrigan that was arranged by her archcompetitor, Tonya Harding, and that occurred before the national championship held just six weeks before the 1994 winter Olympics. Those who have followed figure skating will recognize the names of competitors mentioned in this book and will enjoy following Kerrigan's progress from the Eastern Junior Championship in 1985 to the silver medal in the 1994 Olympic Games. The book is clearly written by fans of Kerrigan; no mention is made of her failure to fulfill the public's expectations that she would become an "American sweetheart" after her second-place finish in the Olympics. The only apology for her behavior following her rise to fame is that she is a shy young woman who wants to be left alone. The last third of the book is devoted to a glossary of figure skating terms, a viewer's guide, and lists of national and international championships and champions.

Lewin, T. (1993). *I Was a Teenage Professional Wrestler*. New York: Orchard Books. 128 pp. (ISBN: 0–531–08627–5). MS, HS.

Professional wrestling currently has a following among young people, many of whom are entertained by the campy and dramatic antics of the wrestlers. Professional wrestling fans, especially those who are middle school–aged, will enjoy this easy-to-read book of narrative, photographs, sketches, and paintings. The author, a wrestler when he was a teen in the 1950s, is also the artist. With his insider's perspective, Lewin is able to provide readers with hints of the ways that professional wrestlers think and live. A short glossary of wrestling lingo and wrestling holds is provided for those who are new to the sport.

Macy, S. (1996). *Winning Ways: A Photobiography of American Women in Sports.* New York: Henry Holt. 217 pp. (ISBN: 0–8050–4147–8). MS, HS.

Described as a "scrapbook filled with anecdotes and photographs, news reports and commentaries" (14), this book is a delight for those who are interested in the progress of American women as athletes—and American sports in general. Macy acknowledges that her interest in women as athletes was fueled by an interview, more than twenty years ago, with legendary tennis star Althea Gibson. Macy uses photographs and narrative to present decades of development, from the late 1800s—when Francis Willard wrote a book encouraging women to ride bicycles despite men's predictions that exercise would cause them to grow small tumors on their ankles—almost to the present. The book closes with a time line of events that are important for women athletes, including mention of women's ice hockey as an Olympic sport for the first time during the 1998 Olympic Games in Nagano, Japan.

Expositions on Athletes and Sports in Contemporary America

Ashe, A. R., Jr. (1988). *A Hard Road to Glory: The African-American Athlete in Basketball.* New York: Amistad. 257 pp. (ISBN: 1–56743–037–6). MS, HS, Adult (A).

This book is the work of the late Arthur Ashe, best known as a Wimbledon champion and civil rights advocate. It includes information from Ashe's three-volume series *A Hard Road to Glory*, in which he covers the emergence of sports in ancient Egypt, highlights contributions of African Americans in the nineteenth century, examines African American athletes between the world wars, deals with the impact of integration on major sports, and chronicles the contributions of African American athletes from World War II to the end of the 1980s. This book provides fifty-one pages of carefully researched narrative devoted to the history of the place of African Americans—as players and coaches—in college and professional basketball. Basketball enthusiasts will also be interested in the charts that fill pages 55–257; included are NBA records, statistics for Hall of Fame players such as Bill Russell and Walt Frazier, and all-Americans from universities and colleges across the nation.

Berger, G. (1990). *Violence and Sports*. New York: Franklin Watts. 128 pp. (ISBN: 0–531–10907–0). MS, HS.

Written for young adolescents, this book explores the serious and growing phenomenon of violence among athletes and sports fans. Berger defines the problem in a way that differentiates between physical actions that are part of a game and those that are incidental to a sport. He then presents information about the growing incidents of sports violence. Next, Berger turns attention to several popular sports, discusses the history of each sport, and looks at particular aspects of those sports that often lead toward violence. The sports covered are: auto racing, baseball, basketball, boxing/wrestling, football, ice hockey, motorcycle/horse racing, and soccer/rugby. The following are examples of the focal points of the individual chapters: in the chapter on baseball, the high incidence of drinking alcohol at games is cited among the aspects that tend to breed violence among fans; in the chapter on basketball, the foul shot is treated with special attention to the association with violent actions of players. This is a sobering book; it ends without any solutions for reducing violence committed and suffered by athletes and fans.

Blais, M. (1995). *In These Girls, Hope Is a Muscle*. New York: Atlantic Monthly. 263 pp. (ISBN: 0–87113–572–8). MS, HS, A.

Blais focuses on one season in which a female high school basketball team reaches toward the championship. The book reveals truths about what it takes to coach girls, beginning with building their confidence, and what it takes to fight the stereotypes and media images of women and athletics that continue to influence expectations related to females who are athletes. This is a book that moves far beyond attention to the sport of basketball itself; it demonstrates how athletics are a part of the culture of entire communities and gives adolescent and adult readers an inside view of a world that they might otherwise get only through actual participation in the sport. This is a book we recommend to all adults who work with adolescents, and particularly to those who work with female athletes.

Brooks, B. (1993). *Boys Will Be*. New York: Henry Holt. 132 pp. (ISBN: 0–8050–2420–4). MS, HS.

Middle school readers will be drawn to funny essays in this collection, like the ones that address whether girls or boys are better ("Chitchat,"

9–16) and the smell of sweat ("Stink," 56–61). However, the best essays in this book are the more serious ones. In "Victory" (102–114), Brooks explains why he believes Bobby Knight is "the best person I've seen at handling victory and values in a college basketball coach" (111) after Knight let the freshmen on his varsity team play an entire game so that they could gain valuable game experience, despite the fact that they were being beaten. Knight defends his decision by saying, "Sometimes . . . having to win is a nuisance. Winning can really get in the way" (114). In "Arthur Ashe" (115–123), written immediately after Ashe's death at age 49, Brooks gives a stirring tribute to the tennis great, praising his honesty, intelligence, and integrity on and off the tennis court. He contrasts the sophisticated, manly Ashe with the "boyish" Magic Johnson, who, like Ashe, has the AIDS virus, and concludes by imploring readers to remember the "complicated heroes" like Ashe. Brooks is the author of the Newberry Honor Medal–winning book *The Moves Make the Man* (1984, HarperKeypoint), a longtime favorite among teen readers, especially those who are drawn to it by its basketball motif.

Guttmann, A. (1988). *A Whole New Ball Game: An Interpretation of American Sports.* Chapel Hill: University of North Carolina Press. 233 pp. (ISBN: 0–8078–1786–4). HS, A.

This collection of essays is appropriate for sophisticated adolescent readers and adult readers. Guttmann, a professor of English and American studies, states that the book is "an interpretation, a selective history of American sports which seeks to set sports within a larger social framework and, simultaneously, to use sports for what they reveal about the larger culture" (1). Guttmann's topics range from "The South's Contributions to Modern Sports" in chapter 4 and "Playgrounds as Social Control?" in chapter 7 to "Residual Racism" in chapter 9 and "The Cocaine Culture" in chapter 11. At times, the tone of the book is loftier than that of many sports books written for young adults, but Guttman's work will hold the attention of those who are serious about understanding sports as a part of American life.

Paulsen, G. (1994). *Father Water, Mother Woods: Essays on Fishing and Hunting in the North Woods.* New York: Delacorte. 157 pp. (ISBN: 0–385–32053–1). MS, HS.

Written by one of the most popular, prolific, talented, and adventurous young adult literature writers of our time, this collection is obviously a labor of love. In each of the carefully crafted essays, Paulsen introduces readers to special, often hidden, nuances of living as true sportsman, as a part of nature. Equally adept at explaining what poor boys know about catfish and describing details of the dying of summer, Paulsen is a master storyteller who grabs his reader's attention and will not let go. Illustrations of streams, fish, deer, and other natural elements, drawn by Ruth Paulsen, further increase the appeal of the book.

Ryan, J. (1995). *Little Girls in Pretty Boxes: The Making and Breaking of Elite Gymnasts and Figure Skaters*. New York: Warner Books. 244 pp. (ISBN: 0–385–47790–2). MS, HS, A.

This powerful book should change the ways readers watch gymnastics and figure skating championships. The chapters focus on aspects of the sports that are often hidden from the public: injuries (and how the females are encouraged to ignore them); eating disorders (common among these elite athletes); image (how coaches teach athletes to trick nature so the athletes can remain as thin as children); parents (as athletic "junkies"); politics and money (those with the "right" image are paid by high rankings, and television adds high stakes); and coaches (with particularly pointed comments about Bela Karolyi's "worship of winning" [192]). This book is one that all coaches and parents of promising female athletes should read. It reminds readers that even females who are gifted in sports are human beings; adults must be aware that many times they are responsible for young girls' sacrifice of their bodies and self-esteem to the sports that, at some point, they excelled in and loved.

REFERENCES

Anshel, M. (1997). *Sport Psychology: From Theory to Practice*. 3rd ed. Scottsdale. AZ: Gorsuch Scarisbrick.

Bennett, J. (1995). *The Square Circle*. New York: Scholastic.

Chandler, S., D. Johnson and C. Riggs. (1998). "Athletic Participation as an Indicator of Domestic Violence." *Medicine and Science in Sports and Exercise* 30 (5): 699.

Crutcher, C. (1995). *Ironman*. New York: Greenwillow.

Klass, D. (1994). *California Blue*. New York: Scholastic.

Kohn, A. (1992). *No Contest: The Case against Competition*. Rev. ed. New York: Houghton Mifflin.

Lynch, C. (1993). *Shadow Boxer*. New York: HarperTrophy.

Lynch, C. (1994). *Iceman*. New York: HarperCollins.

Martens, R., and V. Seefeldt. (Eds.). (1979). ''Bill of Rights for Young Athletes.'' *Guide for Childern's Sports*. Washington, DC: American Alliance for Health, Physical Education, Recreation and Dance.

Mazer, Norma Fox. (1993). *Out of Control*. New York: Avon Flare.

Mazer, Norma Fox. (1995). "Cutthroat." In Don Gallo (Ed.), *Ultimate Sports*. New York: Delacorte, 148–159.

Murphy, S. (Ed.). (1995). *Sport Psychology Interventions*. Champaign, IL: Human Kinetics Publishers.

Naughton, Jim. (1995). "Joyriding." In Don Gallo (Ed.), *Ultimate Sports*. New York: Delacorte, 4–18.

Orlick, T. (1990). *In Pursuit of Excellence: How to Win in Sport and Life through Mental Training*. Champaign, IL: Human Kinetics Publishers.

Powell, R. (1995). *Dean Duffy*. New York: Farrar, Straus & Giroux.

Salisbury, Graham. (1995). "Shark Bait." In Don Gallo (Ed.), *Ultimate Sports*. New York: Delacorte, 118–143.

Snyder. Z. K. (1994). *Cat Running*. New York: Bantam.

Voigt, Cynthia. (1985). *The Runner*. New York: Simon & Schuster.

Wallace, B. (1993). *Never Say Quit*. New York: Pocket Books.

Wallace, R. (1996). *Wrestling Sturbridge*. New York: Alfred A. Knopf.

Weaver, Will. (1995). "Stealing for Girls." In Don Gallo (Ed.), *Ultimate Sports*. New York: Delacorte, 95–115.

Wolff, Virginia Euwer. (1995). "Brownian Motion." In Don Gallo (Ed.), *Ultimate Sports*. New York: Delacorte, 207–235.

CHAPTER SIX

Music and Musicians' Effects on Adolescents

Lawrence Baines, Elizabeth Strehle, and Steven Bell with Josh Murfree

No legacy and recurrence of inhumanity cancels out the *mysterium tremendum*, the benediction of music. It is in music and the indecipherable self-evidence of its effects on our consciousness that reside the lineaments of our possible humaneness. It is music which carries with it the "background noise and radiation" (as cosmology would have it) of creation itself.

(Steiner, 1990, 221)

MUSIC AND MOOD IN THE LIVES OF TWO 11-YEAR-OLD BOYS

It is 7:30 A.M. Saturday morning, and Stephen and Mikie, both age 11, are slowly getting dressed. Friday evening was spent cruising the mall, eating subs, and watching videos until 1 A.M. But this morning is football practice. In the car, Stephen reaches from the backseat to the front seat to turn off the radio station and put on a tape by Sublime. The lyrics express the speaker's problem, and Stephen sings along: "I'm too drunk to light the bong, / I'm too stoned to write this song." Mikie joins in on the chorus, "Got my greatest hits." Stephen shakes his fist and says, "I need to get pumped up!"

Throughout the journey in the car, the tape rocks with themes of anarchy, rioting, and drug use. As the car moves past a wreath, placed beside the road in memory of a 16-year-old who lost her life in a car wreck last fall, Stephen leans from the backseat into the front seat to turn the volume of the tape down. He peers through the window at the white cross and wreath of pink and red plastic flowers. After they pass the site, the volume goes up again. Once they arrive at the practice fields, both boys are all business, as they spend a few sweaty, dirty hours at football practice with their respective teams.

After practice, they visit a sporting goods store. Mikie and Stephen drink big bottles of blue Powerade as they peruse the aisles looking for a small pad insert for a football helmet. Then, Mikie accidentally spills some of his Powerade onto the floor. Mikie and Stephen quickly find paper towels to wipe up the sticky blue liquid sitting in a puddle.

Stephen knows what kind of music he likes but is not sure exactly why he likes the kind of music he does. His favorite bands, right now, are the Dave Matthew's Band, Korn, Sublime, Wu-Tang Clan, White Zombie, the Presidents of the United States of America, Rage against the Machine, and Beck. About his tastes in music, Stephen says, "This is my music and I like it." He listens to music late at night just before going to sleep, when riding in the car, or working around the house. The kind of music he feels like hearing depends upon the time of day and his mood at the time.

MUSIC AND COOL IN THE LIFE OF A 16-YEAR-OLD MALE

Brian, a 16-year-old, likes rock 'n' roll and says that he uses music to "get the adrenaline going." He also claims that listening to music helps him concentrate when he is working. Brian sees the music he listens to as part of who he is. In his journal, he writes about these musicians: Shannon Hoon, the former lead singer of the band Blind Melon, who died of a drug overdose in 1995; George Harrison, formerly one of the Beatles; and Tori Amos, a contemporary female singer:

Shannon Hoon sings with more emotion than most pop rock singers. Every day his death seems more tragic and sad. Tori Amos is the big hit for today. I listened to her album twice and she has a voice of an angel, but [her] words are dark and painful. She was raped as a teenager, and she is involved in a lot of rape prevention programs that reflect her music. It puts you in a depressed mood. I'm now playing one of my dad's CDs. It [*All Things Must Pass*] is interesting, not something I could listen to with friends because they wouldn't get it at all. It's relaxing and cool at the same time. It is amazing how music that was different in its own time

[can] make someone like me groove out to it. It shows what a great composer George Harrison was. This also helps me go into the past and climb inside my dad's head and feel something he felt twenty years ago. It can bring two souls together across age gap or even death. What an amazing thing music is.

When queried about the music of Tori Amos, Brian fidgets a bit and says that he probably wouldn't play her music around his male friends because "they wouldn't get it." But Brian advises that the CD might be brought out on a date. "When most girls see that you have the Tori Amos CD, they think it is cool—a big macho guy with a 'girlie' CD like that."

MUSIC AND ADOLESCENT BEHAVIOR: BAINES' PERSPECTIVE

I attended high school during the mid-1970s. At that time, in my school, cliques were built around musical tastes as much as anything. There were the head bangers (heavy metal, rock 'n' roll, and pre-punk), the disco dancers, and the kickers (country and western aficionados). Head bangers wore jeans and ratty shirts, wore their hair long (both male and female), and simply "hung out." Disco dancers usually dressed well in polyester, wore jewelry, and "went out on dates." Kickers had short hair and big belt buckles, wore cowboy boots, and enjoyed chewing tobacco.

When I go into high schools now, I witness the continuing evolution of musical cliques. Many of the heavy metal folks have gotten into tattoos and body piercing. Some of the disco crowd has gone over to black lipstick and "gothic" apparel. And, of course, the rap look has become almost ubiquitous—boxer shorts visible above the belt, oversized jeans barely hanging on the hips, sunglasses, and backward baseball caps. It is not surprising, then, that researchers have identified a strong connection between an adolescent's musical tastes and: (1) acceptance from peers (Adoni, 1978; Larson and Kubey, 1983); (2) the selection of prospective dates (Zillmann and Bhatia, 1989); and (3) feelings of sexual adequacy (Greenberg, Brown, and Buerkel-Rothfuss, 1993). According to Gaines (1991), among teenagers, "subcultural affiliations are expressed through clothing and music, coded in signs" (92). Indeed, the connection between personal identity and musical tastes has been established for quite some time (Arnett, 1991; Bennett and Ferrell, 1987; Berry, 1990; Rouner, 1990; Snow, 1987).

Csikszentmihalyi (1996) has written that "One song heard on the radio ... can have a more profound effect on a child's future than a thousand hours spent in school" (108), and I think that he is right. I can remember poring over the lyrics to Jimi Hendrix's "If Six Were Nine" for hours at a time as an adolescent in the hopes of capturing some insight into how I should live my life. Recently, a 50-year-old friend confessed that his conception of the "ideal woman" has always been derived from the lyrics to the Beach Boys' "Surfer Girl."

Jerry Deluna, a hulking eighth-grade football player in my fifth-period language arts class used to wear a flannel shirt over a T-shirt every single day to class. His usual routine would be to walk into class with a boisterous "Hey, d-u-u-u-de" acknowledgment to me, slump back in the desk, then begin beating the desk with his fingers as if he were drumming the rhythm to some hypnotic chant. I can remember days, many days, when nothing would come out of Jerry's mouth except the lyrics from Ice-T's "Cop Killer." Over and over, he sang while drumming wildly with his fingers and bobbing his head up and down like a Pogo stick.

Popular rock and rap songs have supposedly been the inspiration for a variety of heinous crimes, and musicians have often been reprimanded for espousing a "sworn to fun, loyal to none" approach to life. The Beatles' "Helter Skelter" was cited by Charles Manson himself as the inspiration for the Manson family's brutal Tate/LaBianca murders. Another Beatles' song, which was later also recorded by Elton John, "Lucy in the Sky with Diamonds," was said to advocate experimentation with LSD. More recently, the Hillside serial killer in California was said to have been "inspired" by "Night Prowler" by AC/DC, which has lines that ask questions to provoke paranoia.

It usually takes a controversy over something such as Ice-T's "Cop Killer," the Hillside killer, or the case of the double suicide attempt attributed to the lyrics of a Judas Priest song to draw attention to the interactions between adolescents and music. While the reception of rap groups such as 2 Live Crew, who have written such songs as "Hey, We Want Some Pussy" and "Booty and Cock," and NWA (Niggas with Attitude), who have written about gang bangs and drive-by shootings, has been hostile in the courts, their albums continue to sell quite well.

In 1995, over twelve billion dollars was spent on music, with teenagers (age 15 to 19) making up the largest group of purchasers. In terms of genre, rock represented 33.5 percent of purchases, while 18 percent of purchases were for urban contemporary or rap albums (Wright, 1997). In *Rockonomics: The Money behind the Music*, Eliot (1989) presents further evidence of the vast commercial enterprise that rock music has become. In reaction to the proliferation of violent and sexual content of contemporary music, organizations such as the Parents' Music Resource Center have been formed to question the wisdom of allowing adolescents unmonitored access to music. Watching only a few minutes of MTV or VH-1 should convince even those skeptical of media influences that lifestyles are being advocated in contemporary heavy metal and rap songs that do not jibe with traditional values. In terms of promiscuity and amorality, there is no question that the goal of MTV is not to educate, but to titillate (Sherman and Dominick, 1986).

According to recent statistics, most adolescents spend five minutes a day or less around adult role models outside of school (Csikszentmihalyi, 1996). Indeed, many adolescents may choose celebrities of the media, such as rock or rap musicians, as role models, simply because they are not exposed to much else.

MUSIC AND YOUNG ADULT LITERATURE

From Procol Harem's "Whiter Shade of Pale," a song loosely based upon a section of *The Canterbury Tales*, to Tchaikovsky's (or Gounod's or Berlioz's or Prokofiev's or Dire Strait's) *Romeo and Juliet*, writers of music have often been inspired by literary works. Conversely, many writers, especially screenwriters, have attempted to utilize music in their writing. For example, in the film version of Anthony Burgess's *A Clockwork Orange*, filmmaker Stanley Kubrick manages to link Beethoven's *Ninth Symphony* to the glorification of violence and rape. The music of the 1960s is integral to the film *Apocalypse Now*, directed by Francis Coppola, which in turn is based upon Conrad's *Heart of Darkness*. In young adult literature, M. E. Kerr frequently uses references to music and contemporary lyrics to help describe a major character's personality and to connect with young readers. Upon their release, each of the novels in the John Fell series—*Fell* (1989), *Fell Back* (1989), and *Fell Down* (1991)—were hot properties with eighth graders of both sexes in my classroom. Repeatedly, my students made remarks about Kerr's frequent mention of popular music. Typical of students' reaction was that of Lydia, a relatively mature eighth grader: "I can't believe that John Fell listens to Phil Collins—that is so cool."

WEETZIE BAT MEETS *COBAIN*

Francesca Lia Block's Weetzie Bat series of books combines sex, fantasy, and scenes of urban life with the adventures of adolescents in the world of rock 'n' roll. A summary of the plot lines of books in this series should help give the reader an idea of their content:

Weetzie Bat (1989). Weetzie's mother and father have some difficulties and get divorced. After the divorce, her father eventually dies of a drug overdose, while her heavy-drinking mother seems bored with her life. Weetzie, a teenager, has a series of unfulfilling sexual adventures with some heavily tattooed, heavily pierced musicians in punk rock bands. Eventually, she has some good sex with a stranger named Secret Agent Lover Man. Secret Agent Lover Man doesn't want children, so Weetzie, who has decided that she wants children, has three-way sex with two gay friends, one of whom may be infected with the AIDS virus. Meanwhile, Secret Agent Lover Man has sex with a Satan-worshiping witch named Vixanne, which results in the birth of another child. Before she leaves town, Vixanne drops off the baby on Weetzie's doorstep. Weetzie names the child Witch Baby.

Witch Baby (1992). The two gay lovers, Dirk and Duck, are still around for this sequel, as Weetzie Bat's adopted daughter, Witch Baby, becomes jealous of Cherokee, Weetzie's blood daughter. After an affair with illegal alien Angel Juan, who is eventually deported to Mexico, Witch Baby seeks out and eventually finds her Satan-worshiping witch mother but chooses not to stay with her. Witch Baby turns out to be a drummer in a rock band and a photographer whose photographs are so powerful and disturbing that they move even the most hardened souls.

Cherokee Bat and the Goat Guys (1992). Cherokee sings and dances, Witch Baby is on drums, Angel Juan plays bass, and Raphael Jah-Love (who is the offspring of a Rastafarian man and a tiny Chinese woman mentioned in *Weetzie Bat*) plays guitar. With parents off shooting movies in South America, these four become a rock band sensation. Having been left in the care of the ubiquitous wise Native American friend, Coyote, the four have lots of sex, do lots of drugs, and then find out most of what happened was only part of Coyote's dream.

Missing Angel Juan (1993). Witch Baby's love, Angel Juan, moves to New York City, and Witch Baby follows after him. Witch Baby meets up with Weetzie Bat's father, Charlie, and they get to check out much of the city, including a time-travel trip to the city of Brooklyn when Charlie was a child. Of course, they also get to meet pimps, drag queens, and various inanimate objects (such as statues) that apparently come to life with some regularity.

Baby Be-Bop (1995). This sequel focuses primarily on Dirk, who becomes comfortable with being a homosexual after a series of visitations from his dead dad and great-grandmother.

One of the most striking aspects of Block's work is the high regard for musicians and the centrality of music in her depictions of adolescent life. When Weetzie encounters a punk rocker named Buzz, who introduces himself to her by roughly grabbing her wrists, then ordering her to go home with him to drink beer, she's enamored with his good looks. She spends the night with him after getting drunk and puts up with his abuse.

In Block's books, sex and drugs are as much a part of rock 'n' roll as black leather and beer. Yet, the rock 'n' roll life depicted in the fiction of Block is worlds away from the real-life story of rock star and suicide victim Kurt Cobain, as rendered by British writer Christopher Sandford in his 1995 biography *Cobain*. In the following paragraphs, I will contrast Block's fictional depiction of certain phenomena of rock 'n' roll life (described under the letter *a*) with the realities as set forth in *Cobain* (described under the letter *b*).

1. Drugs

a. While Weetzie's father takes her out to eat, he tries to buy drugs (*Weetzie Bat*, 71).

On this occasion, Weetzie and her father go to Harlem for breakfast. Charlie is approached by a man in a black hat; the man touches Charlie's shoulder and mumbles to him, calling him "Doctor Man." Charlie walks away, coughing and pale.

b. Kurt Cobain continues to have problems with drugs (169).

Toward the end of 1991, Cobain demanded that his girlfriend give him injections twice a day. This routine created "a cycle of romantic interludes and violent scenes." One time, Cobain kicked down an apartment door, yelling, "Smack—now" to the frightened woman who lived in the apartment. His drug use caused many kinds of problems. He was literally ejected from one house "for illustrating his locally popular nickname of 'Hurler' by throwing up into his dinner," and his drug dealer had to give him mouth-to-mouth resuscitation when Cobain collapsed and turned blue in the middle of a transaction.

2. Sexuality

a. Weetzie decides that she wants to have a baby and talks about having three-way sex with her two gay friends—Dirk and Duck (*Weetzie Bat*, 44).

"Yeah," Duck says. "I saw it on that talk show once. These two gay guys and their best friend all slept together so no one would know for sure whose baby it was. . . . and when someone in the audience said, 'what sexual preference do you hope she has?' they all go together, they go, 'Happiness.' Isn't that cool?"

b. Kurt Cobain tries to have sex with two girls at once—the girls are twin sisters (182).

"After days of haggling, Cobain persuaded two local twins to join him in bed. . . . In the imbroglio that followed, a window was smashed and the entire complex's fire alarm set off." The scene ended when one of the girls ran down the stairs, screaming that Cobain had hit her. She was followed by her twin sister, who had taken Cobain's camera as she fled.

3. Death by drug overdose

a. Weetzie's father, Charlie Bat, dies of a drug overdose (*Weetzie Bat*, 74).

"Charlie was dreaming of a city where everyone was always young and lit up like a movie. . . . He had taken some pills, and this time he didn't wake up from his dream."

b. Kurt Cobain commits suicide (328–329).

"Cobain barricaded himself in by locking one French door and propping a stool against the other. He completed a one-page note addressed to 'Boddah,' his invisible childhood friend, smoked a half-dozen cigarettes and drank from a can of root beer. Reaching into a cigar box containing syringes, burnt spoons and cotton he injected 1.52 milligrams of heroin, three times the normal fatal dose, into the crook of his right arm. Then Cobain drew a chair up to the window, threw his disguising hunter's cap and sunglasses on the floor, laid down two towels and a brown corduroy jacket, and opened his wallet to show his driver's license. . . . [Nothing] stopped him raising the barrel of the shotgun to his mouth and, by using his free thumb, pulling the trigger."

The characters in Block's fantasies remain free from worry about disease, addiction, peer approval, or—amazingly—the source of the next dollar. Indeed, throughout Block's books is the idea that everyone will somehow attain their goals through serendipity, that everyone will be accepted by their peers, that everyone will eventually be happy. Even Weetzie's father, who dies of a drug overdose, manages to resurface in a sequel. Often, when confronted by seemingly insurmountable troubles, Block's characters will pile into an old convertible and cruise the highways and side roads of urban Los Angeles. The only mention of money is in the background—the news that somebody, somewhere is making gobs of cash making low-budget films with the implicit assumption being that the filmmakers are quietly and faithfully sprinkling profits into the bank account of Block's unemployed characters. Block's characters never need money, never go to the bathroom, never hit, never bleed.

Whatever negativity may occur in the stories turns up as a pure matter of circumstance, a silly speed bump on the highway to happiness.

Although Weetzie loses her father to a drug overdose, gives birth to a child whose father may be any of three possible sex partners, inherits the baby of her live-in boyfriend and his witch girlfriend, has no job, has a friend with AIDS, lives with another friend in his deceased grandmother's house, she still feels full of love. She compares love and disease (88).

As a teacher of English, I would be a little concerned about adolescents in my classes who preferred the novels of Block to other kinds of young adult literature. The novels remind me of the time I got into an argument with a 16-year-old boy named Lucas in a high school in South Texas. Lucas planned to marry an obviously pregnant freshman, Stephanie, a 15-year-old who refused to disclose the identity of the baby's father. According to Stephanie, the father may or may not have been Lucas:

> I asked Lucas, "What will you do for money once you are married?"
> Lucas answered, "I already got a job at Taco Bell making good money. Heck, I already pull in almost $1000 a month. An apartment would only cost about $450 or so."
> Then I told Lucas, "When you are a parent, you'll have to trade some of the fun and freedom of adolescence for adult responsibilities, such as raising your child."
> Lucas responded, "We don't do that much out of the ordinary for fun now. We maybe hang out at the mall, drink a beer now and then, go see a movie. I don't see anything changing that much just because a kid is around."

In Block's fiction, Lucas would have found characters in abundance who substantiated his line of thinking—a life of plenty, free for the taking, a life free from unpleasant consequences or dull routines. As a teacher, I'd much prefer my students to read the bluntly shocking *Cobain*, which renders in raw detail the consequences of certain kinds of dangerous behaviors—taking drugs, experimental sex, abject poverty, blind ambition. If nothing else, *Cobain* would help put the rock 'n' roll lifestyle into realistic focus for wannabe rockers and rappers.

THE COUNSELOR'S PERSPECTIVE

Perhaps the key question to ask about the relationship among music, musicians, and adolescents is, Does listening to songs that promote violence and aggressive sexuality, as expressed in the music or the life-styles of musicians, create a certain kind of pathology in adolescent behavior? Beginning with Albert Bandura's work (1965), serious questions have been raised about the extent to which models are imitated. Bandura believed that watching violence committed on television was as provocative as watching it directly and called the imitation of a kind of behavior on television "observational learning." Jerry Mander (1977) noted that the constant stream of sex, violence, and conspicuous consumption advocated on television seemed designed to create a stimulus flow rate so rapid and varied that most television viewers would eventually find it difficult to discern between the true and the fallacious. David Elkind (1981) and Neil Postman (1982) noted that, in days of yore, learning about violence and sexuality was prevented by children's inability to access the printed word. When the printed word was the dominant mode of communication, children who could not read could be temporarily sheltered from certain aspects of adult life by simply "not talking about it in front of the children."

Today, through MTV, television news, commercials, gossip magazines, cable television, and the Internet, detailed information about drugs, sex, and violence is readily accessible twenty-four hours a day for adolescents. Undeniably, opportunities for openly discussing and experimenting with sex, drugs, and violence seem to be increasing at the same time that the traditional constraining forces of American culture, such as religion and family, seem to be on the wane.

Yet, today's adolescents are only products of the culture that previous generations have helped create. From the work of social psychologists, such as Phillip Zimbardo (Zimbardo et al., 1973), to that of Margaret Mead (1928) and Ruth Benedict (1934), research has by now well established that culture serves as the framework for behavior and development.

In this view, the adolescent whose pants are sagging below the belly button and who has the "Nine Inch Nail" stencil on the back of a black T-shirt may not be so different from adolescents of the 1960s or 1970s, who wore psychedelic shirts and bell bottoms, flashed the "peace sign," and wore huge medallions representing an astrological sign. Like the crew-cut, pontificating "Beat Generation" of Ginsberg and Kerouac, the cultural milieu of the moment sets the range for the set of possible personal identities.

When an adolescent hears a song on the radio or sees and hears one on video, the effects of the song, whether positive or negative, depend upon the cognitive wherewithal of the individual at that particular point of cognitive and affective development and at that specific moment in time in relation to that development. Consider understanding of the notion of the "finality of death." While the notion of death may seem like a serious certainty to many adults, children and those with childlike minds often have very different kinds of ideas about what happens when a person dies. When Daffy Duck blows up Elmer Fudd, when the Coyote drives his motorcycle into the mountainside, or when Bugs Bunny gets flattened by a steamroller, they always manage to get up to continue the chase. When a "shopper" in a store is being interviewed by someone off camera about a particular product, it might not occur to some that the person being interviewed might not be an innocent shopper, but a person hired by a corporation to increase sales. The ability to see through "what is" and to understand the metaphorical aspect of lyrical and visual messages is inextricably tied to a student's maturational development and ephemeral mental state at the time of the interaction.

Jean Piaget (1952; 1967) might suggest there are two levels of reaction to observing sexuality and violence. One possible response, typical of males with IQs below 80 or at concrete thinking levels, is that the violence and sexuality of music might be considered to be something real. Those who think in concrete terms are unable to think in abstractions; they cannot, for instance, mentally generate several possible solutions to one problem, use contrary-to-fact reasoning, or understand the intricacies of a second symbol system (such as the use of metaphoric language in song lyrics). In the case of cognitively immature teens, it is possible that an adolescent might be encouraged to imitate these actions in thoughts, if not in behavior. However, even with this "at risk" population, there is no body of evidence that suggests a convincing correlation between listening to violence and acting it out.

A more likely outcome can be seen in the normally developing youngster who listens to lyrics advocating violence and realizes that what is really being glorified are the fancy cars, the plush homes, and the beautiful people hanging around with the band. When adults or adolescents with normal intelligence listen to Brat, Too Short, Run DMC, Easy EZ, Doc, Snoop Doggie Dog, Dr. Dray, Notorious BIG, Big Poppa, Biggie Small, Beastie Boys, KISS, or Nine Inch Nails, they typically see through the public relations propaganda and the audacious album cover art to an understanding of what is truly being peddled—that these rebels from mainstream society have attained a piece of "the good life." Most adolescents realize that outrageous lyrics and thundering music are ploys for the musicians, much like televised matches are for the "professional wrestler"; encouraging violence becomes a means of staying popular and acquiring the accoutrements of wealth and power.

In fact, it could well be that contemporary music has a calming effect, much in the manner suggested by Sigmund Freud (1924)—a catharsis that involves talking through one's early conflicts. Much of psychotherapy as practiced by those who call themselves Gestalt psychologists (Perls, 1969) involves acting out conflict through psychodrama and sociodrama. Of course, in psychotherapy, acting out is supposed to lower anxiety and lessen anger. Two distinguished psychotherapists, Eric Erikson (1980) and Peter Blos (1989), have contended that the psychosocial goal of adolescence is to achieve a sense of identity, and they have stated that experimentation is a critical part of that journey. Listening to subversive lyrics may allow some adolescents to safely experience identity options without becoming susceptible to the real dangers involved in truly acting out what is being advocated. In this way, adolescents may be free to experience a kind of vicarious acting out, a kind of secondhand trial, free from the possibility of irreparable human consequences. Adolescents may also use books as safe vehicles for experimenting with different settings, ideas, personalities, attitudes, and goals.

Bruno Bettelheim (1983) said, "When you are parenting an adolescent, who is developing normally in other ways, put on your seatbelt and hold tight." I suppose a concluding thought is something that one of my adolescent sons told me last year. He said, "Dad, if the music is too loud, then you're old."

QUESTIONS AND ANSWERS

Following are some questions that teachers, parents, and other adults who work with adolescents might have regarding music and teens. Answers are provided by a psychologist, Dr. Steven Bell.

In your opinion, should parents and teachers be concerned about the lyrics and music to which students listen?

Yes, parents and teachers should be concerned, especially if other worrisome behavior traits also are present, such as significantly declining grades, poor hygiene, suicidal thoughts, withdrawal, or moderate weight loss or gain.

Is there a critical age when students' disposition might be more likely to change than at other times in their development?

In general, early adolescence can be an exceedingly precarious time. Early adolescents have increased cognitive abilities, can visualize into a more distant future, can identify hypocrisy, and are seeking an identity independent of and beyond the one established within the family unit.

To what extent do you feel that students' choice of music reveals their choice of lifestyle and values?

Without corroborating evidence in other areas of their life, such as dress, food, and peer involvement, music might not reveal deep lifestyle or values choices.

To what extent should a teacher or parent attempt to influence a student's choice of music?

Attempting to influence a teen or preteen is always risky business. On the other hand, it is a parent's responsibility to provide loving guidance. I would suggest attempting to directly influence choices in music up to the adolescent's resistance point, but not much beyond. Actually, a more subtle attempt to persuade would be more developmentally appropriate. Finding positive peer role models through print and electronic media, identifying wholesome heros, heroines, grandparents, and social and religious leaders, might prove more effective than more direct approaches, which may be perceived to be encroachments upon an adolescent's budding independence.

To what extent could a teacher use contemporary music in the classroom as part of an instructional package? Does bringing in such music for study and analysis in the classroom negate its antisocial themes?

Bringing contemporary music into the classroom should be handled carefully and sensitively. Be sure your building administrators, counselors, coteachers, parents, and community leaders are in on the planning of such an adventure. Evil abhors light. Studying and analyzing contemporary music can reveal much of its sexist, appearance-obsessed, violent, drug-adoring, depraved, suicidal, and homicidal elements. Discussing controversial song lyrics can allow those youngsters who do not engage in subversive activities to possibly influence those who do.

RECOMMENDED READINGS

Nonfiction Works

Ardley, Neil. (1995). *A Young Person's Guide to Music*. New York: Dorling Kindersley. 80 pp. (ISBN: 0–7894–0313–7). Middle School (MS), High School (HS).

This is a book and CD-ROM pair that introduce readers to thirty-one orchestral instruments. It also provides a history of music and a reference section in which seventy composers are discussed and musical terms are presented and defined.

Barber, Nicola, and Mary Mure. (1995). *The World of Music*. New York: Silver Burdett. 94 pp. (ISBN: 0–382–39117–9). MS, HS.

This book covers a broad range of topics, from the history of music in the Western world to a description of individual instruments and lessons about pitch and rhythm.

Chapman, Richard. (1994). *The Complete Guitarist*. New York: Dorling Kindersley. 192 pp. (ISBN: 1–5645–8711–8). MS, HS.

With photographs and instructions on various finger style techniques and how to create chords, this guide provides practice exercises and songs, as well as background information and photographs that reflect the history of the guitar. It includes a glossary of guitar-related terms and is an ideal choice for those who are sincerely interested in the instrument.

Haskins, James. (1993). *Black Music in America: A History through Its People*. New York: HarperCollins. 198 pp. (ISBN: 0–06–446136–X). MS, HS.

Haskins, who has written several books for adolescents about significant and often overlooked African Americans, traces the history of American black music from slavery to the 1980s. Highlights include Haskins's attention to the influence of black music on jazz, the blues, and rock music, as well as biographical sketches of important African American musicians across the years.

Jones, Hettie. (1997). *Big Star Fallin' Mama: Five Women in Black Music*. New York: Puffin. 129 pp. (ISBN: 0–4–037747–6). MS, HS.

The author organizes a history of black music around biographies of five famous African American female singers from Ma Rainey to Aretha Franklin. The inspiring story of each musician includes struggle and triumph.

Jones, K. Maurice (1994). *Say It Loud: The Story of Rap Music*. Brookfield, CT: Millbrook Press. 128 pp. (ISBN: 1–56294–386–3). MS, HS.

Jones tracks rap music to its origins, then gives attention to the reasons that this form of music has created controversies in modern America. The book includes photographs of rap stars and copies of lyrics.

Kosser, Mike. (1993). *Hot Country*. New York: Avon Books. 262 pp. (ISBN: 0–380–77061–X). MS, HS.

This book will appeal to country music fans because it includes biographical sketches of today's favorite country musicians and focuses on the human side of their stories. Kosser also offers his explanations for the recent increase in the popularity of country music.

Monceaux, Morgan. (1994). *Jazz: My Music, My People*. New York: Alfred A. Knopf. 64 pp. (ISBN: 0–679–85618–8). MS, HS.

This short book is a beauty. Following a foreword by Wynton Marsalis, it presents drawings and brief biographical sketches of many of the great figures in jazz.

Silverman, Jerry. (1996). *Just Listen to This Song I'm Singing: African American History through Song*. Brookfield, CT: Millbrook Press. 95 pp. (ISBN: 1–56294–673–0). MS, HS.

With introductions that place each song within a context of historical significance, Silverman presents a history of African American music from the mid-1800s through the mid-1900s. Each of the selections has photographs or illustrations, full lyrics, and piano and voice scores. The songs range from spirituals and folk songs to jazz and blues.

Vernon, Roland. (1996). *Introducing Mozart*. New York: Silver Burdett. 32 pp. (ISBN: 0–382–39158–6). MS, HS.

Like his *Introducing Gershwin* (1996), which introduces the twentieth-century musical legend, this book is a biography and history of the life and times of one of the world's most famous composers. Illustrations, a time line, and a glossary are features of this book.

REFERENCES

Adoni, H. (1978). "The Functions of Mass Media in the Political Socialization of Adolescents." *Communication Research* 6 (1): 84–106.

Arnett, J. (1991). "Adolescents and Heavy Metal Music: From the Mouths of Metalheads." *Youth and Society* 23 (1): 76–98.

Bandura, A. (1965). "Influence of Models' Reinforcement Contingencies on the Acquisition of Imitative Responses." *Journal of Personality and Social Psychology* 1: 589–595.

Benedict, R. (1934). "Anthropology and the Abnormal." *Journal of General Psychology* 10: 59–82.

Bennett, H., and J. Ferrell. (1987). "Music Videos and Epistemic Socialization." *Youth and Society* 18 (4): 344–362.

Berry, V. (1990). "Rap Music, Self Concept and Low Income Black Adolescents." *Popular Music and Society* 14: 89–107.

Bettelheim, B. (1975). *Personal Conversation*. Athens: University of Georgia. Spring.

Block, F. L. (1989). *Weetzie Bat*. New York: HarperCollins.

Block, F. L. (1992). *Witch Baby*. New York: HarperCollins.

Block, F. L. (1993). *Cherokee Bat and the Goat Guys*. New York: Harper-Collins.

Block, F. L. (1995). *Baby Be-Bop*. New York: HarperCollins.

Block, F. L. (1995). *Missing Angel Juan*. New York: HarperCollins.

Blos, P. (1989). "The Inner World of the Adolescent." In A. H. Esman (Ed.), *International Annals of Adolescent Psychiatry*, vol. 1. Chicago: University of Chicago Press.

Csikszentmihalyi, M. (1996). *Creativity: Flow and the Psychology of Discovery and Invention*. New York: HarperCollins.

Eliot, M. (1989). *Rockonomics: The Money behind the Music*. New York: Franklin Watts.

Elkind, D. (1981). *The Hurried Child*. Reading, MA: Addison-Wesley.

Erikson, E. H. (1980). *Identity and the Life Cycle*. New York: W. W. Norton.

Freud, A. (1924). *A General Introduction to Psychoanalysis*. New York: Boni & Liveright.

Freud, A. (1966). "Instinctual Anxiety during Puberty." In *The Writings of Anna Freud: The Ego and the Mechanisms of Defense*, vol. 2. New York: International Universities Press, 152–172.

Gaines, D. (1991). *Teenage Wasteland: Suburbia's Dead End Kids*. New York: Pantheon.

Greenberg, B., J. Brown, and N. Buerkel-Rothfuss. (1993). *Media, Sex and the Adolescent*. Cresskill, NJ: Hampton Press.

Larson, R., and R. Kubey. (1983). "Television and Music: Contrasting Media in Adolescent Life." *Youth and Society* 15 (1): 13–32.

Lull, J. (1985). "On the Communicative Properties of Music." *Communication Research* 12: 363–372.

Mander, J. (1977). *Four Arguments for the Elimination of Television*. New York: Quill.

Mead, M. (1928). *Coming of Age in Samoa*. New York: William Morrow.

Perls, F. S. (1969). *Gestalt Therapy Verbatim*. Lafayette, CA: Real People Press.

Piaget, J. (1952). *The Origins of Intelligence in Children*. New York: International Universities Press.

Piaget, J. (1967). "The Mental Development of the Child." In D. Elkind (Ed.), *Six Psychological Studies by Piaget*. New York: Random House.

Postman, N. (1982). *The Disappearance of Childhood*. New York: Dell.

Rouner, D. (1990). "Rock Music's Use as a Socializing Function." *Popular Music and Society* 14: 97–107.

Sandford, C. (1995). *Kurt Cobain*. London: Victor Gollancz.

Sherman, B., and J. Dominick. (1986). "Violence and Sex in Music Videos: TV and Rock 'n' Roll." *Journal of Communication* 36 (1): 79–93.

Snow, R. (1987). "Youth, Rock 'n' Roll and Electronic Media." *Youth and Society* 18 (4): 326–343.

Steiner, G. (1990). "Struck Dumb." In C. Fadiman (Ed.), *Living Philosophies*. New York: Doubleday, 213–222.

Walser, R. (1994). *Running with the Devil: Power, Gender, and Madness in Heavy Metal Music*. Hanover, NH: Wesleyan University Press.

Wright, J. (Ed.). (1997). *The Universal Almanac*. Kansas City, MO: Andrews & McMeel.

Zillmann, D., and A. Bhatia. (1989). "Effects of Associating with Musical Genres on Heterosexual Attraction." *Communication Research* 16 (2): 263–288.

Zimbardo, P. G., W. C. Banks, C. Haney, and D. Haffe. (1973). "A Pirandellian Prison." *New York Times Magazine* (April 8).

CHAPTER SEVEN

Ethics in Athletics for Adolescents

Chris Crowe and Mel Olson

Though typically they are loath to admit it, adolescents rely on role models to help them navigate the chaos of adolescence. As teenagers struggle to develop an identity, to develop a set of standards and morals, and to find their place in society, they often look to the adults they interact with in some way, adults they admire, as role models. They pattern all or parts of their developing lives on their role models. It is not unusual for adolescents to reject their own parents as role models and turn instead to other significant adults: relatives, such as uncles or aunts, older friends, teachers, professional athletes, celebrities, and coaches.

Many, maybe most, athletes can cite the powerful influence—for good or for bad—a coach has had in their lives. For teenagers, coaches occupy a unique adult role. As athletes or former athletes themselves, coaches are viewed by their teenage athletes in a more favorable light than are most other adults. Athletes develop a closer relationship with their coaches than they do with most other adults because coaches work more often and more closely with athletes than do teachers, parents, and other adults. The stress that comes from competition also creates a bond between coaches and athletes, and when that bond is positive, it also produces implicit trust. These factors make coaches significant and influential role models for teenage athletes and put coaches in a powerful position to hurt or help young people.

The huge growth in men's and women's sports in high schools and colleges since the 1950s suggests just how much American society believes in the value of athletic competition. Today, we realize that participation in sports can provide entertainment, teach lessons about life, and help young people learn about teamwork, commitment, and overcoming challenges. As more and more men and women join sports programs at all levels, the pressures related to competing—and to winning—have grown proportionately. Now, some coaches, too many, are willing to win at any cost. In many situations, the goal of winning has supplanted the traditional values associated with sports: the development of character and of athletic skills.

In our society, we expect our amateur sports coaches to win games and to develop character, and coaches who fail at one or the other (or both) are not tolerated for long by parents' booster groups, school or recreation league administrators, or team support organizations. The pressures coaches feel to succeed cause some of them to resort to unethical behaviors that violate their trusted role-model position. Television, newspapers, and sports magazines regularly report examples of fanatical or unethical coaches who, in their efforts to win games, commit crimes against their players and/or society. Successful high school and college athletes are often exploited by coaches. Star athletes may be given special privileges; often they are excused from academic requirements and protected from punishment. Coaches sometimes shield these players from taking responsibility for their actions by lying or cheating for them, or in some other way covering up an athlete's misdeeds. Such behavior by coaches or others who have stewardship over athletic programs damages athletes by giving them a distorted view of what moral, responsible adult behavior really is. By failing to deal with reality and take ownership of their own problems, athletes who have been exploited or coddled by coaches develop poor character and a warped sense of ethics. The negative impact on these adolescents is exacerbated when, instead of serving as positive, effective role models, their coaches do not establish and insist upon high standards.

Unethical behavior by coaches and/or athletes is nothing new, and it occurs despite school and athletic organization guidelines. In an effort to foster ethical behavior and sportsmanship among participating schools, governing organizations have been established at the high school and college level. The National Collegiate Athletic Association (NCAA), founded in 1906, and the National Association of Intercollegiate Athletics (NAIA), founded in 1951, cover nearly every college and university in America. In 1920, delegates from high schools in Indiana, Iowa, Michigan, and Wisconsin created the Midwest Federation of State High

School Athletic Associations, which in 1922 became the National Federation of State High School Athletic Associations. It now has members from all fifty states and some Canadian provinces. These governing bodies have established clear guidelines for student athletes and their coaches; unfortunately, the organizations have not had much effect on curbing the decline in sports ethics. Media reports are full of real-life examples of players and coaches who have violated ethical and institutional standards to achieve personal success.

Here are some examples:

- The father of a high school football player in New Mexico helped his son sharpen the chinstrap buckles on his helmet so that opposing players would cut their hands on his helmet.

- College recruiters, high school coaches, and even some test proctors have been caught helping student-athletes beat the NCAA academic standards for the ACT and SAT exams. In one case, after a high school basketball player had failed the SAT nine times, he was flown from New York to Los Angeles to take a test rigged for him to pass.

- A high school football player in Utah accused of sexual assault continued to attend school and play in games for several weeks until he was finally arrested by local police.

- More than 300,000 boys and 175,000 girls in grades nine through twelve are reported to have used steroids to build muscle for sports.

- After losing a close match, a high school wrestler attacked the referee who officiated the match.

- A survey of current and former Canadian Olympic athletes revealed that more than 20 percent of them had had sexual encounters with authority figures.

- Former University of Connecticut basketball star Marcus Camby admitted that while he was a college athlete, he took money and gifts from agents and violated other NCAA rules.

- A basketball coach at the University of California paid fifteen thousand dollars to the parents of a student-athlete for every year he played. The coach was found guilty of illegal recruiting, giving extra benefits, and other violations.

- NCAA investigations of Texas Tech found that the school had seventy-six athletes in eight sports who were ineligible.

- Lawrence Phillips, a running back from the University of Nebraska who later played for the St. Louis Rams, had a number of run-ins with the law and with his coaches but continued to play.

• In a widely publicized case, Latrell Sprewell, a star player in the National Basketball Association, attacked his coach during practice, choked him, and shouted, "I'm going to kill you!" Other NBA players used the media to defend his actions by blaming the coach for pushing Sprewell too hard.

These incidents are directly or indirectly related to the coaches the athletes had in high school and college who provided poor leadership and were poor role models. The win-at-all-costs attitudes of coaches combined with their laissez-faire approaches that allow marginal or ineligible athletes to continue to play cause irreparable damage to athletes' character.

ADOLESCENTS AND THEIR COACHES IN CONTEMPORARY LITERATURE

It is not surprising that with the pervasiveness of sports in American culture and the widespread decline in the morality of sports, coaches and their unethical activities have found their way into the background of many books for teenage readers. Some, like the nameless football coach in Robert Cormier's novel *The Chocolate War* (1974), look and act the part.

The coach looked like an old gangster: broken nose, a scar on his cheek like a stitched shoestring. He needed a shave, his stubble like slivers of ice. He growled and swore and was merciless. But a helluva coach, they said. The coach stared at him now, the dark eyes probing, pondering. Jerry hung in there, trying not to sway, trying not to faint. (9)

This coach is as evil as he looks, giving Jerry false hope that he'll make the team and openly allowing other players, members of the school's secret society, to torment and brutalize Jerry on and off the practice field.

There are many more like him. In David Guy's *Football Dreams* (1980), Coach Grupp is the stupid and obsessed varsity football coach. Dan, the protagonist/narrator, describes him this way:

He was a short round man, and stood with his arms behind his back, his belly rested before him like a great boulder. He had a bushy mustache, and a large upper lip that he characteristically pushed up and out in contemplation . . . regularly—I had already heard—he exploded into violent fits of temper. (81)

Grupp belittles and discourages Dan, cheats him out of a starting position, and eventually drives him to quit the team.

The racist basketball coach in Bruce Brooks's *The Moves Make the Man* (1984) is bad in a different way. Jerome Foxworthy wants to try out for the all-white team but is denied permission by the coach. Hoping to impress the coach and win a tryout, Jerome throws up a trick shot; it drops in from twenty-five feet out, but the coach is not impressed. Instead, he insults and criticizes Jerome: "Typical jig shot. . . . Fancy, one-handed, big jump. Harlem Globetrotter stuff. You like the Globetrotters, boy?" (71). Jerome, knowing he's better than any other boy in the gym, challenges them to a two-on-one game. If he wins, he gets a uniform; if he loses, he gives up. The coach accepts the challenge and selects his two best players to face Jerome, but Jerome's experience still gives him the edge. His talent and determination, however, can't overcome the coach's consistently unfair calls that negate every basket Jerome makes. He leaves the gym defeated and cheated.

Other coaches are portrayed as cheaters who have succumbed to the pressure to win, someone like Coach Lednecky in Chris Crutcher's *Running Loose* (1983). Louie Banks, the novel's protagonist, describes him:

And one reason I didn't make it big in football before this year was that I wouldn't cream the little guys in practice. Lednecky always wanted everybody to go all out against everybody, and that meant if you came up against a 95-pounder in the meat grinder, you took his head off. (15)

Hoping to guarantee victory in a crucial game, Lednecky orders his players to injure the star of an opposing team. The team wins the game but loses Louie, who quits in protest of the coach's unethical actions. Because of Louie's insubordination, Lednecky and the principal, who is a former coach, suspend him from all sports. An assistant coach pleads for him to be allowed to turn out for track, but the coach and principal refuse. Lednecky, citing one of the oldest and most popular justifications for sports (which Louie describes as "the Domino Theory of Rotten Apples"), explains his odd reasoning:

"You seem to have missed the point, Coach," he said. "We're not just producing athletes here; we're building young men. Young men we can turn out into the community or send off to college and be proud of. Somewhere along the way we obviously failed in this case, and I don't want it to spread. One person with an attitude like Banks's can destroy a whole team." (155)

These types of coaches are not restricted to the pages of fiction. Works of nonfiction like Robert Lipsyte's *Sports World: An American Dreamland* (1975) also describe the negative effects of coaches. Lipsyte writes:

> A million Little Leaguers stand for hours while a criminally obese "coach" drills the joy of sports out of their souls, makes them self-conscious and fearful, teaches them technique over movement, emphasizes dedication, sacrifice, and obedience instead of accomplishment and fun. (281)

Coaches like these, and those described in Martin Ralbovsky's nonfiction *Lords of the Locker Room: The American Way of Coaching and Its Effect on Youth* (1974), complement the works of fiction that examine the negative effects coaches can have on young athletes.

A CLOSER LOOK AT HIGH SCHOOL FOOTBALL PLAYERS AND UNETHICAL COACHES: *FRIDAY NIGHT LIGHTS*

The single work of nonfiction that provides the most comprehensive insight into big-time high school football is H. G. Bissinger's *Friday Night Lights: A Town, a Team, and a Dream* (1990). Bissinger, an editor of the *Philadelphia Inquirer*, left his job to spend a year living with and observing a high school football team in Odessa, Texas. The football team at Permian High School in Odessa was known as one of the best in the United States, one that had won several state championships, had made countless playoff appearances, and would often draw more than twenty thousand fans to its Friday night home games. It also was known as a place of high-stakes football, where boosters placed unrealistically high expectations on its coaches and players while at the same time lavishing them with attention, support, and money.

The Permian Panthers would be successful only with the intensity and commitment of players and coaches who spent hundreds of hours a year training, practicing, studying game films, and preparing for games. The players possessed a single-minded dedication that is rare in most teenagers. Their lives seemed to revolve around football, and Permian football was so big, so important in Odessa, that for many of the players, life without football would have been unthinkable. Though there were some exceptions, most of the players' devotion to football caused them to neglect school, study, and even their families. The coaches and the boosters, of course, promoted their players' fanaticism because their intense focus on and commitment to football were necessary for success.

When coaches and other adults encourage or even demand "total commitment" to a sport, many high school and college student-athletes willingly comply. For those who are marginal students, sports tempt them with an opportunity for success they might not otherwise have in school. For the talented student-athletes, sports offer the lure of future success and glory. The fantasy of a glamorous and wealthy professional sports career motivates far more athletes than could ever hope even to play at a major college level. But Boobie Miles, a running back for the Permian team had such fantasies. He dreamed of winning state and then making it in the pros. He couldn't imagine a life without football. (56)

Unfortunately for Boobie, a knee injury cut short his high school career. He was immediately replaced by another equally talented player. His hopes for any success in college athletics were suddenly eliminated; because Boobie's dreams for his future never included anything but football, when his football career evaporated, he had nothing left. The damage to Boobie and to other Permian football players, none of whom played a full career at the college level, was that their unrealistic devotion to football and the exclusion of all else left them ill-prepared for life without football.

If this sounds like exploitation, it is. Unethical coaches become more concerned about their own careers and success than they are about the futures of their athletes. After all, the players usually remain in the program for four years or less, but a successful coach's career can last decades. Whether or not the coaches were directly or indirectly involved, Boobie and other football players at Permian were pampered, receiving preferential treatment that normal students could barely imagine. When Boobie was kicked off the sophomore team for missing workouts, the coaches let him back on when they realized that they couldn't expect the same from him as they could other players and still keep him on the team. He and others took dead-end, mindless courses during the season to avoid being distracted from football. On game days, many players would skip classes, and most players weren't expected to do any kind of schoolwork at all. Though the coaches knew better, the student-athletes couldn't appreciate the adverse effects such behavior would have on their future, a future these young men were trading to ensure the success of their coaches.

In Odessa, exploitation sometimes took on an ominous, racist nature. When the coaches realized that Boobie probably would not play again in his senior year, one was asked what Boobie would become without football. Rather than showing compassion, the coach responded that without football, Boobie would be just another "big ol' dumb nigger" (67). After Boobie was hurt, some boosters suggested that they should just do to him what trainers did to lame horses: "shoot him to put him out of the misery of a life that no longer had any value" (67). Of course, most high school athletes remain oblivious to their own exploitation while they are in the middle of it, but more impartial observers have a clearer view of what happened at Permian and other schools. A former minister from Odessa described the situation this way:

> Before, it was take the blacks and put 'em in the cotton field. Let 'em do farm work. Let 'em do share crops. In the twentieth century, because of football, the real smart people use these blacks just like they would on the farm. And when it's over, they don't care about them. Some people say in their mind, that's all they were good for anyway. (109)

Coaches who focus solely on winning typically do not care at all about players—black or white—when the season, the run for a local, state, regional, or national championship, or a short career is over. Their careers are built upon the backs and lives of athletes who succumb to the allure of athletic glory and who rarely realize how fleeting that glory is.

In addition to exploiting athletes, the obsession with winning causes coaches and their supporters to warp the priorities of schools and education. Because of the prominence of sports in American culture, academic success often takes a backseat to athletic success. Of course, the coaches benefit from all the attention and support while their athletes, their teaching colleagues, and the students suffer. One frustrated Permian teacher said, "This community doesn't want academic excellence. It wants a gladiatorial spectacle on Friday night" (147). Though all the attention is rewarding to coaches, it only increases the pressure on coaches to field winning teams at all costs. Coaches know full well the value schools and communities place on sports programs. For example, one of Permian's opposing coaches convinced his principal to schedule a game with Permian by saying, "we can have ten merit scholars at school. But if we beat Permian, we get more publicity" (118). When such statements are true—as this was in *Friday Night Lights*—the goals of a high school become skewed as principals give in to public pressure calling for the promotion of athletics over academics.

This pressure sits even more heavily on the coaches of prominent teams. In Odessa, and in all of West Texas, football was king, and boosters were exceedingly hard to please. For example, the Permian High School boosters wanted to fire the football coach who had seven wins and two losses in his first year: "We'll just get another coach, a coach that can win" (125). During the season that Bissinger chronicled, the city newspaper published a letter condemning the football coach after the team experienced a crucial loss. Earlier in his career, the coach had said, "It doesn't matter if you win or lose if two good teams are playing." The letter predicted he would never be a winner with that kind of attitude (241). Unrealistic expectations like these create unbearable pressure on coaches, pressures that even normally ethical coaches may give in to. In some instances, coaches may rationalize their unethical behavior by saying they were only giving their customers what they asked for: winning teams with no questions asked.

An English teacher at Permian High pointed out another kind of warped values created by the school's obsession with football. The teacher observed, "The Bible says, where your treasure is, that's where your heart is also" and claimed that the school spent more on athletic medical supplies than it did for teaching materials. After a little research, Bissinger confirmed her suspicions. In 1988, the school spent $6,750 on boys' medical supplies and $6,400 on game films, but only $5,040 on teaching materials for the English department. He found other financial inequities as well. The English department chair, a teacher with a master's degree and twenty years experience, earned $32,000. On the other hand, the head football coach, who taught no classes, earned $48,000 and the use of a new car each year. The school and its boosters also lavished money on the program. In the 1988 football season, in addition to the equipment and maintenance expenses for football, Permian spent about $70,000 on charter flights to take their team to away games. A year later, investigators discovered that for more than ten years, boosters had secretly paid the head football coach $10,000 to $20,000 a year in performance bonuses despite the fact that rules stipulated that anything over $300 was illegal. The reason for the rule, said one league official, was that "The coach should have no monetary interest in whether it was a winning or losing affair, and therefore would have no monetary interest in exploiting a player" (359). The explanation sounds logical, but given the financial excesses associated with the "big-time" football program, secret cash bonuses to successful coaches hardly seem a surprise. Of course, the cash incentives and the huge financial investment in the school's football program only added to the pressure on the coach to cheat and to exploit players for the sake of winning.

In order to field winning teams, some coaches stoop to coddling athletes to keep them content and to cheating for athletes to keep them academically eligible. Ultimately, this kind of treatment has a detrimental effect on young student-athletes, creating in them a kind of "welfare mentality" that leads them to believe that they deserve something for nothing. The status and special treatment they receive while they are high school or college stars rarely continues after their short careers are complete, but the attitudes and behaviors the star treatment engenders in young athletes can linger, malignantly, for a lifetime.

One of Permian's opponents in 1988 was Carter High School from Dallas. During the play-offs, a grade scandal rocked the school and its football team. Texas has a strict no-pass, no-play policy; athletes who aren't passing all of their classes at six-week intervals are ineligible for competition until the next grade check. One of Carter High's star football players failed an algebra class, but the principal changed the grade to maintain the player's eligibility. The grade change was based, in part, on the school's "School Improvement Plan," which mandated that half the weight of a student's grade come from class participation. A legal battle erupted, with one side, mostly Carter High football supporters, fighting to keep the grade change while the other side fought to have the player declared ineligible. The battle raged back and forth until a court hearing determined the passing grade would stand and the player would remain eligible for play. The results were immediate; the athlete played a major role in the rest of the play-off games, leading Carter to the state championship. The algebra teacher who had dared to fail a football star had a doctorate and thirty-five years teaching experience; he was reassigned to teach industrial arts in a Dallas middle school.

The decision to change the failing grade to a passing grade probably didn't surprise the football player and some of his teammates who were accustomed to special treatment by the school and community. Carter High School was paradise, said one football star.

> You walk around, you break all the rules. The teachers and administrators, they see you, they just don't say anything to you. It was just like we owned it. Everybody looked up to us, it was just a great life. (291)

Star athletes had it made; they were free to leave class and school, miss exams, and were sometimes even given answers with exams. Another star athlete said, "I loved goin' to school because I didn't have to do nothin'. I just went" (295).

The privileged treatment continued after the season. These same two student-athletes, members of a state championship football team, were heavily recruited by major universities. On their recruiting trips to several big-name schools, they received sex, gifts, and promises of cars and money. At home, restaurant managers gave them free meals; if they were stopped for speeding, the policeman recognized them and let them off with a warning. Having enjoyed privilege, notoriety, and special treatment for so long, the two stars were convinced they were above the rules. Said one, "We were on top of the world. . . . We thought nothing can happen to us" (341).

That attitude cost them dearly. In May, the two Dallas high school football stars joined several other football players and friends on a crime spree, committing seven armed robberies in a month. They didn't need the money; the holdups were just for kicks. Even after they were arrested, they were convinced that their athletic reputation would protect them as it always had in the past. One of the players said,

> we were sittin' in the police car and we weren't even worried. We thought we're gonna go to jail for a little while and our mothers would come bail us out and we'd go back home and it would be over with. (341)

However, for these misguided young football players, the problems were not over with. One was sentenced to twenty years in prison; the other received a sixteen-year sentence. Their friends and former teammates were sent to jail for periods ranging from thirteen to twenty-five years. Finally, life beyond football had found them.

The judge in the case might have been one of the first people who did not grant these high school football stars any special treatment. At the trial, he said,

> I can think of, but will not name, off the top of my head three former Dallas Cowboys and one former Miami Dolphin who have two striking things in common. All four have Super Bowl rings and they all four have been to the penitentiary. . . . When it comes to violating the law, at the courthouse it simply doesn't matter that you can run the football. (342)

After the trial, the prosecuting attorney wondered out loud about the disservice that had been rendered these young men by placing them on a golden pedestal. "You look at how we treat them in high school, and how we treat them in college, and everyone asks why they act like children. . . . How would you expect them to act any other way?" (343).

Knowing the way many athletes are mollycoddled by their coaches and schools, we should not be too surprised when we read of athletes accepting illegal payments or gifts, using performance-enhancing drugs, failing school, or violating rules. The social injustice perpetrated on athletes who labor under unethical coaches is that many of these young people leave their schools with a warped sense of values and personal accountability.

IS *FRIDAY NIGHT LIGHTS* REALISTIC?

Unfortunately, the incidents described in *Friday Night Lights* are not limited to a few schools in the state of Texas; they occur more regularly in schools across the United States than anyone would like to admit. Excessive pressure to win at any level of sports can cause some coaches to believe that they would get fired for losing long before they would get fired for cheating, and so, many coaches are willing to do whatever it takes to win. Sadly, unethical coaching behavior does not affect only coaches. When coaches cheat, they send a message to their players that it's acceptable for players to break the rules or accept special privileges that are undeserved or illegal. This inherited social behavior—the attitude that athletes are above the rules and/or that they merit special treatment—has hurt many athletes.

One example of this is similar to an incident Bissinger reported in *Friday Night Lights* about the football players in the Dallas high school. In the past two decades, there have been repeated cases of high schools or high school employees "enhancing" the academic records of athletes being considered for collegiate athletic scholarships. Several years ago, the NCAA ruled that in order to be eligible for an athletic scholarship, high school student-athletes had to earn a minimum score on the ACT or SAT and earn passing grades in their high school core courses. The test scores could be verified by the National Testing Center, but the student-athletes' high schools were allowed to determine whether or not the core course requirements were met. School principals issued the official verification of core course requirements to the NCAA. In many cases, pressure from athletes, their families, high school and college coaches, and even school counselors convinced some principals to falsify school records in order to make an otherwise ineligible student-athlete eligible for an athletic scholarship. At times, school officials have also given illegal assistance to student-athletes who were unable to earn a passing score on the ACT or SAT. In one case, a talented student-athlete scored an 8 on his first ACT exam, a score that made him ineligible to receive an athletic scholarship. On the next ACT exam, this same student-athlete's ACT score miraculously—or mysteriously—jumped to 24. When falsification of core course reports and cheating on college entrance exams became too widespread, the NCAA created an independent and objective screening service, the National Clearinghouse, to review and then certify the academic records of high school students who hope to earn collegiate athletic scholarships.

The football coach and his assistants at Permian High School worked hard to help their players develop their talents. All young athletes need help at one time or another, and all deserve to have coaches who will, whenever possible and appropriate, serve as advocates for them. Unfortunately, unethical coaches, driven by their desire to win, go beyond mere advocacy for their players. Coaches hold positions of respect in most schools and communities, and many times they compromise their positions when they request special favors or privileges for their athletes. For example, some coaches ask teachers to change grades to help star athletes maintain their academic eligibility. The teachers may change the grades because of their friendship with the coaches or because of the sympathy they have for coaches who labor under extreme pressure to win. When coaches are able to garner special privileges for their athletes, it undermines athletes' attitudes. Some players begin to believe that they don't have to attend classes or complete course assignments because if they fail, all they have to do is let their coach know, and the coach will work with the teacher to change the grade. Unethical advocacy by coaches can also lead athletes to believe that they can violate other school and community standards and escape any consequences. Coaches who take responsibility for their players tarnish their own integrity and character. They also hurt their players by teaching the players that they are not directly responsible for their own behavior and that players who are important to the program will be rescued from any situation by their coaches.

THE COACH'S PERSPECTIVE: REMARKS BY MEL OLSON

In my [Olson's] experience as a coach (Brigham Young University), I have observed that when a coach does not have the overall goals of athletics in proper perspective, the win-at-all-costs attitude takes precedence and rule violations of various kinds occur. In its efforts to curb cheating by coaches and schools at the college level, the NCAA must legislate new rules every year to close the loopholes coaches find to exploit past rules. As more and more coaches sacrifice integrity for winning, the list of schools placed on probation by the NCAA grows annually. Since 1952, more than 390 colleges have been placed on probation for rules violations ranging from illegal payments to athletes, to changing grades, to having athletes participate under assumed names. These are the prices schools and coaches are willing to pay for winning games.

The intensity of big-time sports, the pressure to win, and the unethical behaviors that coaches and schools sometimes resort to in order to win suggest that amateur sports now have more to do with winning than they do with their traditional goal: making athletics part of the educational process. As *Friday Night Lights* suggests, the win-at-all-costs philosophy and the unethical behavior it engenders have trickled down from college sports programs to high school sports programs.

QUESTIONS AND ANSWERS

In the following section, Crowe represents parents and teachers of adolescents as he asks Olson, an experienced football coach, questions.

Friday Night Lights gives a pretty grim view of high school football. How typical are the attitudes revealed in the book? Is this kind of situation unique to football, or do athletes and coaches in other sports fall victim to an almost maniacal devotion like the people in Odessa?

Sports programs with great fan support and money tend to resemble the one presented in *Friday Night Lights*. The coaches face incredible pressure to win and sometimes make decisions that are not in the best interests of their athletes. The area of the country—Texas is notoriously mad about football—has something to do with the pressure applied, but perennial powers in any state in most cases react to the pressure the same way that Odessa's Permian did.

The pressure to win and the mistreatment of athletes tend to occur in the revenue-producing sports, such as football and basketball. This is where the community comes to the event and there is pressure to produce money and to make the play-offs because the better the team does, the more prestige and money the school and community receive. Olympic sports (swimming, track and field, and so on) are competitive and entertaining, but because these sports usually do not receive the same attention and pressures that revenue-producing sports do, they function better in terms of the ways you would expect athletic programs to function in schools. Of course, there are always exceptions as some coaches get things out of perspective.

What are some ways in which unethical practices by high school coaches affect student-athletes academically?

There are several ways that a coach can mess up an athlete in terms of academics. The first would be to advise athletes to take classes that will not prepare them for college. This can prevent an athlete with the talent for college sports to lose the chance to play in college. When coaches are only worried about keeping their players eligible for high school participation, they don't explain the NCAA academic requirements; they allow their athletes to participate even if they are not performing well in class; they may pressure teachers to change grades; they may find ways to give their players academic credit for team participation. The things coaches do demonstrate their attitudes about athletics and academics, and their athletes are quick to pick up the same attitudes the coaches present.

How are high school student-athletes influenced by the behaviors of college coaches and even college athletes?

These coaches and players are role models for young athletes, so when high school players hear of a college athlete violating a rule, the high school players begin to believe that it's okay to break rules—academic or athletic rules—as long as you don't get caught. Often high school players see violations by college athletes and observe that the coaches impose no penalties. They are also influenced by the conduct of college players and coaches they observe on game day. The papers are full of situations where college coaches and athletes circumvent the rules and many times get away with it. Often, their actions are copied at the high school level.

How much blame can be placed on schools for the misconduct of players and coaches?

I feel the schools have a great responsibility. The message is sent early if the tail is wagging the dog. Principals are responsible for their schools; they need to state a philosophy that emphasizes building character and academic talents when they hire coaches, and enforce that philosophy. Athletes should be treated like any other student in the schools. The purpose of school is to educate students and to allow them opportunities to discover and develop their skills. Coaches and athletes who follow the guidelines of their schools can bring honor and recognition to their schools by demonstrating their goal of excellence and that you can win with integrity. Principals who pressure teachers to change grades or who aid coaches or counselors in falsifying transcripts to allow athletes to qualify for college scholarships perform a disservice to the educational community. People, including coaches and athletes, perform up to the expectations of their leaders.

What can high school or college student-athletes do about unethical behavior in their sports?

Athletes can bring to the attention of the people in charge the violations they have observed. High school athletes must not do anything that violates the rules as they know them. They need to express their desire to receive a quality education and to maintain their own integrity in the process. They must desire to win, but they should not violate their conscience in order to win. If athletes report violations to their coaches but do not get a proper response, they should go to the principal or school board. Athletes know what is right and wrong, and they should not violate rules or accept benefits they know violate rules. They need to give a message to their peers and their coaches: "No thanks, I don't cheat, and I can't be bought!"

What can those who aren't directly connected to athletes—teachers and professors—do about sports misconduct in their schools?

Teachers and professors are looked up to as role models by the athletes and nonathletes in their classes. They need to state that they have an interest in the athlete as a student in their class but that rules apply in their class just as rules apply in the athlete's sport. As long as the athlete abides by the rules and does the work of the class, the teacher will be supportive and helpful. But if the athlete cheats or ignores the rules, there will be a penalty, a penalty that may make the athlete unable to play in a game. The teacher needs to let athletes know they will be held responsible for their actions and that while the teacher may be supportive of the coach and sports, he is unwilling to become a part of anything illegal or unethical.

What can coaches do to avoid giving in to pressure from outside sources to win at all costs? Who are some coaches who have managed to be successful and ethical?

Coaches need to maintain a philosophy such as "athletes first and winning second." Coaches should set behavioral goals, academic goals, citizenship goals, as well as athletic goals, and judge the success of their programs based on their achievement in all of these areas. Their sports programs operate under the educational umbrella of the school and should teach educational and life lessons. A good coach can make a man out of a boy and a woman out of a girl. The test of a good coach is whether he prepares his athletes for life, not just for the next game.

There are many great coaches who have been successful and ethical. My high school coach was a great example of a coach who had rules, helped prepare us for life, and still had winning teams. I learned to function within the rules and to work hard to achieve a worthwhile goal. Tom Osborne, recently retired as the football coach of the University of Nebraska, has always been respected for his leadership. Tom is a Christian who practices what he preaches. His graduation rate was 83 percent. He allowed players to make the team if they worked hard. He dealt with discipline problems when they happened and was not accused of cheating to win. His teams have won the National Championship two of the last three years, and he did it with class. He won more games than any other coach in the last twenty-five years and had more academic all-Americans than any other coach. Tom has a doctorate and is a great example to his players of the importance of education.

Joe Paterno, the great football coach at Penn State, was a great example when, during the 1997 college football season, he refused to allow two of his best players to play in a bowl game because of rule violations. Coach Paterno was asked after the bowl game (which they lost) if he felt they lost because they did not have those two players. He replied, "I will not dignify that question with an answer because that would not be fair to my players who played the game and were willing to abide by the rules." I think this is a great example of integrity in a coach and a school. Coach Paterno has always taken pride in playing by the rules, understanding that athletics is a part of the educational process, and still allowing his players to develop the skills to play professional football. His graduation rate is about 85 percent.

Dean Smith just retired as basketball coach of North Carolina and was named *Sports Illustrated* Sportsman of the Year. He was the college basketball coach with the most wins of all time, and he did it with class. He once said, "It's hypocritical to have athletes telling other students to say no to drugs when we say yes to beer ads, and alcohol is a bigger problem." This is an example of the attitude of a great coach: "I judge my team on how they play and not whether we win or lose." He judged his success as a coach on the personal success of his former athletes. He is very proud of Michael Jordan and other players who have gone on to NBA stardom, but he judges his success on the fact that they are good citizens. He lost many times in the Final Four, but his teams played consistently well enough to make the Final Four, and he knew that his players were better people because of their association with his program, not because of Final Four appearances. He was ethical and reaped the rewards of playing by the rules.

We know that coaches feel incredible pressure to win, but what do you think should be the goal of high school and college sports?

Coaches cannot make a great player out of a player who is not potentially great, but they can make a competitor out of any player. There are many successful coaches who focus on different aspects of the game: the coach who does his best to coach the players to success at their sport; the coach who teaches his players to play by the rules; the coach who lives his philosophy of athletics and life; the coach who understands that athletics are part of life but not life itself; the coach who plays by the rules and can live with himself after the game; the coach who is interested in helping the athletes be their best selves in all areas of their lives.

The truly successful coaches not only win on the field, but will see their athletes graduating from school and becoming good citizens in the community. They live by the rules of life and apply the lessons they learned in sports to be successful. The coach who works his hardest and gives his best to his job can walk away, win or lose, knowing that he is successful. Coaches should keep sports in proper perspective, knowing that a loss isn't the same as death, that something can be learned from every game. Good coaches teach that you are not judged on your wins and losses but on how you achieve those wins or endured those losses. A good coach must also be a good teacher, a good parent, and a good member of the community. The best tribute to a coach comes when players play well, are well coached, and are good citizens and students.

Given the attitudes prevalent among athletes, coaches, and sports supporters, what do you think is the future of high school and college sports?

Sports are an important part of society. Despite the problems sometimes associated with school sports programs, it is worth fighting to keep sports in the school system. We need to emulate the ethical successful coaches and eliminate the unethical tactics used by other coaches. We need to do a better job of training moral coaches for the future. School administrators need to take control of sports programs and make sure they are run ethically. Coaches need to take responsibility for their behavior and learn that unethical and illegal activities will not be condoned. Because the media tend to promote the negative aspects of sports, we need to promote the positive things happening in athletics: the athletes who are graduating, athletes who are model citizens, the good examples former athletes learned from their coaches.

I have not given up hope. I am actively involved in coaching education programs, and I work with schools to take back control of their athletic programs. There are lots of problems with sports, but I, like many other former athletes, am thankful that I had coaches at the crossroads of my life to care for and guide me. I will work to guarantee my children the same opportunity for their future. Parents need to get involved, administrators need to address problems, and society needs to demand higher standards for coaches and athletes. There is hope as long as we have coaches like Tom Osborne, Joe Paterno, and Dean Smith in the world. I like the saying "I am only one, but I am one. I can't do everything, but I can do something, and what I can do, I ought to do, and what I ought to do, by the grace of God, I will do." Improvement will only come when each of us becomes involved and makes coaches and athletes responsible for their own actions.

RECOMMENDED READINGS

Fiction Works

Bennett, J. (1995). *The Squared Circle*. New York: Scholastic. 288 pp. (ISBN: 0–590–48671–3). High School (HS).

As a freshman at Southern Illinois University, Sonny promises to be the star who will lead his team to an NCAA championship, but he's not ready for the academic life of college nor for the shady dealings that come with big-time college sports.

Brancato, R. (1988). *Winning*. New York: Alfred A. Knopf Books for Young Readers. 224 pp. (ISBN: 0–394–807–510). Middle School (MS), HS.

Paralyzed by a football injury, a high school athlete struggles to accept his disability and how it has changed his identity, his relationships with others, and his future.

Cannon, A. E. (1992). *The Shadow Brothers*. New York: Dell. 192 pp. (ISBN: 0–440–21167–0). MS, HS.

A 16-year-old Navajo student has spent most of his life in a white, suburban school. When he begins to question his identity, sports provide a helpful outlet.

Crutcher, C. (1986). *Running Loose*. New York: Bantam Doubleday Dell. 192 pp. (ISBN: 0–440–97570–0). HS.

A high school football player quits his team because the coach orders his players to intentionally injure the star on an opposing team.

Crutcher, C. (1991). *Athletic Shorts*. New York: Bantam Doubleday Dell. 160 pp. (ISBN: 0–440–21390–8). HS.

These six short stories cover a range of ethical issues faced by high school athletes: racism, bigotry, violence, anger, family relationships.

Deuker, C. (1991). *On the Devil's Court*. New York: Avon Flare. 256 pp. (ISBN: 0–380–70879–5). MS.

As a new student in school, Seth struggles with his sense of failure when he doesn't make the basketball team. He's willing to sell his soul for basketball success.

Deuker, C. (1994). *Heart of a Champion*. New York: Avon. 176 pp. (ISBN: 0–380–72269–0). MS.

Seth, a high school baseball player, must learn to compete and to deal with his talented but irresponsible best friend and teammate Jimmy.

Draper, S. (1994). *Tears of a Tiger*. New York: Simon & Schuster. 192 pp. (ISBN: 0–689–31878–2). MS, HS.

A night of drinking leads to a fiery car crash that kills the captain of the high school basketball team. Driving the car was his best friend and teammate, who now must deal with grief and guilt.

Gallo, D. (Ed). (1995). *Ultimate sports*. New York: Bantam Doubleday Dell Books. 320 pp. (ISBN: 0–385–32152–X). HS.

These sixteen stories by popular writers for teenagers examine conflicts that arise in a range of major and minor sports from football to racquetball and tennis to cross-country.

Guy, D. (1992). *Football Dreams*. New York: Signet. 288 pp. (ISBN: 0–872–23624–2). HS.

A high school football player must deal with the growing pressures of school and football compounded by the gradual death of his father.

Klass, D. (1989). *Wrestling with Honor*. New York: Dutton Children's Books. 208 pp. (ISBN: 0–525–67268–0). MS, HS.

The captain of the wrestling team, a kid who never uses drugs, fails a drug test and is declared ineligible. He refuses to take a second test because he believes drug testing is a violation of personal rights.

Lee, M. G. (1998). *Necessary Roughness*. New York: HarperCollins 240 pp. (ISBN: 0–06–447169–1). MS, HS.

In an effort to become a part of the new high school he is attending, a Korean American high school student dedicates himself to football and its violence and recklessness.

Lipsyte, R. (1967, reprinted 1991). *The Contender*. New York: HarperCollins Children's Books. 190 pp. (ISBN: 0–06–447152–7). MS, HS.

A teenager in Harlem hopes that boxing will be his ticket out of a life of poverty but first must discover for himself if he has what it takes to be a champion.

Lynch, C. (1994). *Iceman*. New York: HarperCollins Children's Books. 160 pp. (ISBN: 0–06–0233–40–0). MS, HS.

A 14-year-old hockey player loves hockey, especially the violence. His parents, who don't understand that his violence is an effort to please his father, worry that he's becoming a psychopath.

Miklowitz, G. D. (1990). *Anything to Win*. New York: Bantam Double-day Dell. 144 pp. (ISBN: 0–440–20732–0). MS, HS.

A high school quarterback is pressured by his coach to use steroids in order to qualify for a college scholarship.

Myers, W. D. (1983). *Hoops*. New York: Bantam Doubleday Dell Books for Young Readers. 192 pp. (ISBN: 0–440–93884–8). MS, HS.

A young basketball player dreams that his basketball talent will allow him to escape life in the ghetto. His coach helps him see that his dreams are not realistic.

Myers, W. D. (1996). *Slam!* New York: Scholastic, Inc. 272 pp. (ISBN: 0–590–48668–3). MS, HS.

Slam is an inner-city high school basketball star with dreams of NBA stardom who believes he really doesn't need to worry about grades or anything else to make it in life.

Tamar, E. (1993). *Fair Game*. New York: Harcourt Brace. 272 pp. (ISBN: 0–15–2270655) MS, HS.

Several high school athletes, who, because of their status, believe they are above the rules, brutally rape a retarded girl.

Nonfiction Works

Bissinger, H. G. (1991). *Friday Night Lights: A Town, a Team and Dream*. New York: HarperCollins. 368 pp. (ISBN: 0–06–097406–0). HS.

This is the account of the year Bissinger spent in Odessa, Texas, following the Permian High School football team. It provides a detailed and inside look at a big-time, successful high school football program.

Davies, R. O. (1994). *America's Obsession: Sports and Society since 1945*. New York: Harcourt Brace. 192 pp. (ISBN: 0–03–073332–4). HS.

A recent look at the various aspects of sports, including ethics, racism, television, business, women, college athletics, and how sports influence American society. (Also available on audiocassette.)

Ralbovsky, M. (1974). *Lords of the Locker Room: The American Way of Coaching and Its Effect on Youth*. New York: P. H. Wyden. 236 pp. (ISBN: 0–88326–071–9). HS.

Though published in 1974, this is still a scathing indictment of unethical coaches. In chapter three, Ralbovsky writes, "In America today, it is entirely possible that millions of young males acquire their first lessons in cheating in the playgrounds of the neighborhood schools. The coaches do the honors" (35).

Videos

The Basketball Diaries. (1995). Directed by Scott Kalvert. (ASIN: 6303567126). HS.

This movie, starring Leonardo DiCaprio, presents the recollections of Jim Carroll and the drug abuse, violence, and basketball that were part of a New York City high school in the 1960s. Produced by Chris Black-well and Dan Genetti. New Line Pictures.

Hoop Dreams. (1994) Directed by Steve James. (ASIN: 6303413145). MS, HS.

This award-winning documentary film follows the lives of two inner-city Chicago athletes who attempt to use their basketball skills to escape the ghetto. Executive Producer Catherine Allan. New Line Studios.

REFERENCES

Bissinger, H. G. (1990). *Friday Night Lights: A Town, a Team, a Dream.* New York: Addison Wesley Longman, Inc.

Brooks, B. (1984). *The Moves Make the Man.* New York: HarperCollins.

Cormier, R. (1974). *The Chocolate War.* New York: Bantam Books.

Crutcher, C. (1986). *Running Loose.* New York: Bantam Doubleday Dell.

Guy, D. (1980). *Football Dreams.* New York: Signet.

Lipsyte, R. (1975). *Sports World: An American Dreamland.* New York: Quad-rangle; Times Book Co.

Ralbovsky, M. (1974). *Lords of the Locker Room: The American Way of Coaching and Its Effect on Youth.* New York: P. H. Wyden.

CHAPTER EIGHT

Leaving Home: Transitions and Independence

Connie S. Zitlow
with Janet M. Rogers

I have found a new addition to my favorite book list. [The book] made me think, made me cry, made my happy, angry, and guilty. Not every book can evoke so many things. After thinking about [it] for a while, I realized how much it spoke to me as a first semester college student. I am in a new place, knowing no one, and with new experiences, new responsibilities, and a life of decisions . . . before me.

Right now my biggest decisions are pertaining to what I will become, and who I will spend the rest of my life with. However, in the course of one day, many more smaller decisions are placed before me. . . . In addition, every day is filled with simple enjoyments and small pleasures. . . . And every once in a while I am comforted and made to smile by a memory from home. . . . It's not until a person stops and thinks about it that the memories become real again . . . and you realize that many of them are gone and left behind. In this way it seems that any college student is able to relate to Jonas in such a way that a young[er] adult would not be able to. We are like Jonas.

from Jackie's log, fall 1997
(Lowry, *The Giver*, 1993)

The surprising connections that Jackie, a college student, found in Lois Lowry's book *The Giver* (1993) show that a literary work of art has the potential to reach readers of all ages, not just the age for which it might be targeted by an author or a publisher. When we read good literature, we merge with characters and become a part of their experiences. The wisdom and appreciation evident in Jackie's log entry show how readers respond to the moving celebration of the human spirit, which Lowry portrays in Jonas. The age of the protagonist and of the reader, in this case, do not matter. Jackie took on the perspective of another human and made the story her own. Her words are the expression of a person who is in a new place, faced with new responsibilities and decisions to make, a person who looks backward and forward while trying to sort out who she is and who she will become.

For many young adults, the mid to late teenage years involve reworking their relationships with family and home as they define their more adult identity. Often, as older teens sort out who they are, their changing view of self is accompanied by an exploration of parent and family issues from a distance. The distance is a physical one for older teens who go away to college; for all teens, the distance can be an emotional one, brought on by clashes with parents or a change in the makeup of the family. In many books for young adults, issues associated with identity and coming of age are dealt with by a person of high school age, but college students also see the connections between the protagonist in a story and their own lives.

Many of the ideas in this chapter have emerged from book discussions and literature log entries of first-year university students, such as Jackie, who had the opportunity to choose an academic honors tutorial where young adult (YA) novels were read. Ideas have also been included that were noted by college juniors and seniors enrolled in children's and YA literature courses that are a part of their teacher education programs. Regardless of the age of the college reader, they see the literary merit and the timeless themes in YA literature.

It is important to note that books written by "some of today's top YA authors . . . are, without a doubt, as substantive, incisively written, and revealing as many of the best books published for an adult audience" (Cooper and Zvirin, 1998, 792). The college youth are often surprised not only by the literary quality of the books, but also by the way the situations portrayed in the novels parallel their own experiences. In their more independent role, especially as related to day-to-day decisions, college students understand the struggles for identity experienced by younger teens. In addition, some adolescents have experienced, or are living with, some of the difficult issues now dealt with in YA novels. Because all good literature deals with human interactions and events, the classification of a work as a YA novel is not what determines whether its themes seem valid to older adolescents. As their lives are in transition, they experience conflicts and uncertainties that are part of looking at earlier years from a different, more fully independent, vantage point.

RELATIONSHIPS AND CONNECTIONS: LITERATURE AND PSYCHOLOGY

In a moving "narrative vignette" written by a college student in a class taught by Tom Romano, a young woman has found out how a piece of literature can help her understand her world articulate her feelings. She writes. "I, a senior in college seeing herself in a young adult novel, odd, but true" (7). Romano, in "Relationships with Literature" (1998), refers to what Robert Coles has written about "literature's capacity 'to work its way well into our thinking life as well as our reveries or idle thoughts, even our moods and dreams' " (9). After many years of reading, as Romano has noted, it is not unusual for readers to get hold of a book that depicts a part of their identity long dormant (12). This connection between experienced readers and books that revive dormant feelings and ideas is the basis for the focus, within this chapter, on transitions. The discussion that follows includes examples of YA books with themes that relate to the experiences of readers who, like Tom Romano and his students, have "re-experienced the effect of literature" on their lives (9). When they encounter fiction, readers are not likely to analyze their own experiences; instead, the text acts as a vehicle that brings their experiences to life on the page. Because of the changes that occur when young people move away from home, the experiences that are connected to issues of independence, identity, and family are often the ones that are brought alive, for those young people, through literature.

There are terms used by psychologists that refer to the changes involved in achieving an identity and becoming independent. As Sharon Stringer has stated in her book *Conflict and Connection: The Psychology of Young Adult Literature* (1997), even though they can be painful, both conflict and change can create the wisdom that leads to autonomy. In fact those devoted to facilitating the psychological development of college students, such as counselors and other student affairs professionals, would argue that conflict and challenge (and the accompanying emotional turmoil) are necessary for change to occur. "Discovering who we are, developing autonomy, facing conflict, establishing intimacy, and resisting peer pressure are lifelong tasks" (Stringer, 1997, xi). College youth, like their younger counterparts, vacillate between wanting values and decisions dictated to them by others and wanting to think for themselves as they reexamine their beliefs. Although the majority of youth enter college in a state of moratorium, a time of exploration and questioning, students leave home in various stages of identity achievement. Those who think their direction is clearly established, who have not examined various options, enter college in what James Marcia termed identity-foreclosure (Stringer, 1997, 3–6). Some select a negative identity as they rebel against the role defined for them by parents. For college students who come from chaotic or difficult circumstances, the reworking of their relationship with their parents is often especially problematic. Sometimes issues that have not been addressed do not emerge until young adults are away and begin to compare their families with those of others. Most young adults want the opportunity to think critically and develop their own sense of morality and identity, particularly if they have moved beyond the identity confusion that is relatively common during early adolescence.

Reading for themselves about youth in various stages of "sorting out" can be an important part of the internal probing that leads to identity achievement as college students learn to balance self-sufficiency and meaningful affiliation with others (Stringer, 1997, 8–9). As younger teens, and again as college-age youth, they are in a period of transition, experiencing "individuation," the tension between separation and connection. As they become increasingly aware that real life does not offer easy answers, especially if they experience painful consequences from decisions they have made, they admire the compassion, persistence, courage, and honesty of protagonists in YA literature such as Jonas in *The Giver*, Jerry in *The Chocolate War*, Maggie in *Spite Fences*, and Yuki in *Shizuko's Daughter*, among others. Often it is during the college years when young adults develop a new sense of behavioral and emotional autonomy. This new sense of autonomy results in the development of an identity as a distinct, separate person who is able to gradually redefine a more cooperative relationship with parents (Stringer, 1997, 16). But other times what has caused the separation from home results in an emotional distance that cannot be repaired. Some young adults find out that being independent does not bring the happiness they had expected it would.

LEAVING

Whether there is happiness or not when the young adult looks back, the leaving is often a difficult part of growing up. In literature, we have various examples of what the leaving involves; sometimes its significance is not realized until years later. One fine example is the title story in the collection *The Leaving and Other Stories* by Budge Wilson (1990). Set in Nova Scotia, it is told by Sylvie, a 22-year-old narrator who, as a college student, is thinking back to her first leaving, which occurred when she was 12 years old. Sylvie first sees Dalhousie University during the surprise three-day trip to Halifax that was initiated by her mother, who says she plans to do some thinking (108). When the two of them are in the public library, Sylvie's mother tells Sylvie that she has recently finished reading a book she found in a box of clothes from the Salvation Army. From *The Feminine Mystique*, a book that was "real troublin' " but good (115), she learned she "weren't alone" (114). The leaving involves a brief time of freedom from work in a male-dominated home. More significantly, the journey is a symbolic flight to freedom, a release for the mother, who returns with the courage to be more assertive about the oppressive language and daily commands of her husband and sons. And as a result of the leaving, Sylvie gains a new sense of possibilities about who and what she might become.

John Moore, in his book *Interpreting Young Adult Literature* (1997), notes how Sylvie moves in and out of memory and time as she quilts together the events before and after the leaving. She crafts a finished story that circles back and does not really end (131). In his discussion of the book, Moore refers to the quilting metaphor used by Mary Catherine Bateson in *Composing a Life* (1989). This metaphor fits the young adult in college who is in the process of constructing a selfhood, an adult identity, a new quilt. But however new the pattern of the quilt, it must be sewn against a backing. College students can find in YA literature a variety of ways different characters view their moment of leaving and, when looking back as Sylvie does, they consider how they feel about the backing and about what they have left behind.

Molly, a college student, remembered thinking that her leaving would be very difficult for her mother. But when she left, her mother seemed to understand that it was time for Molly to go. As she read Katherine Paterson's YA novel *Jacob Have I Loved* (1980), Molly was struck with the realization that her leaving had been like that of Louise, the narrator of the story. Much of Paterson's novel is about Louise's adolescent years, which are a painful time of uncertainty about her identity and her feelings of rivalry toward her twin sister, Caroline, whom she sees as the favored one. When Caroline leaves their Chesapeake Bay island home to further her music studies, Louise, who loves the sea, stays to work with her father. To Louise, her own identity is like that of the female crabs who just get soft and die (Paterson, 133). Finally the time comes when she decides she can stay no longer. She is surprised that her mother says she understands that Louise must leave, but she will miss her daughter terribly. Years later, with a new perspective and sense of identity, Louise, as the midwife in an Appalachian community, delivers twins. She then understands the circumstances of her own birth when the "weaker" twin must have immediate care. She has achieved autonomy and is able to sort out her past, looking back with new understanding, happiness, and reconciliation.

For some young people, there is no happiness and understanding when leaving home or when looking back. Like the title character in Jamaica Kincaid's *Lucy* (1990), they expect leaving home and arriving at a new place will be accomplished with one swift act. Their initial longing to be back where they came from comes as a surprise, but the longing does not last. While working in New York as an au pair, Lucy comes to realize that untruths in family life do not belong exclusively to her and her family back in the Caribbean. She had planned her separation for many years because she hated how her mother expected great deeds of her sons but not of Lucy, who had been expected to become a nurse and have a sense of duty and obedience to her parents. After Lucy is away from home for one year, she knows "that girl [has] gone out of existence" (133). At age 20, she is inventing herself. She begins to see the past as a line you draw for "yourself, or sometimes it gets drawn for you; either way, there it is, your past, a collection of people you used to be and things you used to do . . . the person you no longer are, the situations you are no longer in" (137). After leaving her position as an au pair, Lucy is free to come and go as she pleases. But the feeling of bliss, of a longing fulfilled, that she thought would come with her freedom, is nowhere to be found inside of her (158).

While Kincaid's novel was not written as a work of YA literature, it portrays what many young adults come to realize about being away from home: that they are never completely away. Their longed-for independence does not guarantee happiness or reconciliation. They find adult independence is really a kind of interdependence between their past and the evolving present, between self and family, self and others.

When Sylvie remembers her first brief leaving, after Louise has left her island home in the 1940s, and after Lucy no longer lives in the West Indies, each looks back through the lives of their mothers. Their achieving an identity, putting together a new pattern, was done against a backing. Similarly, even when the circumstances for the protagonists in Kyoko Mori's works are sad and difficult, and even when the leaving is an emotional separation that occurs before the physical departure, the young women in her works put together new lives, each of which relies on solid backing. For Yuki in Mori's *Shizuko's Daughter* (1993), the backing is made up of the memory of her mother's love of her and of beauty.

NAVIGATING MY WAY: DEFINING SELF

Kyoko Mori's books, including fiction, poetry, memoir, and essays, portray many of the themes associated with being on one's own and sorting out an identity that leads to autonomy. The journey for 12-year-old Yuki, who lives in Kobe, Japan, is very difficult after her mother, who could no longer live with her husband's unfaithfulness, committed suicide. Yuki's father is cold and distant; her stepmother is rigid and uncaring. Yuki feels like an outsider in her home; at school she is separated from peers by her family situation, her intelligence, athletic skill, academic ability, and independence. Where does she belong? How will Yuki develop a sense of who she is and who she will become? Her grandparents love her, but her father will not permit her to live with them. She is, however, strengthened by her visits with them and by memories of times when she and her mother had enjoyed the beautiful shapes of pottery and the flowers whose vivid colors were such a contrast to the drabness and lack of color that characterized life with her father. She remembers what her mother taught her about nature and art and life.

Six years after her mother's death, as Yuki prepares to leave for Nagasaki, she goes to the attic to look through her mother's things. Because she has paid her tuition and a month's rent, she has barely enough money for the train ticket and will not be able to ship anything or send for anything later. Vivid and loving memories accompany each item she unpacks as she wonders what she might fit into the small bag that she will take with her:

> It would be wrong to take any ten or twenty things as though her mother had been nothing but an assortment of dresses, necklaces, and a few pho-

tographs. . . . To save a few things and leave the others was to say that her mother could be reduced to one essence, like the mothballs that disappeared in every way except their smell. She would not do that. . . . These things were not necessary for her to go on remembering. In her sketchbook, she had drawn pictures of the clothes her mother had made for her, and of the pottery they had bought and used together. Even more than that, she had the memory in her mind. . . . My mother and I, Yuki thought, we are moving on. We leave behind nothing but empty spaces—empty spaces turning green as we move away from here. (147–148)

Yuki leaves without saying good-bye and does not plan to return. A week later, her father burns the contents of the boxes.

In a college classroom, when she was discussing *Shizuko's Daughter* with her classmates, Jennie hesitantly said her relationship with her father and her leaving had been like Yuki's. She had not returned home. The art of Mori's book continues to speak to Jennie. It does not matter that she is older than Yuki, has not lived in Japan, or that the beautiful images and vivid details of Kyoko Mori's work are very different from the circumstances of Jennie's life. She understands Yuki's pain and also sees the strength in Yuki's independence and determination. This book, for Jennie, is a means to bring alive an experience and connect to another, because Mori's very personal writing has become what composition theorist James Moffett refers to as *transpersonal*. It has reached outward to blend with others.

Because of the circumstances of many college students' lives, they understand a sense of loss, particularly when they have no control over a situation. Many, like Yuki, know the difficulty of accepting change and the fear of beginning new relationships.

ON THEIR OWN AND MAKING DECISIONS

For some young adults, their independence and searching come about because they have been abandoned in one way or another. Extreme cases of youth being completely on their own include Gary Paulsen's adventure stories such as *Hatchet* (1987), which is set in the Canadian wilderness, and *Haymeadow* (1992), which is set in a mountain meadow in Wyoming. In both stories, ingenuity helps the young protagonists, who are completely alone, survive. Brian emerges from the Canadian woods as a tougher, wiser, more thoughtful and confident person who changes his mind about telling his father "the secret" about his mother. In *Hay-*

meadow, John and his father establish a new relationship after John survives forty-seven days in the mountains tending the sheep.

Although Jerry Renault, in Robert Cormier's *Chocolate War* (1974), lives with his father, he is also alone. The challenges to his survival are a very different kind from those faced by Brian or John, but he is also a young adult who must make his own decisions. Since Jerry's mother died of cancer, his father has been sleepwalking through life. In many ways Jerry's life is like Yuki's in *Shizuko's Daughter*: his mother has died, he is unable to communicate with his father, and he feels like an outsider. His identity begins to emerge when he takes a difficult stand. Jerry finds amazing courage and strength even as he agonizes about his decision not to be a part of the school chocolate sale. This story of the strength of the individual against all the others at Trinity High School, the secret society (the Vigils), and the vicious Brother Leon, shocks readers into realization about what happens when people do not take a stand against evil. Cormier's book has become a standard by which other YA literature is measured, and it offers much to ponder for readers of any age, especially young adults who are sorting out various options and making decisions about their independence.

The title character in Brock Cole's *Celine* (1989) is, in many ways, as alone as Jerry. At age 16, she is not happy about living with her young stepmother while her father is away on an extended lecture tour. He has promised that if she will "show a little maturity" (18), she will be able to spend the summer in Italy. But spunky, funny, artistic Celine is the most responsible character in the story. She cares for her neighbor, 8-year-old Jake, whose parents are getting a divorce. Celine tries to define her identity through her art and is troubled by an assigned essay on *Catcher in the Rye* that she must write. She must destroy her masterpiece, *Test Patterns*, before she can feel free to begin a self-portrait. One example of her emotional growth in the story is her realization, as she looks to the future, that "things don't seem so simple anymore" (216).

Like Celine, Rainbow in Alice Childress's *Rainbow Jordan* is vulnerable, lonely, and confused. Rainbow's parents are divorced, and her mother works as a go-go dancer. Fourteen-year-old Rainbow is left alone so often that the family social worker sends her to live in an "interim home" with Miss Josie. Rainbow makes up stories about her family situation, experiences problems with her girlfriends, and almost gives in to the sexual pressures of Eljay. But she is strong and decides to tell Miss Josie the truth. In turn, Miss Josie faces the truth about being abandoned by her husband. Also like Celine, Rainbow is the most adult character in the novel.

Many novels show that when parents are weak, the young person must be that much stronger. Sometimes the parent is inadequate; other times the parent is absent. Katherine Paterson's *Lyddie* (1991) portrays another strong female who is left alone to find her own direction in the mid-1840s. Lyddie is the head of the family even before her mother leaves. When the family is deserted by the father, and later when her unstable mother leaves then hires out Lyddie to work at a tavern, Lyddie is left alone. She is determined to find a way to reunite the family and save the farm. The same stubbornness that leads Lyddie to become a mill worker in Lowell, Massachusetts, also enslaves her. Lyddie's quest and determination lead to personal growth and independence only when she faces her own selfhood and is willing to decide what she must retain and what she must let go.

At the beginning of Lyddie's story, she saves her family by staring down a bear who enters their home in search of food. At the end of the novel, the bear Lyddie must stare down is inside herself. She has to resolve her internal conflict between freedom and oppression. As Sharon Stringer (1997) points out, significant modification requires thinking through our behaviors, our reflection on action (41). Often during the course of a quest for something, characters in a story learn something that is different from what they anticipated, and they change significantly. This aspect of YA literature is what many college readers see as a clear connection to what they experience.

In Bruce Brooks's novel *Midnight Hour Encores* (1986), 16-year-old Sibilance is smart and self-assured, but lonely. She is glad when her father tells her she can change her flower-child name of Esalen Starness Blue to Sibilance T. Spooner. A world-class cellist, she lives with her father, Taxi, but she longs to know the mother who abandoned her at birth. Together, Sib and Taxi journey across the United States to find Sib's mother. While in California, Sib does find her mother, but she is very different from what Sib expected; she has become a successful professional woman. Sib also surprises herself by realizing what she has had all along in her loving father. Her quest results in a significant change, but that change is quite different from what Sib had anticipated. Her discovery of love for her father is the perfect complement to her complex intelligence. In *From Romance to Realism: Fifty Years of Growth and Change in Young Adult Literature* (1996), Michael Cart refers to this novel as one that can be particularly meaningful for the young adult in transition. Cart describes Brooks as a powerful writer who has sympathy for the outsider and whose words "offer wisdom, art, and enjoyment" (253). His intelligent, complex characters have strong, idiosyncratic voices. Brooks, like Kyoko Mori, has great sympathy for the outsider and great respect for the intelligence of his readers.

In Mori's book *One Bird* (1995), 15-year-old Megumi feels alone and, like Sib, is searching. Life with an unfaithful husband had become so difficult for Megumi's mother that she left to live with her parents in the small village where she was born. Megumi is left to live with her father and cranky grandmother. Again, as in *Shizuko's Daughter*, Mori explores the mother-daughter relationship, the desire to be different and yet wanting to belong, and the search for what life is about. Megumi questions the religious beliefs of her friend Kiyoshi Kato, the pastor's son, but she likes what her teachers at Christian Girl's Academy say about freedom, respect, and love. Gradually, through her friendship with a woman veterinarian whom she helps heal wild birds, Megumi learns how she can become more than a lone bird who barely endures. Her story is an exploration of the complexity of truth and lies, a moral journey like that of many college youth who search for what they believe is truth and who often feel caught and very much alone in their search.

CAUGHT BETWEEN HOLDING ON AND LETTING GO

In YA fiction, there are many stories of young persons caught between what is truth for them and what their parents have dictated. A part of the difficulty of sorting out is determining what to retain and what must change. Some young adults are not aware of the extent of the distance between their parents' politics or religion and their own until they go home after having been away. Others are keenly aware of the differences before they leave. For all youth, at several different points in their life, this carving out of an identity that is linked to their past and yet different is a part of developing a clear sense of individuality.

The questioning about what parents believe and the tension involved in the exploration of how one will be different from them is apparent in the work of Han Nolan, particularly in *Send Me Down a Miracle* (1996). For 14-year-old Charity, who has always been the perfect daughter, the exploration begins when an artist, Adrienne Dabney, returns to her hometown of Casper, Alabama. Everything about Adrienne is an affront to Charity's rigid preacher father: her dress, mannerisms, decisions, and most of all, her artistic experiment of locking herself in her home for a month long sensory deprivation exercise. The exercise results in a revelation that splits the "god-fearing community."

In many ways, including the fact that Charity's mother has left for an undetermined length of time, Charity's moral journey about what is truth for her is similar to that of Megumi in *One Bird*. Both girls question what they had previously accepted as truth and learn they must find their own way. Charity represents what some young people do in the course of their moral journey. Charity tries on another life, one that is very different from what is expected of her. The free-spirited Adrienne is exciting to her, and Charity wants to be like her—even to the point of dreaming about being an artist, too, and following Adrienne to New York.

Charity finds it unbelievable that her father does not understand the response of people in the community, such as "Mad Joe," who need to believe Adrienne really did have a revelation and saw Jesus sitting in a chair in her home. She is surprised about how different she feels about her father than she had ever felt before: "I was mad at Daddy, really mad. I don't think I'd ever felt that way about him before and it was giving me all kinds of crazy thoughts. I was questioning everything. Like why should I stay away from someone who could help me, who could show me how to be a real artist, a real somebody?" (133). Charity defies his orders to stay away from Adrienne, to remain in her room and memorize Bible verses about idol worship and obedience to parents. Her father is holding on too tight, and something is "bound to bust," as Mad Joe says (184). When Charity's father finally realizes he is losing her, as he lost her mother, the tight hold breaks, and Charity learns something about finding her own way. Nolan's story, like those of Kyoko Mori, does not give answers, but helps readers ask questions in a safe place. This balance is also achieved in Anne Fine's *The Tulip Touch* (1997).

NEW VIEW OF PARENTS: CHANGE IN RELATIONSHIP

Charity's new view of her father, whom she had grown up idolizing, leads to a change in their relationship. His reactions to Adrienne's visits and to the surprising responses of "his flock," show Charity a view of her father that she did not see before. When he loses control, it is inevitable that a change will result. Many times the changes that occur in the relationship between young adults and their parents are promoted by sudden, dramatic events. Sometimes because of what young people see about their parents and what they experience as a result of decisions made by parents, the change in relationship cannot be repaired. Robert Cormier's *After the First Death* (1979), a book like his others—one that can be read on many levels, offers one example. Ben is not even a part of the dramatic event when terrorists capture a school bus full of young children that Kate is driving. However, when the terrorists deliver their demands to the army, Ben is sent by his father, General Marchand, to become the substitute hostage. During the interrogation, Ben has to face the fact that his father betrayed him by expecting the capture. Sensitive, trusting Ben sees what his father really is and what he has done. Nothing will be the same again. It is not only Ben's view of his father that is changed; Ben's own selfhood and the life he had come to know are gone.

Realities are not softened in Cormier's fiction, nor are they in Paula Fox's *The Eagle Kite* (1995), another book where truth, parent-child relationships, and coming to terms with change are explored. Liam, like Ben, feels betrayed, as do many college students who face circumstances where they must live with disappointments brought about by a parent. Liam has buried his memory of a scene on the beach in which he saw his father embracing a young man. The scene comes into full view again when Liam learns that his father is dying of AIDS and that he did not contract the disease as a result of a blood transfusion, as his mother claimed. Frustrated by changes after his father moves out to go to the seaside to die, trying to erase the burning image of the scarecrowlike beggar with AIDS who sits across from their apartment, Liam must face the fact that his parent is not the person he thought he was. The illusions he held as a child, like those held by Charity in Nolan's novel, must be abandoned. Healing, for Liam, begins when he visits his father one Thanksgiving. As time passes, Liam and his mother learn to love again the spirit of the man they once knew.

Paula Fox's *A Place Apart* (1980) is another wise and compassionate view of the complexities of human nature. Tory Finch and her mother move from Boston and search for a way to put their lives back together after Tory's father dies suddenly. Tory meets rich, exciting Hugh, who helps her travel a little distance from herself (70); however, Hugh is condescending and manipulative. Tory feels she does not belong anywhere until her uncle helps her find her own place apart.

Tory learns, as does Catherine in Fox's *The Moonlight Man* (1986), that life's happenings may be chance but that what one makes of life is not chance. Catherine finally accepts her parents' twelve-year divorce when she realizes her "moonlight" father is an undependable man who hides from himself as much as from her. During a summer visit with him, Catherine ends up in the role of the adult when she is the one who must drive an old car with her drunk father and his friends in the backseat. Her view of him alternates between seeing him as a moonlight person, who is insubstantial yet able to transform everything he touches, and seeing him as an aging and weak wreck. Her father finally admits there is nothing funny about the way people betray each other. Certainly her view of him and their relationship is changed.

In some books, both the young person and the adult face a change in identity as a result of the events portrayed. In other stories, the significant change occurs in the ways young people view their parents. In Kathryn Lasky's *Memoirs of a Bookbat* (1994), 14-year-old Harper Jessup begins to see how her parents' promotion of censorship, which is their quest for control of how and what people think, is also a means to control her choices and decisions. She must come to terms with the fact that she can no longer bear their perspective; hers will be different.

In Cynthia Rylant's *Fine White Dust* (1986), serious young Pete is also critical of his parents. He is disturbed that they are not more religious. After he goes to a religious revival, he finds he is attracted to the charismatic Preacher Man. His emotions are so overwhelming that he cannot express what he feels to his best friend, Rufus. Pete is determined to go his own way and leave town with Preacher Man, in a way very similar to Charity's decision to follow Adrienne. After Pete is stunned at being betrayed and left behind by the Man, he looks again with appreciation at his parents and his friend Rufus. He also learns to accept the fact that he is different from them. Whether the situation ends with a reconciliation and appreciation or not, when young people face the conflicts involved in making decisions that differ from those of their parents, change toward autonomy results.

Like works of contemporary realistic fiction, the Collier brothers' historical fiction work *My Brother Sam Is Dead* (1974), a favorite of readers of many ages, shows the inner turmoil that young people suffer when their view of their parents and of their own beliefs changes. Tim does not want to be disobedient to his Tory parents, but he idolizes his older brother Sam, who has joined the Rebels. The events of war lead to a dramatic change in the relationship between Sam and his parents. Tim is left to face a different, more complex view of them than he previously held. Tim's feelings of indecision, self-doubt, and confusion, especially as he assumes massive responsibilities, are certainly similar to what Charity, Pete, and Harper experience.

I AM DIFFERENT

Many college students find, like the protagonists in various YA books, that they are different from their parents. Through reading YA books, they are able to explore questions and issues raised in the stories that parallel their own questions and issues. Many know that deciding to take a stand on a difficult issue, particularly if it pits them against their parents, is a painful but necessary part of being different, of achieving independence and an authentic self-identity. College students are often particularly troubled when their interests and desires conflict with their parents' expectations in terms of religion, cultural norms, career goals, or sexual preferences. They find comfort and a sense of companionship when they read about fictitious characters who must deal with similar issues.

College students understand the pain felt by adolescent characters in YA novels. They therefore come to realize why their responses to the YA books that are favorites of readers much younger than themselves are so intense. It is not the age of the protagonist, but the experiences of young people who are in conflict with their parents, that elicit strong responses. For example, Jess in Katherine Paterson's *Bridge to Terabithia* (1977) knows the difficulty of being different from his parents' expectations. He wonders where he fits and whether he is loved. The story of Jess's close friendship with Leslie, who is an intelligent, imaginative, athletic girl, is considered a children's book. Yet many college students, with their newfound complexity in thought and emotion, are moved to tears when they read it, even if they first read it when in fifth grade.

M. E. Kerr's *Deliver Us from Evie* (1994) is an example of a YA book that shows parents' concerns about the different choices their adolescent children make. In Kerr's novel, complications in the family's dynamics lead to change: one child pulls away, friendships cross socioeconomic and religious lines. After losing much of their farm to a flood, Evie's family fears losing her, too. Her lifestyle and choices are very different from what the members of her family and community in rural Missouri expect. Her mother constantly tries to insist that Evie is not homosexual. Ultimately, to be true to herself and her emerging sexual identity, Evie leaves the family and the farm to live in New York with Patsy, the beautiful, rich woman she loves.

Scars left by differences are explored by Michael Cart in *My Father's Scar* (1996). Andy Logan's story alternates between his confused and

lonely days as a freshman in college and his memories of pivotal and painful occurrences from when he was a young teen. It enrages his father, a former football star, that Andy will not play the game or fight the class bully,
Billy Curtis. Andy wonders why the whole world is a bully, why he is so
fat, and why his father hates him (13). Andy overhears his father express
dissatisfaction about Andy: " 'All he wants to do is sit on his butt and
read,' the old man bellows at my mother. 'What the hell is wrong with
him?' " Andy's father actually hits him after trying to force him to teach
Billy a lesson. While Andy is on the ground, his "drunk, furious, frustrated,   failed-by-his-fat-son-who-can't-show-anybody-anything father"
kicks him "in the butt," as if he were a football (15).

Andy becomes a runner, but no matter how fiercely or fast his "feet
might fly, they can never outrun the memories" (17), including memories
of an Easter pageant that resulted in the near-fatal beating of an older
boy Andy idolized and memories of his uncle Charles, who also loved
books and told Andy to value his differences, but who was also bait for
bullies. He also remembers the scene after high school graduation: Andy
tells his father he is gay, and his father demands he leave. Andy walks
out of his home and does not look back (193), but he develops scars.
They are not visible like the one on the face of Andy's father a scar
made by Andy's lover, the former bully, Billy Curtis (195). At college,
after an embarrassing encounter with a professor whose attention Billy
has misunderstood, he finds love. First, however, he realizes that "being
totally alone, completely solitary" is the hell where he has been for so
many years of his life that he cannot stand it anymore (200). Billy finds
a place that feels, for him, like home.

In David Klass's *California Blue* (1994), 17-year-old John Rodgers
feels like he is something "between a nerd and a wimp" because he is
not following in his father's footsteps like his athletic older brothers did.
John, like Andy, finds he prefers the solitude of distance running, something he does frequently to help himself think, particularly after learning
that his father is dying of leukemia. In the midst of all the confusion, he
discovers a previously unknown species of beautiful butterfly, hidden on
the property of the local lumber mill, where most of the community,
including his father, is employed. If the forest is saved to protect the
endangered butterfly, the mill will have to close. John realizes that his
decision about whether or not to tell where the butterflies are located
will have a profound impact on the town's economy and on his relationship with his father. There are no easy answers.

There are many stories that show how difficult it is for young adults to sort out their beliefs when parents do and say cruel things in the guise of being right, such as in Bette Greene's novels *Summer of My German Soldier* (1973) and *The Drowning of Stephen Jones* (1991). Others portray harsh punishment that is inflicted on the youth because the father feels the son must be taught a lesson, as in Chris Crutcher's *Ironman* (1995). Many young people find they cannot accept their parents' prejudices. "Telephone Man" in Crutcher's collection of short stories *Athletic Shorts* (1989) expresses the difficulty: "I got to think a little bit, which is something I don't usually like to do because it makes me feel nervous, and I wondered if my dad would mind if I stopped hating niggers for a while. . . . If dad made a mistake about *them*, I wonder if he could of made a mistake about the other colors, too" (128).

Like Telephone Man, Maggie Pugh in Trudy Krisher's *Spite Fences* (1994) develops a social consciousness that sets her apart from her abusive mother. The mother's prejudice contrasts sharply with the intelligence and kindness of Maggie's courageous friend Zeke and others in the black community. Because her world is Georgia in 1960, Maggie must use her camera to record the things she witnesses but cannot speak about. Her lack of an inner voice that she trusts is like a fence she cannot climb until she confronts the racism and the abuse in her family. To achieve independence and autonomy, Maggie, like young people in college, must sort out how to become separate from parents. Although it is painful, she decides in what ways she will never be like her mother: "I told myself that Mama didn't make sense and never would. Why I still secretly hoped that some kind of peace would come to us I'll never know" (279). But Maggie also knows there will be a connection because she chooses to retain her mother's will. Once Maggie comes to terms with who her mother is, she finds her own voice and begins to sort out her own identity.

CAUGHT BETWEEN CULTURES

It is very difficult for anyone to deal with feeling like an outsider; it is especially hard to be the young adult caught between two places. Through her beautiful poetic prose in her collection of essays *Polite Lies* (1997), Kyoko Mori explores her own memories, hopes, and experiences, and the roles of women in Japan and America. She sometimes wonders where she belongs. Her words echo what many young adults feel: "One of the hardest things about living between two cultures is trying to decide what I can accept as different but well intentioned and what I cannot tolerate regardless of cultural differences" (47–48). For persons of any age, it is not unusual to have this sense of confusion, to experience a feeling of dissonance and restlessness, especially when returning to the once familiar and yet strange place. "I have nothing to hold me anchored to the country of my birth, and yet I feel out of place among people who look nothing like me" (250). The search for one's own voice involves sorting out what to discard and what to keep.

The particular circumstances are different, but Maggie's search and the searches of college youth are echoed in Kyoko Mori's essay "Language": "My whole schooling has been a process of acquiring a voice. In college and graduate school, I learned to speak, write, and think like my favorite writers" (18). It is important for Mori to think the thoughts she has come to value in English. As she leaves from one of her visits to Japan and begins the flight back to her home in the United States, she feels a pull: "But even as part of me feels nostalgic, another part of me remains guarded, and my adult voice talks in the back of my mind like a twenty-four-hour broadcast. *Remember who you were*, it warns, *but don't forget who you are now*" (19).

Even when young people live in the country of their birth, questions about home cause a sense of anxiety and confusion. In "Home," Mori captures the contradictory emotions felt by many college students who are eager to return home for holidays, yet who, when they are there, realize how different they have become: "When people ask me how I could leave my 'home' at twenty and never go back, I remind them that there is nothing unusual about my choice. Many people leave home at eighteen to go to college and end up settling in another state, perhaps across the continent" (251).

For the college student who is away, there are two places: the special place of childhood and a different place where they live, study, work, and often become a part of the community. Where and what is home? Relating her sense of home to Holden Caulfield's imagined rye field in *The Catcher in the Rye*, Mori says her home is "an imagined place that brings together the comforting elements of childhood . . . the paintings and the books my mother taught me to love" (256), even though the place was also a place of sadness, secrets, and lies. Kyoko Mori finds in art, in the beauty her mother taught her to love, a way to connect to home. "I had left home, I was sure, not to forget about my mother but to be closer to her memory. All these years later, my conviction remains the same: I speak her words though I speak them in another language" (258).

The desire to define a life that is not only different from their parents' lives, but different from cultural expectations, is explored in some literature. Notable examples are Victor Martinez's *Parrot in the Oven* (1996) and Judith Ortiz Cofer's *An Island Like You: Stories of the Barrio* (1995). Cofer remembers what if feels like to be caught between cultures. In her book there are twelve loosely interconnected stories about young people coming of age in El Barrio in New Jersey, where they feel trapped by poverty and prejudice. In one story, "Beauty Lessons," Sandi unfavorably compares her own looks to the conventional Latino/Latina ideal of feminine beauty. In another, "Arturo's Flight," the title character fantasizes about what it would be like to leave because his love of poetry is "not a talent that'll get you very far in the barrio" (30). In "White Balloons," Doris tells the story of Rick Sanchez, who died of AIDS. She says, "I thought about Rick's life in the barrio as a 'different' boy. I know from experience that you basically have two choices once you're made to feel unwanted here: to leave home or to try to become invisible like me" (147). For Rick, the barrio was a place that "doesn't forget and . . . doesn't always forgive" (151).

LITERATURE

Art is for Kyoko Mori a way to connect to home. Literature, as art, also gives readers a way to leave home, to view home from a new perspective, and a way to find a new life. For author Chaim Potok, a piece of literature transported him from his home to a world apart from anything he had ever experienced. Until he was 16 years old, Chaim Potok lived in a stable world where values were determined for him. He did not read contemporary novels in school. Then he went to a library and chose a book like none he had ever read. The words came alive, he was immersed in a world not his own, and he became a part of a different place. Potok and all writers of stories remind us that no matter where we live, we are also part of another enterprise—our literature. With stories, we have the opportunity to focus on the confrontations, the tensions of the individual who is caught between a stable, inherited past and an alternate world, between one kind of culture and a contrasting experience. We can read stories about individuals who grow up on the edge or those who have no sense of belonging anywhere. But whatever the experience, we think about the world through story. Literature explores the dimensions of what we are involved in, not to give us easy answers, but to give us the questions to think about.

Inside the world of literature, we live in the experiences of others, see connections, and find words to give voice to our feelings. We find a way to share our pains, explore new possibilities, and develop some insights as we look back and ahead. At recurring times in our lives we, like Jonas in Lois Lowry's *The Giver* (1993), as Jackie reminds us in the log entry that begins this chapter, feel alone and must sort out both painful and happy memories as we go in a new direction and figure out who we are. To achieve and maintain an identity, we must, like Jonas and the young adult who is becoming more independent, face how we are different, find a way to live with conflict, navigate our way, make difficult decisions, and learn to live with changes in relationships and in our lives.

The novels discussed in this chapter have not been written because the authors chose to begin with a specific lesson in mind. They are not books written to teach or to recommend specific moral truths. They are not to be used as if reading them would work as a means of therapy for a troubled youth. They are instead literary works of art in which writers, influenced by aesthetics, have made choices. These works reveal a writer's musings, questions, journeys, thoughts, and possible choices. The books bring to the forefront and clarify issues faced by young adults, because questions young people ask—Who am I? Where do I belong? What is my purpose?—are questions asked over and over in the process of human growth and development. Viewed through the imaginations of both the writers and readers who bring the text to life, the stories broaden the experiences of readers and help them blend more deeply with others.

FACILITATING YOUNG ADULT DEVELOPMENT

Like Jackie, the college student who found personal meaning and connection with her own life experiences in Lowry's *The Giver*, young adults in college are faced with two major developmental challenges: forming a personal identity (Who am I?) and developing relationship intimacy (Whom shall I love?). According to Erik Erikson, these developmental passages, often marked by intense emotion, conflict, and uncertainty, are experienced as "crises" in the sense that a successful resolution is required for the individual to be able to mature and move forward with his or her life. These developmental crises often begin during the high school years and continue even more intensely in college and beyond.

As teachers, parents, counselors, and others who interact with young adults and want to help facilitate their growth and development in meaningful, supportive ways, we might ask ourselves the following questions in relation to literature:

1. What key questions, or choices, is the adolescent or young adult in the story facing? Are the adults in this individual's life aware of the normal "developmental crisis" that is emerging? What are they doing to help or hinder the young person's passage to adulthood?

2. Which of these coming-of-age stories might be most relevant or inspiring to the young adults in your life or with whom you interact? Are the portrayals valid? What connections do you see or experience?

3. From an adult's perspective, is there something universal about the human quest for identity and for love and intimacy during the young adult years? Or is each person's journey unique?

4. Movement into a more mature stage of psychological development is often preceded by a great deal of conflict, confusion, and emotional turmoil as the young adult reassesses his or her current way of thinking and experiencing the world. How can this literature assist you in establishing or deepening relationships with those young adults in the midst of painful struggles?

5. As you read these stories, reflect back on your own coming-of-age experiences with identity and intimacy. What connections can you make to your own life experiences? What is different? How can you use this literature to expand your awareness and understanding of gender, racial, cultural, and other differences and your awareness of how these various influences contribute to young adult development?

RECOMMENDED READINGS

A reader's interest will have a stronger influence over whether or not any of the following books is appropriate for middle or high school readers than will the readability or technical reading challenges of the book. The recommendations at the end of each entry, however, merely indicate a potential range of readability for each selection.

Fiction Works

Being Different from Parents and Expectations

Alvarez, J. (1994). *In the Time of the Butterflies*. Carrboro, NC: Algonquin Books of Chapel Hill. 321 pp. (ISBN: 1–56512–038–8). Middle School (MS), High School (HS).

During the time of the guerrilla revolt by the Caribbean nation of the Dominican Republic against the dictatorship of General Rafael Trujillo,

Thanks to Sarah Goldsholl, senior elementary education major, Ohio Wesleyan University, for her work on the recommended readings.

it was almost unheard of for women to join the revolt. However, the four Mirabel sisters prove themselves to be no ordinary women when they turn against everything that is expected of them and choose to fight for their country's freedom and their own freedom in a world torn apart by conflict.

Bridgers, S. E. (1987). *Permanent Connections*. New York: Harper & Row. 264 pp. (ISBN: 0–694–05619–7). MS, HS.

Rob, 17 years old, rebels against his family, becomes secretive, does poorly in school, and feels alienated and hostile. His parents send him to live at the family homestead in North Carolina with Uncle Fairlee, who has been injured and needs his help, ornery Grandpa, and quirky Aunt Coralee. Rob gradually learns to accept responsibility and begins to find a direction.

Charbonneau, E. (1994). *In the Time of the Wolves*. New York. TOR Books. 180 pp. (ISBN: 0–812–53361–5). MS, HS.

Joshua Woods desires to continue his education at Harvard, although his father opposes it. By using ancestral beliefs that greatly embarrass Josh, his father correctly predicts a strange occurrence known as a "year without a summer" that causes everyone but Josh to forget about the conflict over his education. Josh chooses to run away from his family to the family's enemies. It is there that Josh learns important lessons of loyalty and comes to valuable conclusions about his family.

Cushman, K. (1994). *Catherine, Called Birdy*. New York: Clarion Books. 169 pp. (ISBN: 0–395–68186–3). MS, HS.

Catherine, having been born into a knight's family in the year of 1290, resents her lack of control over her own life and chooses to rebel against the conventions of the day that she finds to be so limiting. Her resistance to "women's work," her sense of humor, and her independent spirit make this book timeless.

Gerber, M. (1990). *Handsome as Anything*. New York: Scholastic. 176 pp. (ISBN: 0–590–43019–X). MS, HS.

Rachael is struggling to decide whom she should try to please. Her parents only hope that she marries a nice Jewish boy. Her sister wants her to explore feminism, and her friend Kataya just thinks she should focus on a relationship with a guy who appeals to her. Rachael gradually realizes that she needs to focus more on herself and becoming her own person. Examining both orthodox Judaism and Zen meditation and choosing to attend an unconventional school during her senior year are the first of many actions that Rachael takes in order to discover who she really is.

Klass, D. (1994). *California Blue*. New York: Scholastic. 199 pp. (ISBN: 0–590–46689–5). MS, HS.

John Rodgers does not fit into the small town where he lives. A runner and a nature lover, he has little interest in football and "the company," which are expected to be the greatest concerns in his life. He discovers a type of butterfly that his biology teacher suspects has not been discovered previously, and John must decide whether to fight to save the butterfly or watch while his dying father's company demolishes the woods where the rare butterfly makes its home.

Namioka, L. (1994). *April and the Dragon Lady*. New York: Browndeer Press. 214 pp. (ISBN: 0–15–276644–8). MS, HS.

April Chen, a 16-year-old girl from a traditional Chinese family, is torn between pursuing her own goals and dreams and attempting to fulfill the goals that her demanding grandmother has predetermined for her.

Naylor, P. (1990). *Send No Blessings*. New York: Atheneum. 231 pp. (ISBN: 0–14–034859–X). MS, HS.

Beth, a tenth grader living in West Virginia, is embarrassed by her trailer park home, huge family, and her family's poverty. She vows not to lead the same kind of life that her mother has, although she gets her chance when a twenty-two-year-old boy proposes marriage to her. Will she choose to escape the confines of her mother's life, or will she allow her heart to lead her to holy matrimony?

Peck, R. (1985). *Remembering the Good Times*. New York: Delacorte. 181 pp. (ISBN: 0–440–97339–2). MS, HS.

Teens Buck, Trav, Kate, and their whole community experience change and violence. Trav is sensitive, intelligent, filled with self-doubt, and feels he cannot live up to the expectations of his affluent and successful parents. But everyone, even Kate's outspoken, shrewd great-grandmother, Polly, who is a part of the circle of friends, is surprised when Trav commits suicide. (The suicide will make the novel controversial for some readers.)

Stone, B. (1988). *Been Clever Forever*. New York: Harper & Row. 304 pp. (ISBN: 0–06–025918–3). MS, HS.

Sophomore Stephen Douglas has been smart forever and is fed up with the unreasonable expectations that his parents, teachers, and girlfriend have for him. He finds solace in his friendship with Mr. Truelove, the biology teacher and former doctor in the Vietnam War, who is struggling with his actions during the war. By working together to help one another, they are able to solve their own personal searches for answers.

Making Decisions about Self-Identity: Balance between Separation and Connection

Avi. (1990). *The True Confessions of Charlotte Doyle*. New York: Orchard Books. 210 pp. (ISBN: 0–531–08493–0). MS.

Thirteen-year-old Charlotte Doyle boards the *Seahawk* to journey across the seas to be reunited with her family. Along the way there is a violent mutiny against the cruel Captain Jaggery, and Charlotte proves herself worthy of being part of the crew. While traveling with the sailors, Charlotte gains a new perspective on life and on her values. She is forced to make tough decisions about her upbringing.

Avi. (1993). *Nothing but the Truth*. New York: Avon Books. 224 pp. (ISBN: 0–380–71907–X). MS, HS.

In Phillip Malloy's high school, it is required that the students be quiet and respectful during the playing of the national anthem. When Phillip gets in trouble for softly singing along with it, a huge, public human-rights controversy involving the entire nation results. Phillip must choose whether or not to continue the battle that has turned his life upside down.

Friedman, I. (1995). *Flying against the Wind: The Story of a Young Woman Who Defied the Nazis*. Brookline, MA: Lodgepole Press. 202 pp. (ISBN: 1–886721–00–9). MS, HS.

Cato, a strong-willed German teenager, is disgusted by the atrocities committed by the Nazis during World War II. She chooses to join the resistance although she knows that she will be condemned by many for opposing Hitler.

Garden, N. (1996). *Good Moon Rising*. New York: Farrar, Straus & Giroux. 229 pp. (ISBN: 0–374–32746–7). MS, HS.

High school actors Kerri and Jan are forced to make difficult personal decisions and face the intolerance of their culture when they realize the truth about their relationship. This unconventional love story highlights the strength of two people facing the cruel prejudices of the world around them.

Hamilton, V. (1995). *Arilla Sundown*. New York: Scholastic. 296 pp. (ISBN: 0–590–22223–6). MS, HS.

Arilla, a young woman with a Native American heritage, reconstructs her twelfth year through the use of flashbacks. Her domineering brother, Jack Sun Run, embraces his Native American roots while Arilla strives to find her place in the white community. Arilla is suddenly forced to choose between her two worlds when Jack becomes desperate for her help.

Jenkins, L. (1996). *So Loud a Silence*. New York: Lodestar. 154 pp. (ISBN: 0–525–67538–8). MS, HS.

Seventeen-year-old Juan is enjoying his visit to his grandmother's home in Colombia when he finds himself caught in the fighting between guerrillas and the army. His perception about who he is and his perception about the importance of family come into question during the conflicts that ensue.

Kerr, M. E. (1994). *Deliver Us from Evie*. New York: HarperCollins. 177 pp. (ISBN: 0–06–024475–5). MS, HS.

Living in a small town in Missouri, Evie meets the wealthy and gorgeous Patsy Duff at a party and is forced to deal with her attraction to Patsy. Rumors fly throughout the town, and when Patsy and Evie leave town together, they manage to change a few of the townspeople's attitudes toward love and relationships. (Homosexuality as a topic will cause the book to be controversial for some readers.)

Lowry, L. (1980). *Autumn Street*. Boston: Houghton Mifflin. 188 pp. (ISBN: 0–395–27812–0). MS, HS.

In this touching and thought-provoking book, Elizabeth Lornier rethinks her attitudes about her responsibility toward herself and toward others after her family is forced, because of war, to move into her grandfather's house. Here she meets the tough, streetwise Charles, and they quickly become close friends. Through experiences that the two friends share, Elizabeth learns difficult life lessons about prejudice, fear, loneliness, lies, secrets, and guilt.

Lynch, C. (1996). *Blood Relations: Blue-Eyed Son #2*. New York: HarperCollins. 216 pp. (ISBN: 0–06–025399–1). MS, HS.

While recovering from the severe beating that he received in *Mick: Blue-Eyed Son #1* after trying to escape from his bigoted brother and friends, Mick gains the confidence and strength that he needs in order to break free from the hold that Sycamore Street has on him. He makes important decisions about his future, including where he will make his new home. (The brutal honesty with which racial prejudices are presented and the scenes in which teenagers engage in drinking and fighting will cause this book to be controversial for some readers.)

Lynch, C. (1996). *Mick: Blue-Eyed Son #1*. New York: HarperCollins. 146 pp. (ISBN: 0–06–025397–5). MS, HS.

Fifteen-year-old Mick has spent his entire life on Sycamore Street, a microcosm of the larger segregated city that surrounds him. After witnessing his older brother spending time getting drunk and terrorizing those who are not white and Irish, Mick decides that he wants to lead a different kind of life. Mick eventually meets people who introduce him to life away from Sycamore Street. In his attempt to get away from his roots, Mick must fight his older brother and his friends, all of whom wish him to stay. (The brutal honesty with which racial prejudices are presented and the scenes in which teenagers engage in drinking and fighting will cause this book to be controversial for some readers.)

McDaniel, L. (1996). *Saving Jessica*. New York: Bantam Books. 191 pp. (ISBN: 0–553–56721–7). MS, HS.

Jeremy is more than willing to donate one of his healthy kidneys to his girlfriend, Jessica, who is suffering from chronic kidney damage and is facing constant dialysis and a severely restricted diet. However, Jeremy's parents already experienced the loss of one child and are unwilling to allow him to participate in the operation. Jeremy must stand up for his rights over his own body and must confront both his parents and the courts.

Paterson, K. (1980). *Jacob I Have Loved*. New York: HarperTrophy. 244 pp. (ISBN: 0–064–40368–8). MS, HS.

Louise has always felt great jealousy toward her twin sister. Through experiencing the cycles of life and death, the powers of the ocean, and life on the water, Louise gradually finds ways to overcome her jealousy toward her twin.

Reynolds, M. (1994). *Too Soon for Jeff*. Buena Park, CA: Morning Glory Press. 222 pp. (ISBN: 0–930934–91–1). MS, HS.

Jeff is a high school senior who has decided to break up with his freshman girlfriend. Much to her pleasure and his dismay, she announces that she is pregnant. She refuses to have an abortion and will not consider adoption, leaving Jeff with weighty decisions about his future plans.

New View of Parent/Change in Relationship

Block, F. (1994). *The Hanged Man*. New York: HarperCollins. 137 pp. (ISBN: 0–06–024536–0). HS.

Seventeen-year-old Laurel's father is dead, and although everyone is telling her to eat, she finds that she cannot. Family secrets being kept from Laurel are haunting her. Why won't Laurel's mom share those secrets with her? (This book portrays adult situations.)

Bridgers, S. E. (1981). *Notes for Another Life*. New York: Bantam Books. 201 pp. (ISBN: 0–553–22605–3). MS, HS.

Thirteen-year-old Wren Jackson and her brother, Kevin, who is three years older, live with their loving grandparents. They must accept the fact that their mother, who works far away, and their father, who is mentally ill, will not return to be with them.

Casey, M. (1994). *Over the Water*. New York: Henry Holt. 246 pp. (ISBN: 0–8050–3276–2). MS.

Mary, a 14-year-old Irish girl living in England, is constantly fighting with her strict mother, who will not allow her to have English friends. During a visit to her mother's family farm in Ireland, Mary and her mother fight bitterly. By talking to her aunt, Mary learns more about her mother and comes to understand her.

Ferris, J. (1996). *All That Glitters*. New York: Farrar, Straus & Giroux. 184 pp. (ISBN: 0–374–30204–9). MS.

Brian is stuck in the Florida Keys for the summer with his boring father. Brian is uncomfortable with his new girlfriend, Tia, and with his father. However, when a hurricane strikes during their search for Spanish treasure, Brian has the chance to come to terms with both his father and himself.

Herman, C. (1994). *What Happened to Heather Hopkowitz?* Philadelphia: Jewish Publication Society. 186 pp. (ISBN: 0–82–76–0520–X). MS, HS.

Heather has never known much about her Jewish heritage until she is left for a month with an Orthodox Jewish family. Fourteen-year-old Heather realizes that she wishes to continue practicing her faith in the Orthodox manner, and she must confront her parents and friends with her decision.

Hobbs, W. (1988). *Changes in Latitude*. New York: Atheneum. 162 pp. (ISBN: 0–689–51385–3). MS, HS.

Travis, a self-centered 14-year-old boy, and his family travel to Mexico for a family vacation. Travis and his mother constantly fight, and Travis's sister worries that her parents are going to divorce; meanwhile Teddy, Travis's 9-year-old brother, is concerned about the horrible treatment of endangered sea turtles. When Teddy's love for the turtles results in a tragedy, both Travis and his mom are forced to face the results of their attitudes toward one another.

Janeczko, P. (1986). *Bridges to Cross*. New York: Macmillan. 168 pp. (ISBN: 0–02–747940–4). MS, HS.

James Marchuk's life of baseball dreams and high-top sneakers comes to an abrupt halt when his mother insists on placing him in a devout

Christian high school, although he strongly voices his objections. Once in the school, James feels that his right to think like an individual is being restricted; frustration and resentment cloud James's every thought. Eventually, his mother comes to realize that James needs room to become an individual, and James himself has an epiphany about the fact that his childhood is over and a new life is about to begin.

Lasky, K. (1994). *Memoirs of a Bookbat.* New York: Harcourt Brace. 215 pp. (ISBN: 0–155–215727–1). MS.

Harper Jessup loves to read. However, her loving parents are, as Harper says, "migrants for God," who travel across the United States promoting the censorship of certain literature. When Harper realizes that they are trying to control and manipulate the choices that she makes, she must come to terms with the new perspective of her parents she has gained.

On Their Own/Personal Growth

Alvarez, J. (1991). *How the Garcia Girls Lost Their Accent.* Carrboro, NC: Algonquin Books of Chapel Hill. 290 pp. (ISBN: 0–945–57557–2). MS, HS.

Alvarez was born in New York but was reared in the Dominican Republic, the island of her family. Her book, which is divided into four chapters, includes the fictional account of four sisters adjusting to New York City and learning to live without the support of extended family.

Barret, E. (1994). *Free Fall.* New York: HarperCollins. 249 pp. (ISBN: 0–06–024465–8). MS, HS.

While her parents are trying to settle their divorce, 17-year-old Ginnie is sent to live with her grandmother for the summer. It is there, after she meets a boy named Kris, that Ginnie learns about love, romance, life, and growing up.

Benedict, H. (1996). *Bad Angel.* New York: Dutton. 293 pp. (ISBN: 0–525–94100–2). MS, HS.

In this sensitively written story, 14-year-old Dominican American mother Bianca Diaz is forced to allow her family to separate in order to save the individual members. Bianca deals with the demands of her infant daughter, her husband leaving her, poverty, and hunger.

Block, F. (1997). *Baby Be-Bop*. New York: HarperTrophy. 106 pp. (ISBN: 0–06–447176–4). HS.

Dirk McDonald does not want to be gay. He knows that it will hurt his grandmother, who has raised him. Although he tries to deny and change his sexuality, he is unable to. One night, Dirk is playing with an antique lamp when images of his ancestors (including his mother and father, whom he never knew) appear and tell him stories of his past, present, and future that allow Dirk to finally be at peace with his homosexuality.

Coombs, K. (1996). *Sarah on Her Own*. New York: Avon Flare. 212 pp. (ISBN: 0–380–78275–8). MS.

After a horrible sea journey that claims the life of her only relative, 14-year-old Sarah Douglas lands in colonial Virginia. Her only goal is to return home to England. During the many conflicts that she experiences while trying to earn money for her fare home, Sarah learns lessons of strength, courage, and love from the colonial land.

George, J. (1972). *Julie of the Wolves*. New York: HarperCollins. 170 pp. (ISBN: 0–06–021943–2). MS.

When 13-year-old Miyax is given the choice between facing an arranged marriage or traveling by herself across the frozen Alaskan tundra, she chooses the journey. Miyax faces many challenges and heartaches in her journey and is eventually adopted by a pack of wolves, who become her new family.

Kerr, M. E. (1989). *Night Kites*. New York: HarperCollins Children's Books. 192 pp. (ISBN: 0–06–023253–6). MS, HS.

It is Erik's senior year of high school, and he has just learned that his older brother has AIDS. He must consider his principles and decide whether he wants to be part of the "in crowd" or be a "night kite" and branch out on his own.

Lynch, C. (1994). *Iceman*. New York: HarperCollins. 179 pp. (ISBN: 0–06–023340–0). MS.

Fourteen-year-old Eric is obsessed with searching for a way to discover himself. Unable to turn to his unemotional family, Eric searches his world for a way to discover the answers while he takes out his aggressions on the ice.

O'Dell, S. (1980). *Sarah Bishop*. New York: Houghton Mifflin. 184 pp. (ISBN: 0–590–44651–7). MS.

During the American Revolution, Sarah finds herself orphaned after a vicious attack on her home by patriots. Taking only what she could scrounge from the rubble, Sarah leaves her homeland and plans to move into the wilderness and settle there. Using only her instinct, skill, and musket, Sarah must fight for her survival.

Paterson, K. (1991). *Lyddie*. New York: Puffin Books. 183 pp. (ISBN: 0–14–034981–2). MS, HS.

Lyddie Worthen is on her own, and she is searching for a way to reunite her family. She sees an opportunity when she hears of a mill that is hiring young women. While she works to earn enough money to re-unite her family, she has to make the decision whether to risk her job to protest the working conditions in the factories or to remain silent in order to reach her goals.

Platt, K. (1993). *The Ape inside Me*. New York: Bantam Books. 117 pp. (ISBN: 0–553–14825). MS, HS.

Ed Hill has a voice inside his head that is continuously giving him messages of violence and destruction, resulting in Ed's violent temper and many fistfights. On the brink of disaster, Ed is saved by the auto-shop manager for whom he works and the boxing pro at the local gym, who help Ed to control his temper and convince him to remain in high school.

Santiago, E. (1993). *When I Was Puerto Rican*. New York: Addison-Wesley; Vintage. 274 pp. (ISBN: 0–679–75676–0). MS, HS.

The eldest of eleven children, Santiago shares unique personal expe-riences that show the universality of growing up. This book, which in-cludes early years in Puerto Rico and teen years in Brooklyn, expresses what it is like to be a part of the United States, yet somehow detached.

Comfort/Support Away from Family

Avi. (1995). *Sometimes I Think I Hear My Name*. New York: Avon Flare. 139 pp. (ISBN: 0–380–72424–3). MS.

Conrad travels to New York in order to see his parents, who aban-doned him years earlier. When he becomes involved in a strange relationship with a girl from New York who helps him identify and resolve personal issues of acceptance and love, he comes to discover the true meaning of parents and families.

Banks, R. (1996). *Rule of the Bone*. New York: Harper Perennial. 390 pp. (ISBN: 0–06–092724–0). MS, HS.

After 14-year-old Chappie leaves home to escape his abusive stepfather, he finds himself immersed in drugs, sex, and crime. Just as his situation is getting too out of control for him to handle, he is befriended by an old Rastafarian man. Will he allow himself to accept his new, more peaceful situation, or will Chappie again go back to his life of crime and drug abuse?

Holland, I. (1993). *The Man without a Face*. New York: HarperTrophy. 158 pp. (ISBN: 0–06–447028–8). MS, HS.

Chuck is 14, confused, lonely. He misses his absent father and wants to escape his dominant older sisters and his mother's preparation for her fifth marriage. He slowly develops a friendship with Justin, who is physically and emotionally scarred. Initially confused by their intimate encounter, Justin later realizes the rarity of their relationship.

L'Engle, M. (1983). *And Both Were Young*. New York: Delacorte. 241 pp. (ISBN: 0–440–00264–8). MS.

Flip was prepared for an awful winter when her father left her at a Swiss girls' school while he went to sketch refugee children. However, Flip (real name Phillippa) discovers love, a talent for skiing, and many new friends during her stay at the school.

Morpurgo, M. (1995). *The War of Jenkin's Ear*. New York: Philomel Books. 171 pp. (ISBN: 0–399–22735–0). MS, HS.

Toby is terribly unhappy at Redlands, the boarding school where his parents sent him. His luck begins to change when he meets a young kitchen worker named Wanda and an exceedingly calm boy named Christopher, both of whom he befriends. Together, they face the hatred between the wealthy and poor classes of students at the school. When Christopher admits to believing that he is Jesus and would like to make Toby his first disciple, things begin to get interesting for everyone involved.

Nonfiction Works

Holliday, L. (Comp.). (1995). *Children in the Holocaust and World War II: Their Secret Diaries*. New York: Pocket Books. 409 pp. (ISBN: 0–671–52054–7). MS, HS, Adult (A).

Excerpts of the diaries of twenty-three children who were in ghettos, on the streets, and in the concentration camps of World War II are included in the book. The children, whose ages range from 10 to 18, tell firsthand tales of suffering, torment, bravery, and courage.

REFERENCES

Bateson, Mary C. (1989). *Composing a Life*. New York: Grove Atlantic.

Brooks, Bruce. (1986). *Midnight Hour Encores*. New York: HarperCollins.

Cart, Michael. (1996). *From Romance to Realism: Fifty Years of Growth and Change in Young Adult Literature*. New York: HarperCollins.

Cart, Michael. (1996). *My Father's Scar*. New York: Simon & Schuster Books for Young Readers.

Childress, Alice. (1982). *Rainbow Jordan*. New York: Avon Books.

Cofer, Judith Ortiz. (1995). *An Island Like You: Stories of the Barrio*. New York: Orchard Books.

Cofer, Judith Ortiz. (1995). "Arturo's Flight." In *An Island Like You*. New York: Orchard Books.

Cofer, Judith Ortiz. (1995). "White Balloons." In *An Island Like You*. New York: Orchard Books.

Cole, Brock. (1989). *Celine*. New York: Farrar, Straus & Giroux.

Collier, James L., and Christopher Collier. (1974). *My Brother Sam Is Dead*. Madison, WI: Demco Media.

Cormier, Robert. (1979). *After the First Death*. New York: Pantheon Books.

Cormier, Robert. (1974). *The Chocolate War*. New York: Bantam Books.

Cooper, I., and S. Zvirin. (1998). "Publishing on the Edge." *Booklist*, January, 792–793.

Crutcher, Chris. (1995). *Ironman*. New York: Greenwillow Books.

Crutcher, Chris. (1991). *Athletic Shorts*. New York: Bantam Doubleday Dell.

Fine, Anne. (1997). *The Tulip Touch*. Boston: Little, Brown.

Fox, Paula. (1980). *A Place Apart*. New York: Farrar, Straus & Giroux.

Fox, Paula. (1986). *The Moonlight Man*. New York: Dell.

Fox, Paula. (1995). *The Eagle Kite*. New York: Dell.

Greene, Bette. (1991). *The Drowning of Stephan Jones*. New York: Bantam Books.

Greene, Bette. (1973). *Summer of My German Soldier*. New York: Dial Books.

Kerr, M. E. (1994). *Deliver Us from Evie*. New York: HarperCollins.

Kincaid, Jamaica. (1990). *Lucy*. New York: Farrar, Straus & Giroux.

Klass, David. (1994). *California Blue*. New York: Scholastic.

Krisher, Trudy. (1994). *Spite Fences*. New York: Delacorte Press.

Lasky, Kathryn. (1994). *Memoirs of a Bookbat*. New York: Harcourt Brace.

Lowry, Lois. (1993). *The Giver*. Boston: Houghton Mifflin.Martinez, Victor. (1996). *Parrot in the Oven*. New York: HarperCollins

Martinez, Victor. (1996). *Parrot in the Oven*. New York: HarperCollins.

Moffett, James. (1983). "On Essaying." In Patricia Stock (Ed.), *Forum: Essays on Theory and Practice in the Teaching of Writing*. Upper Montclair, NJ: Boynton/Cook.

Moore, John Noell. (1997). *Interpreting Young Adult Literature*. Portsmouth, NH: Boynton/Cook.

Mori, Kyoko. (1993). *Shizuko's Daughter*. New York: H. Holt & Co.

Mori, Kyoko. (1995). *One Bird*. New York: Holt, Henry & Company.

Mori, Kyoko. (1997). "Home." In *Polite Lies*. New York: Henry Holt & Co.

Mori, Kyoko. (1997). "Language." In *Polite Lies*. New York: Henry Holt & Co.

Mori, Kyoko. (1997). *Polite Lies*. New York: Henry Holt & Co.

Nolan, Han. (1996). *Send Me Down a Miracle*. San Diego: Harcourt Brace & Co.

Paterson, Katherine. (1980). *Jacob Have I Loved*. New York: Crowell.

Paterson, Katherine. (1995). *Lyddie*. New York: Puffin Books.

Paulsen, Gary. (1987). *Hatchet*. New York: Simon & Schuster.

Paulsen, Gary. (1992). *Haymeadow*. New York: Doubleday.

Romano, Tom. (1998). "Relationships with Literature." *English Education*, February, 5–18.

Rylant, Cynthia. (1986). *Fine White Dust*. New York: Simon & Schuster.

Stringer, Sharon. (1997). *Conflict and Connection: The Psychology of Young Adult Literature*. Portsmouth, NH: Boynton/Cook Publishers.

Wilson, Budge. (1990). *The Leaving, and Other Stories*. New York: Philomel Books.

Index

About the Editor and Contributors

PAMELA S. CARROLL is Associate Professor and Coordinator of English Education at Florida State University, where she has received three university teaching awards. A former teacher of middle and high school English, she has been active in the National Council of Teachers of English (NCTE) and the Assembly on Literature for Adolescents of NCTE (ALAN) for the past 20 years. Currently, her research interests include the place of young adult literature in middle grade classrooms, and the psychosocial realities that today's adolescents face and that they find reflected in contemporary young adult literature. She has published articles in, among others, *English Journal, The ALAN Review, Middle School Journal,* and *Journal of Adolescent and Adult Literacy* and chapters in the *Writers for Young People* and *Adolescent Literature as a Complement to the Classics* series. She co-edited, with Gail P. Gregg, *Books and Beyond: Thematic Approaches for Teaching Literature in High School* (1998). She has presented at conferences including the NCTE, ALAN, and International Federation of Teachers of English. Currently she serves as editor of *The ALAN Review.*

LAWRENCE BAINES is the Green Endowed Chair in Education at Berry College, where he teaches adolescent literature, research, and secondary methods. Baines is interested in the ways that transformations in American culture—economic, demographic, social and technological—affect student learning. He has publications in *Phi Delta Kappan, English Journal, The ALAN Review,* and other journals, and is the co-editor of

Language Study in Middle School, High School, and Beyond (1998). He has given presentations at the state, regional, national, and international levels.

ELAINE BEAUDOIN is a licensed clinical social worker in alcohol and drug abuse. She is currently employed as a school social worker at New Britain High School, Connecticut, where she also has a private practice.

STEVEN BELL holds a Ph.D. in School Psychology, University of Georgia, 1976. He has completed post doctoral studies at Johns Hopkins. Bell has been a licensed professional counselor and certified learning disability specialist.

M. LINDA BROUGHTON taught English for over twenty years before returning to earn a Ph.D. in English Education at Florida State University. Now an Assistant Professor of English Education at the University of South Alabama (USA), she incorporates young adult and children's literature into courses for practicing and pre-service teachers of English/ language arts. Dr. Broughton has also served as co-director of the North Florida Writing Project (Tallahassee, Florida) and currently works with the USA chapter of the National Writing Project.

STEVEN B. CHANDLER is a Professor of Health, Physical Education and Recreation at Florida A&M University (FAMU), Tallahassee, Florida. He is a Certified Health Education Specialist and an ACSM Health/ Fitness Instructor. At FAMU, he teaches courses in sport psychology, human sexuality, anatomy & physiology, and sport management.

MAE Z. CLEVELAND, Ph.D., is a nutrition counselor at the Student Health Center of Florida State University. Drawing on a master's degree in psychology and her doctorate in nutrition, she works with a team of health care professionals, helping college students recognize and deal with the physical and emotional problems associated with eating disorders and body image problems. Her research interests include the growing incidence of young girls who use extreme measures to be thin; she is particularly concerned with the increasing number of athletes whom she treats for eating disorders.

CHRIS CROWE is a Professor of English at Brigham Young University (BYU). Prior to working at BYU, he taught high school English and coached football and track in Tempe, Arizona. He is an active member of the National Council of Teachers of English (NCTE), and editor of the Young Adult Literature column of *English Journal*. He has published *Presenting Mildred D. Taylor* (1999), for the Twayne Young Adult Authors series along with several articles on sports and young adult literature.

LaSHAWNDA EGGELLETION, earned a B.S. from Howard University and a M.S. degree in Clinical Psychology, with specialization in Human Development and Family Studies, from Pennsylvania State University. She was employed in Broward County, Florida, as a family counselor in a clinical setting. Her primary interest as a psychologist has been working with survivors of sexual abuse and with adolescent mothers. Now a consultant for Hewitt and Associates in Lincolnshire, Illinois, she spends time volunteering for non-profit organizations that devote attention to adolescents and their development.

GAIL P. GREGG who earned a Ph.D. in English Education at Florida State University, is an Assistant Professor of English Education at Florida International University (FIU). A former teacher of high school English in Miami, and graduate of Florida State University, she has recently won three teaching awards at FIU for her work with students as they study the teaching of young adult literature, written composition, and reading at the secondary level. An active member of the National Council of Teachers of English and its Assembly on Literature for Adolescents (ALAN), she also currently serves as Assistant Editor of *The ALAN Review*. Dr. Gregg has served as chair and co-chair of the Multicultural Commission of the Florida Council of Teachers of English, which has twice won the Affiliate Multicultural Program Award of the National Council of Teachers of English. With Pamela S. Carroll, she co-edited *Books and Beyond: Thematic Approaches for Teaching Literature in High School* (1998); her articles include those that have appeared in *Florida English Journal*, *The ALAN Review*, and *Journal of the Art of Teaching*.

KATHRYN H. KELLY taught English at Shawsville High School in Shawsville, Virginia for twenty years. She is currently an Assistant Professor of English at Central Connecticut State University, New Britain, Connecticut. She teaches courses in writing, young adult literature and English education. Kathy is also on *The ALAN Review* editorial board.

MAUREEN KENNY is an Assistant Professor in the Community Mental Health Counseling Program at Florida International University. Dr. Kenny has conducted research, published, and spoken in the area of psychopathology, child maltreatment, and professional psychology issues for the past six years. After obtaining a Ph.D. at Nova Southeastern University, she completed a post-doctoral residency in Child Clinical Psychology. A licensed psychologist in private practice, Dr. Kenny currently works primarily with children and their families. In 1997, she received the Early Career Contributions Award by the Florida Psychological Association, and in 1999 served as President of the Broward County (Florida) Psychological Association.

JOSH MURFREE holds a Ph.D. from Howard University. He is currently the chairman of the Psychology Department at Albany State University in Georgia. Murfree is the national educational consultant for 100 Black Men.

MEL OLSON is a member of the Physical Education faculty at Brigham Young University (BYU). As part of his doctoral work at BYU, he developed a Physical Education and Coaching program, which he now directs. Mel also serves on a national committee of the National Association of Sports and Physical Education, with the goal of helping accredit coaching education programs. He is committed to training quality coaches to work with youth.

JANET M. ROGERS is currently the Coordinating Director of Student Life at Columbus State Community College. Previously she was the Director of Counseling Services at Ohio Wesleyan University. Dr. Rogers has worked in higher education for over 12 years and focuses her areas of research interest and practice on college student development.

ELIZABETH STREHLE is the director of university-school partnerships at Northern Illinois University in DeKalb, Illinois. Her interests are in developing field-based practices that connect students and teachers in school contexts.

ELIZABETH L. WATTS is the Assistant Supervisor of Multicultural Education in Broward County, Florida, while on leave from her position as Assistant Professor English Education at University of South Florida. Dr. Watts has been active in the National Council of Teachers of English and the Assembly on Literature for Adolescents of NCTE (ALAN) for several years. She completed her Ph.D. in English Education at Florida State University after teaching English at the high school level in Fort Lauderdale, Florida. Her research interests, publications, and presentations focus on, the student reader as meaning-maker, the use of young adult literature in literacy programs, and ways to include non-native speakers of English in regular classrooms. She has a chapter in *Books and Beyond: Thematic Approaches for Teaching Literature in High School* (1998).

CONNIE S. ZITLOW is an associate professor at Ohio Wesleyan University, where she teaches courses in young adult literature and content area reading, and directs the secondary education program. Her publications about young adult literature have appeared in the *Adolescent Literature as a Complement to the Classics* series and *The ALAN Review*. Dr. Zitlow's work with young adult literature includes serving as the president of the Assembly on Literature for Adolescents of NCTE (ALAN). She is also the co-editor of the *Ohio Journal of the English Language Arts*.